"Practical theologians leading parishes and organizational development practitioners can find each other's languages difficult to master. Anderson bridges that gap. He adroitly fosters a conversation providing insight for the organization specialist into the unique relational economy of a church system, and for the pastor into a broader understanding of the human undercurrents operating in a church which hopes to breathe the Gospel into its own mission context."

—Wilson Gunn, Rev. Dr. G. Wilson Gunn, Jr., General Presbyter, National Capital Presbytery, PCUSA

"In the prolific world of church leadership and changing resources, Loosing Control is the one I am recommending . . . as it focuses on the primary function of a church—to disciple people in the way of Jesus through self-organization, resulting in ongoing transformation. Ron Anderson masterfully weaves profound theory, real-life story, and skillful practice into a dynamic source of revitalization for spiritual communities."

—Steve Shive, General Presbytery (PCUSA), Presbytery of Wyoming, and Organizational Relationship System Coaching Coach

Loo∧sing Control

Lo^o^sing Control
Becoming a Pastor/Leader
with **Influence**

Ronald D. Anderson

RESOURCE *Publications* · Eugene, Oregon

LOOSING CONTROL
Becoming a Pastor/Leader with Influence

Resource Publications
An Imprint of Wipf and Stock Publishers
199 W. 8th Ave., Suite 3
Eugene, OR 97401

www.wipfandstock.com

ISBN 13: 978-1-4982-1932-7

Manufactured in the U.S.A.   06/01/2015

Brief portions of Chapter One appeared in a previously published article. (Anderson, Ronald D. "Change: Spontaneous or Designed in Advance," *Congregations*,
Volume 2, 2011). Appreciation is expressed to Alban for permission to reprint this
material.

Contents

Preface | vii

CHAPTER 1   Systems—Everywhere Systems | 1

CHAPTER 2   Emotional Systems | 16

CHAPTER 3   Self-Organizing Happens | 26

CHAPTER 4   Goals Are Determinant | 52

CHAPTER 5   Essential Principles | 65

CHAPTER 6   Discipling—the Central Goal | 81

CHAPTER 7   Systemic Thinkers | 90

CHAPTER 8   Leverage Points | 105

CHAPTER 9   Everyone a Minister | 121

CHAPTER 10   Measures of Success | 139

CHAPTER 11   Worship | 151

CHAPTER 12   Communities of Disciples | 168

CHAPTER 13   Bottom-up vs. Self-Organizing Change | 182

CHAPTER 14   Associations of Churches | 204

CHAPTER 15   Church Start-ups | 219

APPENDIX A   Essential Principles | 239

Bibliography | 243

Preface

WE ARE SCHIZOPHRENIC WHEN it comes to change. Much of the time we are resisting it, "But we've always done it this way." Other times, we are fighting *for* it, "If only I could get them to wake up." Depending upon the context, both tendencies have their place. It is possible, however, to get locked into one of these tendencies; some people have a strong inclination in one particular direction. Some people seemingly always resist change; they want everything to stay just as it is. Others seemingly are always dissatisfied with what exists and are pushing for something different, sometimes without really knowing what change they are seeking.

But resisting change or striving to make it happen are not the only alternatives. This book makes a case for *embracing* change. Change is going to happen whether we want it or not. The old shibboleth, "The only constant is change," has the ring of truth. So what are we going to do about it? The case being made here is for taking advantage of the flow of change, neither resisting it unduly nor pushing too hard to make it be something it cannot be. But this embrace of change is not a fatalistic or passive notion of "whatever happens is." It should be an *adventure* in discerning what God has in store for us.

This sense of embracing change is tied to *purpose*—one's personal purposes, the purposes of our faith community, or the purposes of the kingdom of God. The purposes with which we embrace change have a powerful influence. To productively embrace change requires having a clear sense of purpose. Who am I and why am I here? What is the place of this particular congregation? What do the scriptures tell us about the reign of God? With clarity of purpose we can assertively embrace the adventure of change.

Such an embrace of change is part of our heritage. It is an obvious part of the New Testament record. The Protestant reformation was about change and the Catholic counter-reformation had within it a strong renewal element. The slogan, "Reformed and always reforming," is apt. The pietistic movement of nineteenth-century Northern Europe (part of my personal heritage) was the embrace of change within a "reformed" context that had become static and resistant to change. Embracing change was the way to renewed life, vitality, and fulfillment.

A church where the leaders are embracing change can be an exciting place. The church has leaders of many kinds—pastors, elders, deacons, and men and women with no official office at all. In fact, every person within the church has some influence on what it becomes. Our understanding of this influence, however, depends on what we conceive the church to be. Two different conceptions of the church are common. For some it is an institution, while for others it is an organism. Taken in their pure form, these two conceptions of the church lead to very different understandings of the degree and form of influence of such leaders.

So what understanding of the nature of the church is most accurate, useful, or informative? Is it one of these two, some combination of the two, or yet some other conception? Our answer has important implications for how we approach life in the church. What is our basis for choosing a conception of the church? There are many such bases, of course, but two prevalent sources are our understanding of the biblical picture of the church and conceptions drawn from the social sciences.

The understanding of embracing change presented here is grounded in two sources: modern understanding of organizational dynamics as portrayed in the societal and organizational literature, and our understanding of the life of apprenticeship to Jesus found in the Bible. The two sources come together to provide insights on how to embrace change in our faith communities; both are foundational.

More specifically, the aspect of organizational dynamics central to the presentation of this book is the concept of complex adaptive systems and the corollary notion of self-organizing change. While these concepts may be less familiar to the typical reader than the biblical narratives, both are important to the portrayal found here. As an aside, if this organizational terminology is foreign to you, the reader, have no concern; it will be explained early on.

Even before explaining these concepts, however, it should be noted that self-organizing change is *not* presented here as a guide for specific actions by church leaders, but as a way to understand church dynamics. In other words, *any church is self-organizing and our understanding of this reality is key to being an effective leader in this context.* This thesis is elaborated in many ways in the story presented in this book.

This book is for church leaders and people who prepare others to exercise leadership. The intent is to focus on the practical aspects of these endeavors, but to do so in a manner fully grounded in appropriate conceptual and theoretical understandings. These two groundings—the practical and the theoretical—are sometimes difficult to maintain simultaneously. Some readers may be inclined toward the practical with a degree of impatience with theoretical conceptions. Others may be distrustful of action without a thorough sense of the rationale for it or an understanding of the expected outcomes.

Such tensions between apparent polarities are among the reasons for the approach chosen for this book. Its message has been embedded in dialog and interactions among people, people involved in shaping the life of the church. As such, it may appear to be a folksy presentation of leading the church which has little grounding in well thought-out conceptual frameworks. This possible appearance, however, is not the case. There is a thorough grounding in multiple conceptual frameworks, in particular—as already noted—those drawn from biblical sources and applied social science.

The coming together of these sets of understandings is provided here through the story of the interactions of Kevin Aabard, a pastor, and Swen Quesoda, a church consultant, who develop a relationship based on friendship rather than the typical pastor/consultant professional collaboration. The growing understandings of Kevin are the heart of the story. The threads connecting the chapters of this book are his interactions not only with Swen, but several other people and resources as he gains an increasing understanding of his role as a leader of change in his church.

Because of the progression of understandings found in this portrayal, it probably is best to read it in the order presented. Some authors advise readers that the several parts of their book can be read profitably in a variety of orders. In contrast, since the story in this book emerges over time, and because some of the concepts will be unfamiliar to most readers, it probably is best that the default approach be a straight-through read.

Each chapter begins with a brief section labeled "Waypoints," which is a brief summary of key concepts addressed in that chapter. This section is intended as sort of a table of contents to aid the reader in locating sections of the book where these concepts are in the narrative of the story of Kevin, Swen, and others.

A reader deserves some information about what has brought an author to a particular orientation and perspective. My outlook has grown out of decades of participation in two realms often thought to be quite dissimilar: a large research university and local church congregations. Active participation in academic research on public school education and lay leadership of congregational life have converged on the matter of fostering purposeful change. The cross fertilization of ideas from these two settings has been fascinating and productive.

Activities within the university context have been many and varied, including teaching graduate courses on educational reform, coaching individuals in the art of teaching, conducting research on educational reform efforts, and consulting with people engaged in reform endeavors. They have centered on a role as Professor of Education at the University of Colorado at Boulder, but have extended into short term assignments with the National Science Foundation in Washington, DC, a research institute in Germany, and speaking engagements in the Netherlands, England, Israel, Venezuela, and Taiwan. These activities have resulted in books and research articles on educational change and evaluation reports for various school districts and state education agencies.

Involvement in the church has been long-term as well, ranging across differing church contexts reflecting both evangelical and mainline expressions. Early experience as an elder within a congregational polity was followed years later by becoming a Commissioned Lay Pastor, and still later the Executive Presbyter for the Presbytery of Pueblo which encompasses the Presbyterian (PCUSA) churches in the southeast quadrant of Colorado.

The acknowledgments which follow serve the usual purposes of giving appropriate credit, but they also may give further insight as to what has shaped this book. Within the university world, I have to acknowledge the insights gained from countless interactions with student and faculty colleagues. Of particular note, are those doctoral students and others with whom I worked on a variety of endeavors, including my externally funded project that sent us coast-to-coast studying change in schools.

A similar situation pertains to the local church context where the people who have influenced me are innumerable and deeply appreciated. One person has to be singled out, Ken Bekkedahl, who as pastor of the church where I found myself as an adult with a young family, drew me into church leadership and opened my eyes to what could be. Putting ideas into practice with him and a team including Jim Cessna and John Sparks was the beginning of a new stage in my life of faith.

The many ideas that have come from innumerable sources are impossible to appropriately credit, but since it is recent and influential, I must acknowledge my current context within the Presbytery of Pueblo where I have executive responsibilities. My colleagues have been delightful to work with and I need to acknowledge specifically Randy Schade's demonstration of an excellent group process. Thinking about this professional setting brings up images of a large number of faces of people who have been so supportive of me. Thanks all!

Thanks are also due colleagues who have given the gift of reading all or portions of the manuscript for this book and offering their comments and suggestions, including J.E. Blanton, Kathy Goodrich, Matt Guy, Pat Jessup, Eunice McGarrahan, Brad Munroe, Lisa Nelson, Beverly Parsons, and Steve Shive. Their support is deeply appreciated and, of course, they have no responsibility for inadequacies remaining in the book.

Given the nature of my work and my approach to life, it should be no surprise that the reading of articles and books has been a huge and decisive influence on me. The numbers of such in the academic realm is in the hundreds as would be apparent from the citations in my academic work, but I want to identify three whose writing about educational reform—mostly through their books—has been especially important: Ted Sizer, Michael Fullan, and Seymour Sarason. They have managed to cut through the hype, over simplifications, political machinations, illusions and pessimism of this arena to deal with reality.

A similar comment could be made about the influence on me of articles and books pertaining to theology and the Christian life. My most influential mentors have reached me through the printed page—partially a reflection of the age in which I have lived. Of the hundreds of books consumed over the years, two of their authors stand out: Dallas Willard and N.T. Wright. The books of Dallas Willard (many, but particularly *The Spirit of the Disciplines* and *The Divine Conspiracy*) occupy a special place because of their profundity and the fact that they were backed up by a life that exemplified what he taught. More recently, the writing of N.T. Wright has become important. The scholarship of both is outstanding and, especially important, it relates to how one lives. They truly have shaped my thinking; I hope that this thinking has played out, in some measure, in the way I live.

Some more personal acknowledgments are required as well. This book grows out of decades of life experiences and as such it is impossible to recognize and give adequate thanks to the family members, friends and other apprentices of Jesus who have influenced me through our life together, but I feel a need to pinpoint a small number of this legion for specific mention. In my early life, my father and grandfather stand out, specifically, my grandfather's years of commitment to being a lay leader in our country church and his witness, which had a profound impact on some of the small number of people who found themselves living, at various times, on that family farm in northern Wisconsin. Only decades later did I realize his impact on people I hardly knew.

My sister, Beverly Parsons, occupies a special place in these acknowledgments because of her influence on my professional thinking. We have had distinctly different careers but there have been enough commonalities that we have had occasion to collaborate a bit in our research work. More significant, however, are the many conversations over the years about change and reform. Without these conversations, I would not have come to realize the importance of complex adaptive systems and self-organizing change—the very themes of this book—nor found important resources.

My son Tim is a part of this picture as well. His work as a minister, and as a resource for people in ministry, are evidence of the potential in this arena. Sharing in the operation of a Christian retreat center with him and his wife, Lee Anne, and the fostering of spiritual formation have been one of life's pleasures.

Finally, much of the theme of this book is tied to the life I share with my wife, Sandy. We live in and operate a Christian retreat center together, but possibly more important in terms of this book, is that she is happy to put up with—and be truly supportive of—a guy who finds more fulfillment from spending his time thinking about church change and being a church executive and consultant than from giving attention to "golden year" activities thought to be common to people of our vintage. I am truly blessed.

Ronald D. Anderson
Beulah, Colorado
November 8, 2014

chapter 1

Systems—Everywhere Systems

Waypoints

Both New Testament churches and modern day churches have included events that could be considered attempts to initiate change; some probably would be considered what are commonly called "top-down" initiatives, and in other cases, "bottom-up." Such situations are dynamic with multiple complexities; nothing is simple.

Understanding these situations requires looking at them as *systems*. All systems can be understood as being made up of three aspects: *elements*, *interconnections*, and a *function* or *purpose*.

1. The *elements* of a system are both tangible and intangible, such as people, buildings, doctrines, people's wants and needs, as well as spiritual influences.

2. *Interconnections* are diverse in nature, including physical interconnections and information interconnections.

3. *Functions* or *purposes* are sometimes hard to ascertain; the true functions of a system are deduced from the behaviors observed in the system.

Family systems (emotional systems) theory has been applied successfully to churches and is fairly widely understood by church professionals. It is but one example of systems-thinking and in reality is a specialized sub-set of general systems ideas. Fully understanding systems requires looking well beyond this one example.

KEVIN AABARD, AGE 47, is a pastor of a Midwestern suburban church. At what he has come to accept as both mid-life and mid-career, he has a mix of contentment and mild dissatisfaction with his life as pastor and family man. His wife, Susan, has been a math teacher at the local high school for the past seven years, ever since they moved here for Kevin to become pastor of Trinity Community Church. Between their two incomes, they live comfortably enough, although having their oldest two in college this year has led to a bit of stress—and some reflection on what it means to be content with what one has. Their two careers combine to connect them rather deeply with the community, since both school and church are in the same neighborhood—the one in which they live. In spite of a few of the common marital tensions—and the challenges of raising three children who have to live with the status of being "preacher's kids"—life has been good; he is content with life with Susan and how their kids appear to be turning out.

The mild dissatisfaction he feels is related to his church and his role as pastor. By most measures, the church is strong and he is well-liked by the people. For this status he is thankful and also pleased with the way he is able to minister to "his flock" through preaching and engaging them in other contexts. The mild dissatisfaction arises because the congregation does not seem to extend its influence out among other people in the community as much as he would like, and the level of commitment among members of the church to living as disciples of Jesus does not come all that close to the ideal he strives to portray in his preaching. The congregation does have some outreach, but, on the whole, the manner in which congregants relate to other people outside the church does not have the depth and self-revelation for which he yearns. The pressures of their lives in the world outside of the faith community seem to suppress, to a considerable extent, the potential life with Christ and their fellow disciples that he would like to see.

According to the last annual report, average Sunday attendance over the last year was 147, up from 112 the first year Kevin was pastor. Their building is adequate for who they are and what they do, but certainly wouldn't be considered ideal. The congregation was "planted" fifteen years ago and met in a school on Sundays for a number of years before—under the leadership of the founding pastor—purchasing their current building from another church that was moving to a new site with a new building. Since Kevin succeeded the founding pastor, he has watched the congregation grow somewhat in size, become stable and harmonious, and become not only content but probably complacent. Kevin is pleased that the congregation is functional, rather than dysfunctional, but at the same time he hopes for more. Reflecting on the life cycle he knows congregations go through, he is convinced that his congregation is not in decline, but in many ways it feels like it has plateaued.

A recent development gave him hope that the complacency may not be as pervasive as he thought, but, at the same time, caused him a bit of unease. Three people from the church—a retired teacher, the mother of two young children, and a man who operates a local fast food establishment—had zeroed in on the idea of the church "adopting" the elementary school that was across the street and down a block from the church. The three of them got to talking about the idea at a recent social event after one of them described what she had been hearing about such an endeavor at a church in another city. They started talking about the fact that the neighborhood where their church building and the nearby school were located was not the most upscale part of the city and, in fact, had a relatively high number of low income families. In the language of school people, a lot of the kids were on "free or reduced lunch" when it came to the school lunch program. "Adopting" the school would include having a "work weekend" during the summer when volunteers could do some painting and other fix-up work the school seemingly couldn't afford, giving a backpack with school supplies to each child at the beginning of the school year, and providing volunteers to help throughout the school year in roles such as tutoring. The three thought this endeavor would give them a connection to the people working at the school as well as with families living in the neighborhood of the school.

Their mutual enthusiasm about the sudden idea was such that they quickly started talking to their friends in the church and recruiting others to join them. Kevin was delighted with this sudden interest and initiative, although there was one bit of unease as well. The church board had not yet had an opportunity to talk about the idea and already it seemed that the train had left the station.

The board was having its monthly meeting the very next week and Kevin put the matter on the action agenda for discussion. The church board was a good one, at least Kevin felt it was a cut above average. The classic board-pastor conflicts seemingly common among so many churches were not reality here. The board mostly did not micro-manage everything he did and they tried to operate at a policy level. Nevertheless, they had a lot of questions. Where was the money coming from for all of those backpacks and school supplies? It certainly wasn't in the church budget, which had been rather tight of late. Who would be in charge to make sure this program operated appropriately and wouldn't sully the good name of the church? And there was one board member who took exception to some things done at the school and wasn't sure the church should be linked to everything done there. Two others had been interested in a different outreach idea during the board's recent planning retreat and were concerned that the new venture would displace their preferred initiative. These two felt the board was responsible for the programs of the church and suddenly it seemed that things were happening outside of their control.

Other questions were raised but it was a quite civil discussion. It was decided that the people behind this sudden initiative would be invited to meet with the board at their next meeting. Kevin was asked to communicate with them and try to strike a balance between encouraging them and also letting them know that the board needed to approve anything done in the name of the church. Kevin was sure he would be encouraging them, but he hoped he could do so while letting them know they needed to talk to the board as well.

This rather sudden development caused considerable reflection on Kevin's part. The people in the congregation who said they wanted to reach out to others beyond their own circle rarely seemed to do it, so this new spark was really exciting. He realized he did not know what many of them may be doing in their individual lives, but when it came to doing anything with others, almost all seemed to be waiting for someone else to take the initiative in getting started, thus his pleasure with what had happened. In those pensive moments when he reflected on such matters—not that there were many such moments in his busy life—a lot of questions would come sweeping through his mind. Was their level of discipleship simply not high enough that they were ready to pursue the kingdom in this manner? Were their lives just so busy that there wasn't much room for anything else? Did they just not see the possibilities for ministry around them? And how did all of this relate to what he and the board were trying to program at the church?

Kevin was reflecting on such questions as he drove downtown to attend a one-day conference (9:30 a.m. until 3:00 p.m.) on social conditions in the greater metropolitan area, an area having a population of about one and a half million people. Sponsored by the regional council of governments and several of the social service agencies in the area, the conference would address many of the social issues that tend to make the newspapers. He didn't expect to see many of his fellow pastors from the area at the conference, but he thought it would be a good setting in which to think about how he and his congregation could be disciples outside the confines of their building's walls.

During the lunch break, he struck up a conversation with another fellow attending the conference and was surprised to find he also had an interest in churches. It turned out that this other person, Swen Quesoda, was a church consultant who worked with congregations not only locally but also in other states. Both Kevin and Swen are outgoing people who meet others easily and they seemed to have "good chemistry," so much so that not far into the conversation Kevin felt comfortable saying to Swen, "So you are a church consultant, hey. Well, does that mean you are one of those guys who 'blows in, blows off, and blows out,' never to be heard from again?" Swen laughed easily and responded, "You should talk. Every week you have a captive audience where you can "blow off" however you see fit, and each week they pay you to come back and do it again."

The banter was comfortable for both of them but quickly became a more substantive conversation. Swen indicated that his key interest in attending the conference was to understand more about how various societal agencies operate. He had been developing a growing interest in understanding how various organizations, including churches, foster change and improvement. In particular, he was interested in how change is facilitated from the top-down in organizations as compared to fostering change from the bottom-up. Swen was convinced that both types of change occur in healthy organizations, both are good and he wanted to understand more about facilitating both. He explained that he didn't really expect to learn much about the two forms of implementing change at the conference, but he was thinking about them as he was learning about the work of various agencies.

Kevin's curiosity about this matter of top-down and bottom-up change certainly had been aroused and he said, as the next session was about to begin, "I really find all of that interesting. Do you have a few minutes when the conference ends at three to get a cup of coffee and explore all of this a bit more?"

"Sure," Swen responded. "My calendar is open the rest of the afternoon. Let's meet here by the registration table after the last session."

As they met after the last session, Swen said, "I need to stretch my legs at least a little bit. There is a coffee shop across the street in the next block. Why don't we walk over there? They have a lot of different kinds of coffee drinks if you are into that sort of thing."

"Sure," Kevin responded, "Sounds good to me."

They did a bit of debriefing on what had occurred at the conference on their way, but even before they got there, Kevin launched into what had been on his mind. "You said you were interested in how change is initiated from the bottom-up as well as from the top-down in organizations, including churches. I got to wondering about that. It brought to mind not only recent events in my own church but a church that I know a bit about that has a lot of programs and seems to be growing fairly rapidly. Its pastor tells me all of their programs are managed from the top down. I don't think he is blowing smoke when he tells me he calls the shots on all major program decisions. I don't think anyone else has been around when he has said it, but more than once he has said to me, 'The sheep don't tell the shepherd what to do.' He is persuaded that is the New Testament pattern."

Kevin heard a little chuckle from Swen and thought he may have heard a bit of a sigh as well. "Let's order and then maybe I can offer my perspective. I am going to indulge in a large latte; that coffee in the hallway of the conference center was pretty gruesome stuff."

As they pulled their chairs up to a small table—Swen with his latte and Kevin with a decaf coffee—Swen began, "Like you and your pastor friend, I attend to the patterns I see in the New Testament, so before saying anything about what social science research or contemporary organizational theory has to say about top-down or bottom-up change, let me talk about what I see in the New Testament, specifically the book of Acts.

"Chapter six of Acts describes the situation where some 'widows were being neglected in the daily distribution of food' and the Twelve initiated a process of selecting seven men to administer this distribution so the Twelve 'could devote ourselves to prayer and to serving the word.' These actions are analogous to actions taken in congregations today by individuals and groups in leadership positions: pastors, bishops, boards, councils, sessions, consistories, vestries, etc. This situation in Acts chapter six is clearly a change initiated by the leadership in what we probably would call today a "top-down" manner. The seven men at the center of this change included Philip.

"Two chapters later in Acts we find Philip in a totally different context. The account of Philip's encounter with the Ethiopian eunuch begins with these words, 'Then an angel of the Lord said to Philip...' A bit later at the end of this encounter with the Ethiopian, the text says, 'the Spirit of the

Lord snatched Philip away...' and Philip 'was passing through the region proclaiming the good news to all the towns until he came to Caesarea.'"

As Swen spoke, Kevin was thinking to himself, "I'm not sure if he is quoting from memory or paraphrasing, but this guy seems to know this part of Acts." He didn't interrupt, however, as Swen continued.

"Notice a couple things about this second account of Philip. First, in contrast to the first situation where he was operating under the direction of the leaders of the church, here it appears he was operating under the direction of the Spirit, totally independent of the direction or supervision of the church. Second, this situation was seen as completely natural and good as evidenced by its being reported with favor in Acts. Both "top-down" and "spontaneous" change are part of a healthy church context."

At this point Kevin interrupted, "I suspect my pastor friend probably would say that this second example of Philip is not that relevant in that his experience in chapter eight of Acts is not part of a corporate activity but simply an individual portion of his life lived out while outside the congregation."

Swen was not persuaded at all. "If you look on further in Acts, you see numerous instances of Paul and others living and working together in a rather spontaneous manner. Their lives often ebbed and flowed together under the direction of the Holy Spirit on an ongoing basis largely independent of a plan or direct supervision exercised by the 'church hierarchy.' Obviously, there were other instances of direct connection, as in Acts fifteen, when Paul and Barnabas and some other believers made a trip from Antioch to Jerusalem for the explicit purpose of having the apostles and elders address the question of the extent to which Gentile believers should be expected to follow the Law of Moses. The overall picture portrayed in Acts, however, is of groups of believers operating under the principles and general guidance of the church, but within that context, operating in smaller collections of people in a rather free-flowing manner under the direction of the Spirit."

Kevin responded, "Well, I'm certainly convinced in terms of the biblical perspective, but I want to go further into what you were saying about social science research and organizational theory with respect to top-down and bottom-up change. I think I'm right in the middle of a situation where these thoughts are really relevant."

Swen was ready to keep going. "I would start by saying that both top-down and bottom-up change can happen in the same congregation and this is good. It is the way it should be. And I think we can get many valuable insights about this both from biblical study and modern day research. But let me start by going back to some very basic ideas if you have the time."

Kevin did not hesitate. "Sure, charge ahead."

"Let me start with the fact that most everything we are dealing with here is part of a system, or an intertwined set of systems that have within them various subsystems. This is why I am tempted to take exception to the approach of your pastor friend who is so committed to making all the major decisions about what goes on in his congregation. Obviously, I don't know how he understands what is taking place there, but I do know that there are some people among those committed to this level of control from the top who see everything in a very linear manner, as if there is a simple cause and effect relationship between the various parts of each situation they are encountering.

"By contrast, I don't think many situations are that simple." And as if to be sure Kevin got the point, Swen scrawled on a napkin with his pen, NOTHING IS SIMPLE.

"Let's look at the basic idea of what constitutes a system," he continued. "Systems theory can get really complex, involving mathematics and computer-generated models, but we don't need to go there. The basic ideas are not that involved. A few ideas will suffice."

At this point, Kevin was thinking to himself, "Okay, he seems to be saying every situation is complex, but a few basic ideas will make the complexity understandable. Let's see."

"Think of a system as having three sorts of things called elements, interconnections and a purpose or function." Again, Swen was scrawling on his napkin, ELEMENTS, INTERCONNECTIONS, FUNCTION.

"The elements are organized in some way such that the interconnections achieve some outcome; they serve a purpose. Systems are everywhere. The human body is a system that is made up of a lot of other systems. The circulatory system and digestive system, for example, are appropriately named. When you think of the circulatory system, the elements and the interconnections are fairly obvious, but don't forget the function, which is to pass nutrients to and from cells in the body. All its various systems combine to make up a stupendous total system which is the human body."

At this point, a loud, boisterous conversation about the local college basketball team at a nearby table stimulated Kevin to say, "I suppose a basketball team is a system too."

Swen jumped on it. "A basketball team is an excellent example. Elements include the court, ball, and players, and don't forget the coach. The interconnections include the strategy of the coach, the rules of the game, and players' decisions. The purpose of the team could be to have fun, to win, get exercise, make money for the athletic department or some combination of these purposes."

"And I suppose this college basketball team is part of a larger system as well," Kevin added.

"Of course," Swen responded. "This team is part of a college, which is a very complex system. And here is an example of that. My comment about one of the functions of the basketball team being to make money for the institution is probably wrong. Most such programs lose money. But within the system we are calling a college, it serves several functions which may include a monetary one. In some cases, a popular sports team is important for bringing alumni contributions into the college."

"And since we are talking about a college," Kevin threw in, "I'm sure each of the classrooms is an important system."

"Sure, each classroom is a system with elements that include the students, the prof, the syllabus, the required textbooks, and more." Swen was really engaged at this point as he continued. "The interconnections are probably obvious, but don't forget about purpose. The purpose may seem obvious, that is, to give the students an education, but how the system actually operates is dependent upon how the purpose is understood by everyone involved. The purposes of the student who is in college to have a good time may be quite different from the serious student wanting to be admitted to a post-graduate degree program or get a job in a competitive field. And the purposes of professors are not all the same. The purpose of the one teaching his favorite area of research is not the same as the one who got stuck teaching this course for one time only because no one else was available."

At this point Kevin said, "I've got the idea. I imagine you could go on to explain in a similar fashion a tree, a forest and an ecosystem as a set of systems within systems within systems."

"Sure, and probably thousands of other illustrations. But a key point I need to emphasize is that without a function, you don't have a system. You just have a collection of stuff. A dozen people located in the same space don't necessarily constitute a system. If these people just happen to be the ones located seemingly at random on the sidewalk of a given city block, they don't have a common purpose that joins them. They just happen to be the ones on that sidewalk at a given point in time. There is no function or purpose that serves to constitute them as a system. They are just a collection of people with nothing that makes them an identifiable group or system. Without a function or purpose, an interconnected set of elements is not a system."

I'm getting the sense," Kevin interrupted, "That systems have an aspect of wholeness and integrity to them."

"Exactly," Swen agreed, "But you also have to recognize that they can change over time. They can adapt, evolve, and respond to outside influences in a way that is determined by the system itself. A group of people who originally formed as a system for a particular purpose may, over time, shift their purpose. They are a different system, even though they are the same people, because over time they have come to have a different purpose for their existence. They are just as much a system as before, but they are a different system."

"And that applies to churches, I assume," noted Kevin.

"Certainly," Swen said. "It applies to congregations and groups within congregations. Often without realizing it, a group or congregation can come to have a somewhat different purpose than it did originally, either for good or ill. When you look at examples of congregations that either have surged forward or gone into decline, you often find that their purpose for being has shifted, in many cases without people realizing it, especially in the case of decline."

"All of this makes me think about what you church consultants often are trying to do. My sense is that you commonly go into a congregation with the intent of changing them, but if the congregational system is determined by the purpose the people themselves have for their existence, how are you going to accomplish much?" Kevin was not sure if he was making an insightful comment or just trying to yank Swen's chain, but he felt good about saying it.

Swen smiled a bit as he said, "We could go off on a long discussion about what role we church consultants hope to play, but for now I'll simply say that you are on target. Behaviors typically are determined by a system itself, so as an outsider I can't simply come in and give them a different purpose. Don't discount another outsider though; I've seen instances of the Holy Spirit strongly influencing the purpose of a faith community."

Kevin also smiled a bit at this point and said, "Now if I am understanding all this correctly, doesn't this mean the Holy Spirit is an element in this system?"

"But of course! Elements can include what some people would call intangibles. Don't leave out things when you think about a system. When you think about a congregation, take account of such intangible elements as people's need for friends and their desire to assuage their loneliness."

Swen continued. "In addition to all the elements and sub-elements and sub-sub-elements, there are innumerable interconnections as well. I know you are anxious to talk about church settings, but let me give some other examples first. Here is one from nature—the interconnection between the amount of sunlight and color change in some mammals. Reduction in the amount of sunlight in the fall triggers mechanisms that cause the color of the coat of a snowshoe hare or weasel to change from brown to white and then reverse when daylight increases in the spring. Although we may not fully understand everything about these mechanisms, this interconnection is present.

"Besides these physical interconnections, there are information interconnections, both formal and informal. A good example is the communication on a football team. You have the conversation in the huddle, followed by signals called out by the quarterback, followed by information acquired through the eyes of the quarterback as he 'reads the defense,' all of which influences the action the quarterback takes within this system."

At this point Kevin said, "Am I right in thinking that in looking at a system, elements are the easiest to see, interconnections are harder to identify and functions or purposes are hardest of all?"

"You are so right! Functions and purposes are clearly the hardest to figure out. They need to be deduced from the behaviors observed in the system, not from statements of goals or other talk. For example, how often can you depend on a politician's rhetoric to identify why he or she voted in a certain way. Okay, maybe I am being a bit cynical, but there is a reason why we have disclosure laws and why you hear the phrase, 'follow the money.' Even so, pinning down purposes can be difficult in all arenas."

"But in a system involving people," Kevin noted, "you may have different people with different purposes. How does that work out in terms of a purpose or function for the system itself?"

"Key point," Swen said. "The purpose of a system may not be what any single actor in the system intended. The function of a system may end up being something none of the actors wanted."

"How about an example?"

"Sure," Swen responded. "Think about a family involving a mother, father and teenager. In this particular family, you have a teenager who wants some independence and engages in various risky behaviors for a variety of reasons, including gaining acceptance from his peer group. You have a mother who is overly permissive, loves her son and is afraid to set boundaries. You have a father who also loves his son but is overly harsh and always coming down on his son for any little deviation from his expectations. The son reacts against his parents, at least in part, because of the mixed signals he is getting from his parents. The parents are fighting with each other because they can't agree on how to deal with the son. Nobody is happy with the other two people in the system and it does not function in the way anyone really wants it to. Obviously the situation is far more complex than I have portrayed it, but you get the idea."

"Yeah, that makes sense. But moving on and looking at these three things that make up a system—elements, interconnections and purpose—which of the three is the most important?"

"Well, Swen responded, "I'm not sure I like the question the way you put it. No one of the three is more or less important than another. That is not the way systems are. The purpose of a system, however, is the least obvious part and often is the primary determiner of how the system behaves. A change in purpose often will change a system profoundly."

"I'm sure you have examples of that in church situations."

"Oh, yeah. Lots of them. The ones I see tend to be gradual. The purpose shifts over time and often the shift isn't recognized by the people included in the situation. Given the number of churches that seem to be plateaued or in decline, you probably won't be surprised when I say that a lot of my examples are negative, but let me give you a positive one."

"Sure. Let's be upbeat."

"A church I have worked with recently has a Tuesday morning men's group that meets at six forty-five. They end sharply at eight because most of the guys have to get to work. The group has been around for a long time and has had a quite stable mode of operation and membership—usually about fifteen guys. While billed as a Bible study, the group probably has persisted over the years because of the social aspect. These guys like each other and have been reasonably open and honest with each other. About a year ago, a couple things happened that impacted the group. Three of the guys went on a 'Walk to Emmaus' weekend retreat that had a powerful impact on each of them. About the same time, four other men were part of a week-long mission trip to aid the recovery effort in a disaster area in a neighboring state. In the process, they were confronted with the poverty of some people in the area and also the spiritual dimension of life. Seven of these guys had what some of my secular friends would call a 'religious experience' and it spilled over into the men's group. Without any overt decision, the purpose of the group shifted. The amount of talk about sports, hobbies and recreation diminished and talk about the 'with-God' aspects of their lives increased. It became much more of what you might call a 'spiritual formation group.' The people who made up the group—the elements—and the way they related—the interconnections— were the same as in the past, but the purpose shifted. And as one of the guys in the group said, 'It just happened.'"

"I like your example," Kevin said. "And it points out how important the emotional side of all this is. It also makes me think of something that came to mind when you talked about the mother, father and teenager in conflict—family systems theory."

"Oh, yeah; that's another illustration of how pervasive systems are. I have a therapist friend who specializes in working with adolescents and she insists on working with the parents—and often siblings—at the same time. She says it is pointless to try to work with a troubled adolescent in a solitary setting. The kid is part of a system and you have to deal with the system—not just one element."

"And this applies to churches as well," Kevin added. "I attended a workshop a few years ago that was built around the ideas in a book by Peter Steinke called *How Your Church Family Works*. It was all about looking at congregations from the perspective of family systems theory."

"That's really important stuff," Swen said. "This way of thinking seemed to begin with a guy named Edwin Friedman who wrote a book called *Generation to Generation* that focused on family processes in churches and synagogues. He was basing much of his work on the family systems theory developed by a guy named Murray Bowen. A few years after Friedman wrote his book, Steinke expanded on his ideas and wrote the book you referred to, and as you know, it has had a wide influence—at least among people who theorize about such matters. I hope it is having a real world impact as well."

"Our conversation makes me realize how much connection there is between all of your systems ideas and what Steinke wrote about. But I'm getting the idea that you are moving beyond the emotional aspects of family systems to look at organizational matters more broadly."

"That's true," Swen noted, "but I want you to know that I am a real fan of what Steinke is promoting. It's just that there is even more to the story."

"I'm sure there is, and our conversation is making me think about Steinke's stuff. I wonder if I would see his approach differently after your input about systems?"

"Well, let me think about that connection some more, too," Swen said as his eyes drifted off to the side. "Whenever you look at a very involved situation, such as a congregation, you are looking not just at a system but at a complex mix of many intertwined systems and subsystems. And remember, we are talking about systems-thinking—that is, a way of thinking about what is occurring. You might say it is a mental model of what is going on—not a mechanical model." At this point Swen's pen was writing again, MENTAL MODEL. He obviously wanted to emphasize the point.

"It seems to me that Steinke's approach is to look at the emotional dimension of the total system," Swen continued. "As such, it is just one part of what is going on, but it is such a critical aspect that examining the situation from this perspective can yield powerful results. So I use this approach in what I do as well, but it is still just one aspect of the overall picture I am dealing with."

Kevin jumped in somewhat abruptly, "Oops, you said your calendar was open for the rest of the afternoon but unfortunately, mine is not. I need to leave to pick up my youngest from soccer practice and that's a bummer because we really haven't gotten into the issue we said we were going to talk about—how change can occur in a church from the top-down and the bottom-up?

"Sorry," Swen said, "I get carried away. But this may mean we need to get together again sometime and continue our conversation."

"That would be great. How about having lunch some day before long?"

"I would like that. I'm off on a trip next week, but there are some possibilities the following week."

Kevin was quick to agree. After a check of his calendar he said, "How about Wednesday?"

"Works for me. How about Goolsby's down on the corner of Main and Grand?"

"Sure, that's everybody's favorite. Could we make it eleven-thirty and beat the lunch crowd?"

"That's a plan," Swen agreed. "But before we head off, let me take thirty seconds to defend why I have pushed so hard on all this systems talk. In my mind, it is the key to making change in a church—in any organization for that matter—especially the bottom-up sort of change.

My men's group example is especially relevant here. You may recall that I said the group experienced a rather profound change and one of the members said, 'It just happened.' And that is probably true; it was not a planned change. That is the way systems are. Some systems people like to talk about *self-organizing systems*; others use the label *complex adaptive systems* to refer to the same thing. Whatever the label, it is about how systems can change—sort of from the inside-out—in ways that often are unpredictable, yet can be influenced from the outside. So, when we get together in a couple weeks I am ready to start right off talking about top-down and bottom-up change, mainly, of course, using the language of what I usually call *self-organizing systems*."

"I'll hold you to it," Kevin said and with a few quick affirmations of their new friendship and mutual interests, they headed off in their separate directions.

chapter 2

Emotional Systems

Waypoints

Emotional systems (a special case of systems-thinking) are a powerful tool for *thinking* about the dynamics of a church family. Among key concepts are the following:

Free-floating anxiety in a congregation is destructive and problematic but anxiety also can be a stimulator of positive change.

Thinking systemically (including attention to emotional dimensions) is crucial for guiding positive change in a congregation.

Triangulation within a congregation is a negative factor that should be avoided.

A pastor in the role of leader must be a keeper of the vision for the congregation.

IN THE THREE DAYS following his time at the conference, Kevin encountered a whirlwind of activity, much of it unanticipated. The conference day had been a great break from the usual responsibilities, including the budding friendship with Swen and the stimulating discussion about change in congregations. The unexpected death of a middle-aged parishioner the next morning required his immediate attention and, given the congregation's size and this woman's role in it, had a ripple effect on most everything else.

A few days later Kevin had a bit more time for reflection and began thinking about his discussion with Swen, particularly all that he had to say about systems. They had not gotten to the place he hoped to reach—a focused discussion on top-down and bottom-up change—but Swen had promised they would talk about it the next time they got together, so that was okay. His thoughts kept coming back, however, to the brief mention of emotional systems and the application of these ideas to families and congregations. In particular, he thought about the workshop he had attended a couple years ago that was focused on the ideas of Peter Steinke as described in his book, *How Your Church Family Works*. Obviously, Swen had read the book, not just attended a workshop about it, and Kevin was pleased that Swen had a similar positive response to Steinke's work on emotional systems in churches.

At this point Kevin probably would have started reading the book, but he didn't have a copy, and besides, he was more inclined toward getting ideas from presentations and conversation. It was a personal preference. When he did get into such a book, it went well but somehow other matters seemed to take precedence over such serious reading. Conferences, workshops and seminars, however, seemed to find their way onto his calendar more easily—and he did save the materials he acquired at such events. He remembered the notebook he received as part of the workshop and pulled it off the shelf. The workshop had been presented by someone other than Steinke, but the presenter was touting the "master's" ideas and had been effective in engaging the participants. Kevin reviewed the ideas in the notebook and began thinking anew about congregations as emotional systems.

As he browsed through the opening pages of the notebook, he was reminded of what Swen had said about emotional systems being just one of the many systems and subsystems operating within a congregation, but that they were especially important ones. He also reflected on what had been said about systems-thinking being so different from straight-line thinking. They are not the same whether you are talking about emotional systems or any other dynamic situation.

A key idea jumping out at him was that churches operate as emotional systems whether anyone recognizes it or not. In that sense, they are like family systems. People living together relate to each other on an emotional level; which is just the reality of any collection of people who interact with each other on a continuing basis. And what happens with any individual or pair of people is related to what is going on with everyone else who is part of the picture. What happens between person A and person B is related to what is going on with person C as well. It seems obvious when you say it, he thought, but so often people fall into thinking that the interaction between persons A and B constitutes the entire picture for those two people.

He was also reminded that churches are much more than their emotional processes, even though the emotional aspects are a very powerful portion of the whole. There are other processes including financial, intellectual, theological, and a host of others. And they all relate systemically.

The notebook reminded Kevin that the first part of the workshop had dealt with the nature of emotional systems—beginning, of course, with the notion that systems theory looks at the whole with a focus on the interrelatedness of the parts. They had spent considerable time contrasting straight-line thinking and systems-thinking.

The aspect of emotional systems that had intrigued him at the time—and still did—was the development of patterns of interaction. A dynamic is set up between a pastor and associate pastor, or between a music director and worship committee, or any other combination, that settles into an established form of interaction. They become repeated or patterned. As his mind moved from the pages of the notebook to his personal church situation, he thought about how he and the church board related to each other. Yes, there was a pattern to how they related to each other.

The next part to leap out at him from the notebook was the assertion that emotional processes are influenced by two forces—the need for people to be both separate and close. Certainly, this was the case for him and Susan. A good marriage obviously has many aspects of being close but at the same time there is a need for separation. The needs exist at the same time and part of having a good marriage is maintaining a balance of the two needs. The two needs are held in tension which leads to anxiety.

At this point, he recalled that this word, anxiety, had been prominent all through the workshop. He chuckled to himself as he thought that if Swen had been giving him this information over coffee, he would have been writing the word in bold letters on his napkin: ANXIETY. Anxiety is inherent in any relationship.

The workshop had a word for a person's capacity to maintain the two forces in balance: self-differentiation. Again he could imagine Swen's pen scrawling on his napkin: SELF-DIFFERENTIATION. This word was mentioned often during the workshop. Obviously a lot of the focus had been on this need for personal balance to keep anxiety at bay.

Kevin recalled that at first in the workshop he had been reluctant to buy into the idea that anxiety could be so central a concept in understanding human relationships, but by the time they had worked through lots of examples over the course of the day, he was on board. He thought about how he personally defined himself yet stayed in touch with others, how in his interaction with others he worked at maintaining their well-being without feeling inferior himself, and how he tried to be responsible for himself while simultaneously being responsive to others. He saw that it was an important balancing act and that a lot of people around him often did not do a good job of it. In particular, he thought of Henry in the men's group who always seemed to focus on himself.

As he looked more closely into the section on anxiety in the note-book, he saw again the claim that all systems of relationships become anxious. Somehow this seemed to be an overreaching claim, but he could not think of any counter examples. At a minimum, it had to be a very useful working hypothesis.

The next point was even less intuitively obvious. Anxiety was de-scribed as being free-floating. It can slip off from its place of origin and settle somewhere else. Here again, what was not immediately obvious in the abstract had numerous validating examples in his personal expe-rience. This page noted that the most likely place for this free-floating anxiety to settle was on people in the relationship network who were the most vulnerable or responsible. Within the congregational network, there were many vulnerable people, but the label of being responsible probably belonged to him as senior pastor more than anyone else and ex-amples were not hard to come by. Just last week, Jennifer, whose husband, Danny, has been slowly declining for the last two years with a combina-tion of diabetes and liver disease, suddenly launched into him about the deacons' lack of care for people in the congregation and his personal lack of leadership for this ministry and apparently for the church as a whole. It was especially disconcerting because she had always been one of his big supporters and suddenly it seemed like she had turned on him and would like to see him leave. He realized that the years of being the major care-giver for Danny were taking their toll. Her anxiety to some considerable extent was free-floating and had landed on him.

A related point was one he would want to talk about with Swen since it dealt with change in congregations. The point was that anxiety provokes change. Right on, he thought, but he knew anxiety is not always helpful when trying to lead change. The workshop materials agreed with this point, and in fact focused on it. They emphasized that though anxiety provokes change, when it reaches a certain level of intensity, it gets in the way of change. When the level of intensity in a system is high, a leader wanting to guide productive change has a tough job.

Attention also was given to chronic anxiety. In some instances, anxiety becomes a part of someone and is habitual. It is not helpful to the person who is fostering change, and inevitably is an obstacle to tackle. People with chronic anxiety typically are quite reactive but the contentious issue at hand is not the source of their anxiety or the reason for their reactivity. Kevin would have been happy to never see this kind of anxiety in the congregation ever again, but he knew that was unrealistic. The attack from Jennifer had produced a lot of anxiety for him, but he recognized that he understood much better the dynamic of the situation than he would have a few years ago. It was not just about him and Jennifer. He had to get beyond Jennifer's definition of the problem and look at the situation much more broadly.

The concluding point in this section of the workshop materials was key. When the focus is on blame and problems, personal relationships cannot change in a positive direction and heal. Imagination and redefinition of problems and issues is necessary to override the instinctive reactivity and automatic blaming. Thinking has to take over and replace the automatic processes. Given his experience with pastoral counseling, relatively limited though it was, he had no difficulty with this concept. People who are hung up on their problems and related feelings toward others have a great difficulty breaking out and moving in a positive direction.

The big insight from the workshop for him, however, had been the application of this concept to congregations. Examples had been presented of churches in decline that were so focused on their loss in numbers of people and dollars that they did not have the imagination to think positively about how to move forward and be part of advancing the kingdom. Their anxiety over the loss they were feeling was such that they focused on preserving everything in its current form—or attempting to return to some golden time in the past—and failed to be proactive and address a positive future.

The examples included descriptions of consultants working with churches to help them get beyond this barrier. Kevin was sure Swen would have been able to describe such examples as well. In fact, he could imagine him giving a detailed description of a congregation going through such a process. He knew these examples would include attention to the message of the New Testament and prayerful attention to how the

congregation could imagine a new future—not focused on their problems, but on how to advance the kingdom.

Kevin made a mental note to run some of these ideas by Swen
when he saw him again to be sure, but from the brief comments Swen
had made about related matters, he suspected Swen would agree with
the techniques Kevin learned in the workshop. One example had been
of a consultant working with twenty-four leaders of a church who were
caught in this problem mode. These leaders were placed in groups of four
or five people, asked to cite two or three problems in the church, and then
asked to redefine the problem without focusing only on the person or issue they had stated in the original problem. This approach helped them to
see matters as a whole and think about everything systemically. Again he
imagined Swen's pen scrawling on his napkin: THINK SYSTEMICALLY.

The workshop example included a list of nine questions that had
been posed to this group of leaders to help them move into the process of
self-definition. Four of the questions seemed especially helpful to Kevin:

Who in the congregation are the really motivated people?

If I were satisfied and happy, how would this situation look?

What is your vision?

What would it take to get you excited about investing yourself here?

Once they had completed this process of redefinition, they spent
time making plans for specific changes. Kevin recalled the workshop emphasized making specific plans. Vagueness was portrayed as a friend of
the status quo and an enemy of productive change.

At this point, Kevin's mind again drifted to the topic he wanted to
discuss with Swen: top-down versus bottom-up change. When redefining problems to have a proactive focus on positive solutions and to have
specific plans for achieving them, is change initiated in one of these two
directions more effective than the other? The more he thought about it
the more he concluded these principles probably were very important
whether you had a top-down or bottom-up focus. Yes, he thought, these
principles are important no matter which direction you are moving, but
it is worth seeing if Swen will want to argue about it with him.

As he flipped on to the next section of the notebook, Kevin was
struck again with how prominent the theme of anxiety had been in the
workshop. In this section, it was tied closely to the idea of reactivity. Reactors are problematic people because they are operating so much out
of their anxieties. They have difficulty controlling their anxieties. These
reactors are problematic in church families, of course, because they tend

to exercise a lot of control, usually in a negative way, limiting positive movement forward.

A big issue is the passivity and permissiveness of so many people who live side by side with the reactors in the church family. There are reasonably kind yet direct ways to address this negativity, but most people seemingly hold back and just let it go. Kevin thought of Warren who expressed his opinions quite freely in the Tuesday morning men's group. His negativity was fairly strong and he had no hesitation about expressing it. Others in the group were aware of it but rarely challenged him about it in any direct way. They didn't seem to let it influence them much on an individual basis, and if someone happened to mention it, it was usually dismissed with a comment such as, "Oh, that's just the way Warren is." In the interest of peace and harmony in the group, a live and let live approach prevailed. Yet, to some degree, it put a damper on new ideas and collective initiative about new outreach beyond the group. As Kevin thought about the dynamics within the group, he realized as a reactor, Warren had more of a commanding influence on the group than he had first thought—especially since there were a couple of other men in the group with similar attitudes. The others were not nearly as expressive, but their collective outlook had been a long-term constraining influence.

As he looked through this part of the notebook, he was reminded of his personal limitations in this regard. He did not like to confront people, in fact he dreaded it. He had a strong desire to be liked and confronting someone raised *his* anxieties. He also realized he had passive-aggressive tendencies and his way of dealing with conflict definitely did not lean toward direct confrontation. He sighed as he thought about it, realizing he had made some progress in this arena but still had a long way to go.

An item on *over-focus* jumped out of the page at him. He thought again of Jennifer. Certainly she was an example of someone who had over-focused. The notebook used the label *pursuit behavior* to describe what she had been doing. Yes, Jennifer's pursuit behavior was over-focused on him.

The materials noted that pursuit behaviors take various forms—not just behaviors like Jennifer's—the most obvious of which is rescue. This over-focus is manifest in efforts to rescue someone from some form of difficulty. Caring for others is of high value in any church family so it is easy to overlook the fact that reaching out to others—when motivated by the rescuer's anxiety—easily becomes counterproductive.

The form of pursuit behavior that grabbed Kevin's attention, however, was criticism. It was described as the most difficult form to recognize. He had not thought of criticism as a possible form of pursuit behavior, but as he considered Jennifer and her criticism of him, it was obvious that she was over-focused on him. Her anxiety had landed on him.

Attention was also given to secrecy as a form of anxious reactivity—private conversations that hold some things back from public view. Obviously, the material was not referencing the secrets of an intimate relationship—the sort of private discussion he and Susan had. But he thought of the parking lot conversations that were common after the board meetings at his former church. People who were not totally open during the meeting would air their thoughts and feelings with an individual or two who shared their perspective. They reinforced each other's views in opposition to the stance of the rest of the board. Such secrecy destroys trust.

The presentation on secrecy was tied to the idea of triangles. Here Kevin was on board—and had been well before attending this workshop. When he caught on to this idea, he saw triangles seemingly everywhere—both in his extended family and the church. One person having an issue with a second person would not go directly to this person to address the issue, but instead would go to a third person to address the matter, often with the hope that this third person would take responsibility for the matter.

Just last week, Gloria, their volunteer music director, came to him complaining about the way, Frank, the youth group leader, failed to encourage the youth to involve themselves in the church music groups. When Kevin asked Gloria if she had talked to Frank about it, he heard what he expected—the answer was, "No." When he suggested that she talk directly with Frank about it, she said, "I can't. He is so sure he is right about everything that he will just blow me off."

Recognizing how fragile Gloria was, and how brash Frank could sometimes be, Kevin approached the matter differently than in many other situations. He said he would be willing to be present when the matter was discussed but she would have to address the matter directly with Frank. Kevin said he would not be present for the purpose of taking either her side or Frank's, but if his presence made her more secure, Kevin was happy to help their communication. Gloria's anxiety probably was relieved a bit, but she was not totally comfortable with the appointment she would now have to arrange.

Kevin's mind jumped back and forth thinking about all the church situations he had faced that involved secrets, gossip, and all too often someone talking about an issue with a third person not party to the matter at hand. All of a sudden he was seeing in his mind Swen's pen scrawling: TRIANGLES, and because they are such a big deal, he could see him adding the word twice more for emphasis: TRIANGLES, TRIANGLES. Kevin was thankful that the issue of triangles and how to deal with them had come to his attention long before taking the workshop about emotional systems, but the workshop had helped him see how deeply embedded they are in typical church life.

After taking a phone call and getting a fresh cup of coffee, Kevin moved on to a new section of the notebook; it had to do with church leaders, particularly pastors, and the matter of vision. The focus on vision caused Kevin to think back on an early part of his initial meeting with Swen when he laid out the general notion of a system and said every system had elements, interconnections and a function or purpose. It was the function or purpose part of a system that came to mind when Kevin thought about vision. While vision could relate to new elements or interconnections within a system, in most cases, it centered on purpose. He thought of churches taking on a new sense of mission or a new direction in ministry. He also was keenly aware that vision is essential for a church to be all it is meant to be.

The central assertion in this part of the notebook seemed to be that the leader of an organization is the keeper of its vision. The vision has to be shaped and maintained by the leader. For a long time, Kevin had thought of a pastor as the vision-keeper for a church; this was not new. But the systems notions he had gotten from Swen had broadened this understanding a bit. Function or purpose was an essential part of a system and clearly the vision established and nurtured by the leader shaped this purpose. These concepts all integrated well with each other.

The concept of the leader as the vision-keeper had been expanded a bit for Kevin during the emotional systems workshop. The leader who performs this role successfully must be self-differentiated. There was that big word again. Such people manage their own anxieties well, maintain connections with others in the system, channel resources where they are most effective, and keep a steady course. Such a leader, largely as a result of his or her *position* in the system, is able to establish focus, maintain calm, and affect change in a desired direction. They are the key to positive change, whether top-down or bottom-up.

Because of the strength of their convictions, such self-differentiated leaders know themselves and where they are taking the organization. The reactivity of others does not shake them up easily. They establish realistic and specific goals. The strength of their convictions curtails their own anxieties.

One aspect of technique in this section caught Kevin's eye—the power of questions as an intervention in a system needing leadership. The right questions can bring out new insights, lead people to release their imaginations to see new possibilities, and challenge them to reach beyond where they thought they were stuck. Questions were also promoted as a way to get beyond group thinking and release the potential found in individuals. Kevin could see the potential of questions for himself as a pastoral leader and, as he thought about Swen playing the role of consultant in a church, it occurred to him that Swen probably used this technique often.

Suddenly another systems idea jumped out at him, although Kevin quickly realized that it was but a slight variation on earlier ideas. The point was made that if someone—the leader or another person—changed their behavior, it changed the system as well. How people function is a product of their personality and the environment in which they are located; they are interrelated. If they change how they function, the environment will change in some way as well.

Coming to the last section of the notebook, he saw a lot of attention to forgiveness, certainly a biblical concept. As addressed here, it was about restoring relationships. A caution was given about offering forgiveness to someone for the purpose of relieving our personal anxieties; it had to be more authentic and offered with a desire for a renewed relationship. The result is not just personal relief, but positive change for someone else and thus improvement in the system.

Kevin was reminded of a quick comment that Swen had made about his work as a consultant. He said he routinely asked the people with whom he worked to think about biblical concepts or stories that fit their situation. He wanted to bring theological concepts to the forefront and though he said he usually didn't see strong responses from people, he kept at it because it was so critical to life in a faith community.

After Kevin put the notebook back on the shelf, he leaned back in his office chair and began thinking about ideas stirred up by perusing the notebook that he would like to bounce off of Swen. Systems-thinking was powerful, and when applied to the emotional systems within a congregation, one was dealing with real potency.

chapter 3

Self-Organizing Happens

Waypoints

Self-organizing happens—including in social relationships. Wise leaders make use of this reality and are comfortable with the fact that these changes are not totally predictable. They deal with change as it emerges. Change on the micro level is especially important.

Relationships are key to making change. Tensions within these relationships, and differences between people, are productive sources of positive change. Differences are good. Patterns within these human systems are continually changing in unpredictable ways.

Three modes of intervention in a system are particularly useful for the person wishing to promote positive change:

1. One mode is to find points of influence such as people's sense of self-identity, their sense of purpose, and collective processes of relating to each other.

2. A second useful mode of intervention is to focus on significant differences. Where there are differences, change comes more readily.

3. A third mode of intervention is to focus on emergent interconnections, that is, ones in the process of changing. It is easier to channel change that is underway than it is to get change started.

A valuable leadership approach is loosening control of events and instead attempting to influence them as they are ongoing.

WHEN KEVIN STEPPED INTO Goolsby's and looked around, he spotted Swen sitting in a booth on the right side. He waved off the hostess headed toward him with some menus and headed over to greet Swen. After the usual pleasantries and getting their orders placed, Kevin launched into what was on his mind.

"When we agreed we would meet for lunch we also agreed that the first order of business would be talking about top-down and bottom-up change in a church, but there is another matter I would like to get out of the way first. Since we last talked, I went back and reviewed the materials from that workshop on emotional systems in congregations I attended. There's really a lot of good stuff there. I ended up making a list of what seemed to me to be some of the key points related to promoting change in a congregation and I wanted to run them by you to see what you thought."

As Kevin pulled out a sheet of paper and placed it on the table between them, Swen responded, "Sure, let's see what you have." The paper had a numbered list.

1. Think systemically.

2. Emotional systems are a special case of systems-thinking.

3. Anxiety can be a positive prod for change in a congregation.

4. It helps to focus on positive matters, not blame and problems.

5. The leader must be the keeper of the vision.

After studying the list for a while, Swen said, "I noticed that you said these were important items for you regarding fostering change in a congregation. Since I'm sure there was a lot of other stuff in the workshop, I'm trying to look at it from this perspective of change."

"Oh, yes," Kevin responded, "There were lots of other ideas such as the big ones about how anxiety is at the root of many relationship problems and how self-differentiation is necessary for a person to be effective. And besides these biggies, there were others such as the notion that anxiety can be free-floating and jump out and grab you, that openness and transparency really help a relationship, that passivity toward reacting people encourages their counterproductive behavior, and maybe most important of all, the need to avoid triangles."

"Yeah, triangles. Triangulation causes so many problems in churches." Swen went on, "I like your list. I especially like that at the top of your

list, you identify thinking systemically. That is the foundation of everything else."

"I figured you would appreciate that one. That one really doesn't
need any more comments. The one I thought you might want to comment on is the second one about emotional systems being a special case
of systems-thinking."

"Yes," Swen responded, "I occasionally encounter difficulty in getting people to relate the two, probably because the people who talk about
systems in a general sense tend to use different language and symbols
from the emotional systems people. The language I usually use in talking
about systems is elements, interconnections and function, as I described
last time. You can describe most any system that way. The language of the
emotional systems people tends to be different because they are zeroing
in one facet of a system to address the emotional interconnections. And,
of course, since anxiety is such a big part of how they understand emotional systems, they use symbols to describe this aspect of the interconnections between the elements in the system, that is, the people."

"I get it," Kevin said, "Although at first it took me a bit to tie it all
together. What I thought would be helpful to talk about is the role of
anxiety in the efforts you make to produce productive change in congregations. As I worded it on my list, anxiety can be a prod for change, but
I know it can also produce resistance to change. How do you handle the
fact that it can be both positive and negative?"

"It certainly can be both. I guess my experience as a consultant really helps me to see what is happening. Sometimes it can sneak up and
surprise me, but usually I can sense where anxiety is a help and where it
is a barrier, and deal with it accordingly. The helpful anxiety arises from
people's fears about the decline or stagnation in their congregation and
they are anxious for new life. It can be a powerful motivator for making
proactive changes."

"Yeah, I see that," Kevin said, "But what about the negative influence
of anxiety?"

"Well, that sort of anxiety is the hard stuff. This is especially true
for people who are stuck in the past. They often are quite happy with
their church as it is or they want it to return to some golden age of the
past. Their anxiety actually grows out of a sense of loss. They are griev-
ing over their loss and they fear that the changes being promoted will
produce even greater loss. They don't understand that they can't return
to a previous era and that the only way to keep or regain much of what

they want to have is to make some significant changes. Making change in this climate and reassuring people with these sorts of anxieties is a real leadership art."

"I'm sure these are real issues for you as a consultant, but the person who really has to deal with all that is someone like me—the pastor leading the congregation pursuing change."

"Right on," Swen acknowledged, "you guys have the tough part. In this case my role as an outsider is more that of a coach. Because of my experience I often can help a pastor better understand the dynamics of their situation and help them consider alternative actions to take. I do so especially through the questions I ask them in a coaching session."

"I'm sure this is helpful to a pastor-leader," Kevin said. "Being a lead pastor can be a lonely role at times and it is unsettling to deal with reactive people and the uncertainty of initiating change." Then stabbing his forefinger at the list, he asked, "What about the fourth item—focusing on the positive?"

"I couldn't agree more. Somehow, focusing on problems and setting out to fix them creates a difficult emotional tone. It seems to me it raises the level of anxiety—something the emotional systems people tune into. Focusing on positive matters seems to generate positive feelings about what potentially could be; it introduces an element of excitement."

Kevin nodded affirmatively, but added with a frown, "I easily see how this can be, but how do you focus on the positive when you are dealing with a church that is in decline? If they've got problems, how do you go positive?"

Swen smiled. "This is one of those places where I really feel good about what I can do when I come in from the outside. I like to get people to redefine their problems and focus on positive possibilities. It feels good to people to be able look to the future with anticipation for what God may be ready to do in their midst."

Kevin interrupted, "I can see that, but why do you have to come in from the outside to do that? Why can't the pastor do the same?"

Swen smiled again as he said, "Certainly a pastor can play that role. It is just that most pastors haven't had that much experience with introducing big changes and they usually find it beneficial to have an outsider like me help in the process."

"Well, could you say more about what you do in this role?"

"I already noted that one approach I use is to help people redefine their problems. Another approach I often incorporate into my work with

a congregation is something that has come to be called appreciative inquiry. In a nutshell, it is asking a congregation to reflect on their past and
identify times when they were excited about what was happening in the
life of their church. From there, the process goes on through several steps
to produce plans that have the potential of getting similar results within
the current context. It is a useful tool within a larger overall process. I
could talk a lot more about such work, but I think you have other matters
on your agenda today."

Kevin readily agreed, "Yes, so any comments about my last item—
the one about the pastor being the keeper of the vision?"

"Absolutely. This is one of the pastor's main jobs as a leader. Often
I see pastors help their leadership group develop a vision statement and
think their job of creating vision is done. They come up with a vision
statement that may be good—maybe something like 'serving and proclaiming Christ in the heart of the city'—but a statement of this sort—
even one more complete and eloquent—by itself isn't much of a start."

"So you are telling me that developing a vision statement was a
waste of time?"

"No, no," Swen insisted. "It's just that by itself it doesn't really create
vision. First of all, a vision really has to be specific if it is to be helpful.
It has to include specific goals. Secondly, everyone in the congregation
must come to understand what this vision is and have a sense of where
they personally are part of it. Someone in your role—the pastor—has to
be communicating this vision in multiple ways in all kinds of settings. It
must be included in comments from the pulpit—almost weekly—and in
various meetings, such as committee meetings, and in hallway conversations. The pastor needs to have thirty-second, three-minute and thirty-
minute versions of what some have come to call the 'stump speech' to
provide on a moment's notice. Obviously, such speeches are not possible
if the pastor does not have a detailed, sound vision."

"Well, that certainly goes beyond anything I have been doing to
promote vision in our congregation." Kevin was hesitant and suddenly a
bit more subdued.

Swen paused before responding, "Remember where I'm coming
from. I'm in the business of helping congregations change and set a new
course. You were summarizing some of the key principles of people
who try to understand congregations as emotional systems. My rather

assertive approach to vision grows out of my focus on change. Such assertiveness is not inherent in an emotional-systems understanding of a congregation."

"Okay, so let's get on with talking about change, but first, was there anything I left off my list of emotional systems principles that seems important to you from your perspective as a change agent?"

After a long pause, Swen finally responded, "Well, there is one thing that emotional systems people talk about that is of significance to me as a change agent; it is the fact that particular patterns of interaction develop among individuals in the system. Over time, people in a particular setting establish a certain way of relating and communicating with each other. These patterns appear to develop spontaneously. What is of special interest to me is that some such patterns tend to extend into other parts of the larger system. But talking about this is getting beyond what you were putting on your list, so let's hold that for later."

"In that case, maybe we are ready to move on to the topic we originally had in mind—top-down and bottom-up change." Kevin was showing a tad bit of renewed enthusiasm.

"Okay, I'm ready to go there," Swen said as he shifted position. "To address this topic in any depth, I need to talk about *self-organizing systems* or what some call *complex adaptive systems* and that will take a bit of explanation."

"I seem to recall you throwing out those labels before, but you didn't really explain them."

"Okay, I guess I better explain just what such a *self-organizing* phenomenon is. There are many examples in nature, such as ant colonies, but my preferred example, because it is so visual, is a flock of hundreds or thousands of birds, such as starlings, swarming through the sky as you actually may have seen for yourself or in a program on the Discovery channel. The flock stays together and moves as a unit even though it moves in seemingly unpredictable directions. The key point here is that this "system" has no leader of any kind. As the swarm moves around in the sky, birds that at one point are near the front of the flock are soon at the sides or back. And as the flock moves in an apparently random pattern, the leading edge of the flock keeps shifting. In all of this movement, however, the flock continues to move as a single unit in a highly coordinated manner. The complexity of such self-organizing as found in nature is far greater than can be conveyed with this one illustration, but it has been studied in detail and described in books and articles. One such book written in a popular or journalistic style is *Emergence: The Connected Lives of Ants, Brains, Cities and Software* by Steven Johnson."

"You said a couple of times that all systems have three sorts of things: elements, interconnections and function or purpose. If this huge flock of birds is a system, where is the purpose? It seems rather purposeless to me," Kevin insisted.

"Maybe you don't like the word purpose because it implies for you that someone or something external to the flock is controlling it—which of course is not the case. If you don't like the word purpose in this instance use function."

"Okay, so what is the function of this system?" Kevin wanted to know.

"Well, the birds stay together and operate together as one unit. That makes them very different from the same birds scattered randomly across the landscape. In that case, these birds would no longer constitute a system. You may be wondering why they operate this way, which is an entirely different question. Sticking together probably has some survival value for the birds so they operate as a system. For example, if a predator such as a falcon attacked, the flock probably would break apart as the falcon passed through, but the flock would immediately come back together again. But—and this is my key point—they operate together as a system and we don't really have to know why."

"Yeah, I think I get that," Kevin said, "and I guess you brought up this example because it is what you call self-organizing."

"Exactly," Swen responded. "There is no leader and no outside influence that makes them function as a system in this manner. The system organizes itself."

"Okay, so where does the other label come from? I think you said it was complex adaptive systems."

"The word complex should be fairly obvious in my example, although if we started talking about a colony of ants or a hive of bees, the complexity would be even more obvious. The word adaptive simply means that the system—all by itself—adapts to whatever circumstances come along. The falcon in my bird example, or a hive of bees adapting to changing food supplies. One variety of plants with nectar for the bees may have been located in one direction from the hive and now—a bit later—the plants that are in season for the bees are located in a different direction and most of the bees are going in this new direction to get nectar. It all happened without some leader bee saying it was time to change. And what happens next is unpredictable."

"Okay, that's simple enough," Kevin acknowledged, "but what does all of this have to do with people, or more specifically, congregations?"

"This is where it gets interesting," Swen insisted. "Research shows that this phenomenon is present in human social contexts as well—and these contexts include congregations. Changes occur that are not instituted by the formal leadership, but result from actions that take place at the "grassroots" level, yet become *systemic* changes. Changes may emerge that permeate a congregation, for example, yet were not initiated by the church leadership, and such changes may be positive shifts that enhance the health and spiritual vitality of the congregation."

Kevin jumped in quickly, "That pastor friend I mentioned last time—the one who says 'the sheep don't tell the shepherd what to do'—I think would be very nervous with what you are describing."

"You are probably right," Swen said with a chuckle, "but he probably squelches positive events in his congregation more often than he realizes."

"I think I see where you are heading. You are connecting the idea of self-organizing systems and bottom-up change!"

"Right on," Swen responded. "I think it is an excellent way to think about bottom-up change. As you are sensing, having change emerge in this way without being planned out by leaders at the top does make some leaders nervous. There are other leaders, however, who capitalize on it and that is what makes this topic so fascinating to me—and also very useful if I can get the pastors I work with to understand it. It is not something to be afraid of. It is something to use."

"It seems to me that somewhere I have heard of self-managing teams in the business world. Is that idea related?"

"I guess it would be," Swen responded. "My understanding of what is meant by that label is groups of people in manufacturing, development, or some other sector who are asked to work as a team and are given both resources and a charge to operate a process or develop a new approach. In other words, they are expected to work on their own without a lot of direction from above. So it probably is a matter of business leaders understanding that self-organizing happens and trying to capitalize on it."

"So you are just trying to apply this idea to churches?"

"I suppose so," Swen continued, "but for starters I was just trying to explain that self-organizing happens in systems without anyone trying to capitalize on the fact—or even recognizing that it occurs. Of course, as you seem to have sensed, I am big on making use of the phenomenon. Smart leaders recognize that it exists, is powerful and can be utilized for productive change, even though they do not know exactly what the end result will be."

"And I suppose that is what makes my control freak pastor friend nervous."

"Sure, he has a strong need to know in advance what will happen, but it can become self-defeating for a lot of reasons. It is hard to control a lot of people processes. Control can thwart a lot of positive events he is not even aware of, and leaders can't really know all the possibilities available within the people they are trying to direct."

"But I suspect this pastor would also have some questions you would have to take seriously." Kevin hesitated and continued, "I can imagine him asking if congregations are really complex adaptive systems, and if he became convinced that they typically are so, he would go on to ask if they should be."

"Those certainly are appropriate questions," Swen responded and then paused before continuing. "There probably are few institutions more top-down than the military, yet people who study organizations such as the U.S. military find within it a lot of self-organizing behavior. By contrast, people who study organizations would describe a congregation as a loosely-coupled organization. After all, it is mostly made up of volunteers and leaders who don't have a lot of leverage on the volunteers."

"That's for sure. There have been many times when I thought one of our programs would really take off if I could just give some orders with people responding, 'Yes, sir.'"

"So I don't think there are many people who would argue that actual congregations are tightly controlled in a top-down manner." Swen paused for a moment and added, "I imagine some people would argue that the Roman Catholic Church is a top-down organization, but in reality it is more loosely-coupled than most of us Protestants realize. Doctrinal statements certainly come from the top and personnel decisions may start there. Bishops are appointed from Rome and bishops try to control the process by which individuals become priests. Furthermore, even though most parishes have a council of lay people, they are only advisory to the local priest. The priest can make financial and personnel decisions as he sees fit. In spite of all of that, however, there is a lot of self-organizing that occurs within a given parish. Anyone who doubts this should talk to some lay people who are significantly involved in a parish, or talk to some women—you know, nuns—in one of the Catholic orders."

"I know enough Catholics that I don't doubt you on this one, but this still leaves the question of whether or not congregations should be so loosely-coupled."

"Let's be real," Swen said somewhat impatiently. "How could it be otherwise given human nature and how we connect with each other? God created us this way. And remember when we got together last time, I gave you my little spiel about Philip and others in the book of Acts. In the New Testament church, things happened both top-down and bottom-up."

"I sense I touched a bit of a sensitive point there," Kevin chuckled. "But I'm not one of those top-down control freaks, so we can move on. I think I may have kept you from getting where you were headed a moment ago, which seemed to me to be related to how you make use of the self-organizing character of congregations as you help them make positive changes."

"Exactly, and it is important stuff."

"So don't let me keep you from what you have to say about this self-organizing," Kevin interjected.

"Not a problem at all," Swen quickly said. "This was only a slight digression from where I was headed and it is all stuff I often have to address with pastors and congregations when I work with them. So I am used to it and also ready to move on. First of all, I wanted to make sure I was communicating the basic idea that self-organizing happens in essentially all human systems, aside from top-down direction. Self-organizing happens even in places where there is a lot of top-down control, although obviously a lot of top-down control limits it. But you are sensing where I am headed. My conviction is that a person who is leading change in a congregation must understand that the self-organizing phenomenon is fundamental to what is occurring and the leader of change needs to work with it."

"That sounds like a very firm conviction and one that is a building block for your approach as a consultant."

"Yes, and I make use of it all the time in my work as a change agent," Swen asserted.

"You know, the last time we met you had your pen out and were making notes about key points on a napkin," Kevin said. "Isn't this a point where you would normally be making notes for emphasis?"

"I guess it is," Swen chuckled as it pulled his pen from his shirt pocket. He took the paper with Kevin's list and wrote on it: SELF-ORGANIZING

HAPPENS. And then below it he wrote in scrawling letters: WISE LEAD-ERS USE IT. "I guess that summarizes a lot of what I have been trying to say."

"As I said before, I now see that self-organizing happens. After all, lots of unexpected things happen in our church. Unpredictable things happen in spite of all of our structures, committees, by-laws and what not. As I think about it, it seems that many of our procedures and much of our culture act to suppress self-organizing. But in spite of these re-straints, self-organizing happens."

"My experience says that what you sense is true of other churches as well," Swen noted as Kevin continued.

"I'm really interested in what you have to say about wise leaders using it. This is a new idea to me and I get the sense that it is really im-portant for you."

Swen pondered a bit before saying, "I tend to think of it from the perspective of an outsider—someone who comes in to help the leader—the pastor—use these ideas. I am using them myself as a consultant and, at the same time, trying to help the pastor incorporate them into the on-going leadership role."

"Yeah, I get that this is how you see your role and this is the way you operate, but I don't have much of a clue as to what this involves. You need to tell me more."

"Okay, we probably are at a good point for me to try to explain my-self in this regard, but it requires looking at some underlying ideas. To start with, I probably should distinguish between looking at what goes on in a congregation from the macro level and the micro level." At this point Swen had his pen out and was writing on the paper again: MACRO VS. MICRO and Kevin noted that micro was underlined.

"I see that you underlined micro; I take it you put your focus there."

"You got it. I think most church consultants tend to look mostly at the macro level, but I am convinced that the most effective and power-ful change processes are at the micro level. We are dealing here with the many relationships between people, the patterns of interaction unique to this particular congregation, the various new little ideas people try, and the customs that people follow. All of these things are interconnected and change can be introduced by influencing things at this level."

Kevin was frowning as he said. "I don't see how you can come into a congregation and start impacting all these little things and hope to get anywhere."

"This could get to be a fairly long story but I'll take a shot at it. I'll have to lay out some ideas that may be a bit involved. I'll start with my model of change, in other words, how I think about change. It is not a specific plan of action that I follow as a consultant, but how I think about what is going on in a congregation and how it can be influenced." At this point his pen was on the paper again, scrawling MENTAL MODEL.

Swen continued, "In contrast to a more traditional model of change in which it is assumed that a few variables determine what will happen, my model assumes that the variables are essentially innumerable and I need to look at this situation holistically. I am assuming that the direction the congregation takes is not determined by a few leaders but is mostly determined by the participation of lots of people and by what emerges from their interconnectedness. This means that what is about to happen is unpredictable and beyond my control. Relationships are key to what transpires, not because relationships are important so people will follow directives from above, but because relationships are empowering and are the source of so much of the new vitality that will emerge."

"Whoa, there is a lot packed into what you just said," Kevin interjected.

"Yeah, I know, but let me throw a couple other points into my model of change before I stop. Decisions are not just made on a rational basis— you know, data and facts—they grow out of the tensions in the congregational system and the emerging patterns of interaction. Finally—and with this I will pause—the leader cannot expect to control everything that is happening, but should set about to influence it."

"Okay, now that you have come up for air, how about using your pen again to list the key points on paper."

"Sure," Swen replied as he wrote: INNUMERABLE VARIABLES. "This is just another way of saying that reality is complex, thus that label I have used many times, complex adaptive systems."

As he wrote HOLISTIC on the paper, he said, "I'm saying you have to look at the whole system, not just some part, such as new programs you want to introduce: maybe a welcoming program, or a new management process, maybe a reconstituted board and a new committee structure, or a new target population you want to reach. You have to look at the totality."

"That makes me think of various new things we have tried or that some fellow pastors have tried in their churches. Often they don't make a big splash. You mentioned in passing a welcoming program. We started one a couple years ago—we like it and it continues—but I am not sure it has had a big measurable impact."

"Not surprising," Swen said. "There are so many other variables involved. For example, did visitors just find your church to be friendly, or did they make true friend there? You have to take account of the complex system holistically."

"Okay, what else did you list off when you described your model?"

"Well, let's see. I'm going to write CHANGE EMERGES. I think the next thing I mentioned was that you shouldn't expect the important changes to emerge because of directives from above; you should expect them to emerge from the interactions and relationships within the congregation."

Kevin interrupted, "This makes me think about the language you used last time to describe systems. I assume you could use those words here."

"Certainly, I talked about elements, interconnectedness and purpose. Any change in the elements—including people, the building, and intangibles—and the way in which they are interconnected, or any change in the purposes of the system, result in change in the system as a whole. In my model, change emerges."

"Okay, what's next?"

CHANGE IS UNPREDICTABLE, wrote Swen. "I think this one makes a lot of people a bit nervous—especially leaders of the take-charge type. They want to know ahead of time what to expect, most likely because they want to be able to control it. I like to encourage people to consider the possibility that the Holy Spirit is ready to do great and unexpected things in their lives. Although most people think this is how it should be in theory, in reality they often are afraid of it."

"Well," Kevin sighed, "I'm afraid this is part of the human condition—or maybe it is ingrained in our culture. I don't have many people in my congregation who talk that way."

"Sad, but true," Swen said as he wrote: RELATIONSHIPS ARE KEY. "As I said earlier, I am not talking about having good personal relationships in the congregation so people are ready to follow directives issued from the top. What I'm referring to are relationships that empower everyone and produce a new vitality that helps realize the purpose of the system. When I say that I do so with full realization that the purposes driving many congregations are not always the biblical ones we may claim in theory. So, one important role of pastors—and consultants—is encouraging these relationships to focus on appropriate purposes."

"So true," Kevin agreed. "That is a key aspect of my preaching and teaching and individual encouragement of people."

After a pensive pause, Swen went on. "The next item, as I recall, was that tensions are one of the causes of the emerging patterns of interaction in congregations." He scrawled: TENSIONS ARE GOOD.

Kevin looked closely as Swen wrote and exclaimed, "I'm not so sure about that. I'd prefer less tension in our congregation."

"Well, maybe it would help if I used the word 'differences' instead of 'tensions.' When everybody is the same, things can be pretty dull. Differences in people produce some of the most fruitful outcomes. A richness of outcomes often results—and they also usually are unpredictable. And wherever you have differences, you have some tensions. That is why I said tensions are good." With that, Swen crossed out tensions and wrote differences in its place. The scribbled paper now said DIFFERENCES ARE GOOD.

"Yeah, I like that better, but I do get your point. As I recall you had one more point, something about control."

"Actually, it may be more accurate to say it was about not controlling." This time the pen left these words on the page: INFLUENCE NOT CONTROL.

"Somehow I imagine this is a big one for you," Kevin said.

"Yes, it really is. It is key to understanding how to promote productive change in a self-organizing system. Most people seem to have bought into the idea that you make change by creating specific plans and then setting the wheels in motion to produce those specific outcomes. The control idea seems to be deeply embedded in our culture, including the church culture."

Kevin asked, "So, how is influence used to make change?"

"Let me give you one example. We talked earlier about the pastor being the keeper of the vision in a congregation. This one is key. The pastor influences change by keeping the vision of the congregation in front of them. That is one part of a much larger picture. There are lots of ways to influence change without controlling it."

"You have convinced me that change can be influenced, not just controlled," Kevin said, "But somehow it seems we are talking about a matter of huge dimensions—this business of promoting change from your perspective of seeing congregations as complex adaptive systems. I'm not sure I've got much of a handle on it."

"Well, being an agent of change is not simple, but maybe I could give a thumbnail sketch of how I go about promoting change from the perspective of understanding congregations as complex adaptive systems— or as I have sometimes labeled them, self-organizing systems. Is it okay to start from sort of a theoretical perspective? I think I need to explain an underlying rationale before going into specific actions."

"Sure," Kevin responded. "Go for it."

"I'll start by looking at one of the three components of a system, namely interconnections. Patterns develop in the interconnections of a system. You may recall that when we were talking about emotional systems, I said I was especially interested in the fact that patterns develop in the way in which any two people interact with each other. I went on to say that my interest in such patterns went far beyond the patterns that emerged for two individuals and extended into the entire web of such patterns with a broader system such as a congregation. Within a congregation, of course, such interconnections are almost innumerable. Second, there are numerous elements in a congregation and they are of many types. Such elements include people, physical space, rules of behavior—both informal and formal, such as bylaws—church income and intangibles. All of these elements change over time. In addition to the ongoing changes in the elements of the system, the third component of a system, purpose, can change as well. Most congregations have multiple purposes—both in the total system and within its various subsystems— and, as with elements, they are not constant over time. So my basic point is that patterns inevitably develop in congregational systems and these patterns are not constant." As Swen had been talking, his pen had been active as well. He had started by writing one word on the paper and he now added a second word so it said: PATTERNS CHANGE.

"Somehow this makes congregations sound very fluid, but my experience makes me think of them as being quite static."

"I hear you," Swen responded. "Many congregations are relatively static, especially those that are plateaued or in decline, but even in those cases, changes in patterns are taking place. To a lesser or greater degree it is going on all the time."

"Somehow I am beginning to think that this business about ongoing change in patterns is related to the work you do—what you seem to want to call being a change agent."

"You've got it," Swen replied with obvious enthusiasm. "I like to think of myself as being an agent of change by influencing the patterns in the congregational system and helping the pastor and other leaders do so as well. Note that I said influence the patterns, not control them." As he said it, he pointed to the paper where earlier he had written: INFLU-ENCE NOT CONTROL. "As a change agent I am attempting to influence these patterns; I can't control them."

Kevin quickly pointed to the place on the paper where earlier Swen had written: CHANGE IS UNPREDICTABLE. "You have emphasized how so much is unpredictable here and now you are emphasizing again that you aren't trying to control things, only influence them. How can you go into a congregation and assure them that if they take you on as a consultant that they can count on getting certain outcomes?"

"I can't and I don't want to," Swen said quickly. "People who think that way commonly are thinking of change as being a top-down process and like to think in terms of control rather than influence. Certainly I do some things at times that tend toward the top-down direction, but by and large, I am approaching things in a bottom-up manner. First off, I need to help the people employing me understand the dynamics of change so we can set expectations together that are realistic."

"I imagine it is not easy to establish this as the basis for a working agreement. After all, we have had a lot of conversation in getting to this point."

"True indeed. A common way for a consultant to work with a con-gregation is to come in and do something often called a church health survey, or simply a church survey, to help them understand who they are at the moment. I think this is a good beginning point and I often do it myself, although what I use is more sophisticated than a lot of such surveys. But that is only a beginning point for me and to go much beyond it we have to start dealing with systems ideas and begin our work together on that basis. "

"Wow," Kevin said as he leaned back. "This is giving me a new per-spective on change in congregations, but it is also raising a lot of ques-tions. I guess a lot of them boil down to one simple question. Given how you understand congregations and change, how do you go about making change, or I guess I should say, influencing change?"

Swen seemed to take a deep breath and he paused a bit before con-tinuing. "You are moving this conversation on to another huge topic. I think I have to begin by being somewhat theoretical or abstract again."

"Fine. That approach has been helpful so far."

"As I've already at least hinted, I set out to influence the emergence of new patterns in a congregation, but before I go there, let's be sure I have given a sound definition of a self-organizing system. It is a system in which there is a tendency to form new patterns and even structures—for example, changes in some of the elements in the system—simply as a result of its own internal dynamics. These new patterns are not the result of something that happens outside the system. They just emerge from what is going on inside the system itself."

"Okay," Kevin said, "that's consistent with what you said before, but how about a specific example within a congregation?"

"Sure, how about this. The youth director of a church has a growing conviction that it is important for the youth to become mission-minded and decides to pursue setting up a week-long summer mission trip next year. The youth director was the source of the idea and takes steps to initiate plans with the potential of realizing the desired results. Of course, the youth director is part of a system and there are lots of possibilities as to the origin of this conviction. It may have come from listening to many weeks of sermons, or from studying the scriptures, or spending lots of time in silence and contemplation, or any one or more of several other possibilities. Going forward, lots of other things will happen, such as seeking the support of the senior pastor, taking a plan to the board for its approval, getting the support of the youth and their parents, beginning a fund-raising process for the trip, and the list goes on. It is possible that this mission trip could become an annual event. The inner dynamics of a system can lead to new patterns."

"It is easy to see that all kinds of things of this sort could be happening in a congregational system," Kevin added. "I'm with you."

"Well, I also should note," Swen continued, "that even as a new pattern is emerging, the interconnections in the system are being influenced by old patterns such as board authorization, parental permission and support, insurance requirements and so on. These new patterns are both the result of old patterns and the cause of some future ones, depending, for example, upon the outcomes of this youth mission trip."

"Okay, I'm with you. This seems pretty obvious. My question is about how you use all of this to make changes in the system. You say you are a change agent, but how do you do it? Or does that come under the category of trade secrets you can't divulge? "

"Hardly," Swen laughed, "But after I describe more of what I do, I can imagine you saying that I just go into a church and muck around and hope for the best."

"What, you don't have a detailed, scripted plan?" Kevin feigned shock.

'Oh, I have a plan alright. It's just that it is quite fluid with lots of options."

"Okay, let's hear about your loosey-goosey approach then," Kevin responded with a chuckle.

"Well, in all seriousness, given the dynamic and evolutionary nature of self-organizing systems, the path forward for the change agent is not crystal clear, but I can describe what I usually call modes of intervention. They are modes of attack, or entry points, for influencing the emergence of new patterns and structures. I put them in three categories. These modes of intervention are not mutually exclusive so it may be best to think of them as three different perspectives on intervening."

Kevin noticed that Swen's pen was out again and he was writing on the paper: POINTS OF INFLUENCE, as he continued, "The first one I describe as finding points of influence in the system, places where change potentially will occur if I exert the right influence. Some call them containers, but I usually don't use this term. These points of influence are not just physical things, thus my dislike of the other term."

"I'm sure you aren't surprised that I would like some examples."

"Of course," Swen went on. "I've got lots of them. I'll start with a couple of physical ones, such as a suite of offices. How the offices are configured with respect to each other influences the interconnections between people. Or think of a classroom. You would expect the nature of the interconnections in a classroom where all the seats are arranged in rows facing forward to be quite different from one where all the seats are arranged in a circle."

"I have a hunch there are other points of influence you are more interested in."

"Yes, how about someone's sense of self-identity? There are many sorts of professional identities that people have and they may interact with other identities they have as family members. And to what extent is the sense of self-identity that of a disciple, or follower, or apprentice, of Jesus?"

"This could be profound," Kevin said, "And I imagine there are lots more points of influence."

"Sure. Think about the culture of a congregation, that is, their values and beliefs, not just doctrinal beliefs, but beliefs about how life should be lived and all kinds of other things." After a pause he continued. "There are organizational points of influence. The church board that operates a committee structure under themselves will be different from one that instead has ministry teams reporting to them."

"And there are more?"

"How about procedures and rules as points of influence? An intervention point may be the financial rules followed or it could be the procedures in place—or not in place—for protection of at-risk persons."

"Another one occurs to me," Kevin interjected. "Given our earlier discussion of purpose and your emphasis on pastor as vision-keeper, I imagine those are places you would sometimes want to intervene."

"Absolutely. Such points of influence are important ones for me. Helping a congregation to clarify its purpose and coaching a pastor on how to be a keeper of the vision are important points of attack."

"That's enough that I can't really expect more examples. These help give me the picture."

"Okay, but let me say something about how points of influence vary. Some points of influence, such as the central purpose of a congregation, or a dynamic leader, tend to pull in other elements or interconnections so the influence of this point may be large. Likewise, similarities in gender, culture, and various commitments tend to strengthen a system. On the other hand, some points of influence tend to constrain the system and limit the emergence of new patterns. So a change agent tries to be very discerning in selecting key points of influence."

"The picture I am getting," Kevin said, "is one with lots of components. In fact, it seems that these points of influence may overlap each other."

"Absolutely," Swen responded. "Potential points of influence are not mutually exclusive."

"You warned me that this would be a little theoretical or abstract, but it is not that bad. Even so, how about an example of a point of influence you selected and worked with in a congregation?"

"Sure," Swen said and paused to think. "Here's one. I was working with a congregation that seemed to have considerable difficulty getting off the dime and getting new ideas implemented, even though they had a lot of innovative and imaginative people. Putting a new idea into practice seemed to be really hard. The point of influence we looked at was the decision-making process in the congregation. I'll skip over everything that happened along the way, but the outcome was a reorganized governance structure that included replacing the committee structure under the board with ministry teams—no more committees made up of people not directly involved in a particular ministry that approved the decisions of other people who were doing that ministry. The ministry teams were made up of people—again mostly volunteers—who were directly involved in doing that ministry. Collective decisions were still made, but they were made by people with a direct stake in them. That change by itself did not revolutionize everything, but it was a key part of an important climate shift."

"Your point of influence in that case seemed to be the place where the key change was made. Is that typical?"

"I'm not sure, but probably not. And on top of that, changes do not always have the expected outcomes, and furthermore, just giving attention to an issue often causes the system to adapt in subtle ways that don't involve formal decisions."

"Am I right in thinking that you must have a lot of tolerance for ambiguity?" Kevin asked with a smile.

"Probably so," Swen laughed. "It may not be an essential characteristic of a person in my business, but I think it helps me be more effective."

After both of them resisted the server's attempt to entice them to order the dessert special, peach cobbler, but allowed her to refill their coffee cups, Swen continued. "I said I would describe three modes of intervention that I use and so far I have only mentioned one. Here is a second one. I like to focus on significant differences within the system." At this point, his pen was on the paper again writing: SIGNIFICANT DIFFERENCES.

"What kind of differences are you talking about?"

"These are differences within a system between elements, interconnections or purposes, but more often elements. The bigger the differences, the more likely they are to cause adaptive changes. So I am looking at them as points of intervention."

"I'm sure you are surprised that I would like some examples."

"Of course," Swen continued. "Many of the most important ones are value issues, but let me first give you examples that are more obvious. You may have differences in the educational level of your ministry staff, one with an M. Div. degree and another possibly with only a high school diploma. And you have differences in level of expertise—a worship leader with great musical ability, for example, and someone else who is tone deaf. And you have differences in power level—the senior pastor on one hand, and the leader of the youth volunteers on the other."

"Hold on here," Kevin objected. "The pastor doesn't always have that much power. I really came to realize this about a year after I came to this church. There is a woman—Martha is her name—who wields enormous influence. Others seem to take a cue from her and if she is not supportive of an idea about a matter of substantial importance, it probably is going nowhere. She was a key member of the group that formed this church with the founding pastor. She is highly respected and has strong opinions, even though she is not obnoxious about how she expresses them. It took me a year before I came to understand this."

"So what else is new?" Swen laughed. "Doesn't most every church have an informal power structure of some kind? When I talk about power levels, I'm talking about both formal and informal power. My point is that such differences may be worth the attention of a change agent. And these differences are not bad; they just exist and are worth attention."

"I'm surprised you didn't say something about the fact that this particular person is a woman."

"Could it be the fact that this person is so powerful—and smooth about it—caught you unaware because she is a woman? No, you don't have to answer that," Swen added with a laugh. "But it does bring up another example of a significant difference, gender. And of course, we can throw in others such as the socio-economic level of people, and race. I know we like to think that such factors should not influence what happens in a church but we are human, plus—and I think this is important—such differences do exist. Again, they just are—not necessarily good or bad."

"You are making me think about race because our church—like most churches—does not have a lot of diversity in this regard. Our community is much more diverse than we are."

"And where you do have such diversity in a congregation," Swen added, "this diversity is often both one of the strengths of the congregation, as well as one of the points of tension. So it shouldn't be surprising that such a difference would be significant to the change agent who is looking for intervention points where adaptive change can be fostered."

"I think I'm getting the message, but I'm waiting for you to say something about values. You seemed to indicate they were of great importance, but you haven't gotten there yet."

"Sure," Swen said, "I think I can illustrate their importance with just one example—differences in people's preferences regarding style of worship."

"Oh yeah. In a previous church, the music war was in full swing. These differences were a big deal."

Swen sighed and paused a bit before continuing. "Obviously, you were experiencing differences there that had negative consequences, but such differences aren't always bad. I want to look for significant differences whether they are problematic or not. Let me give you an example of a positive episode related to worship."

"Go for it. After my experience in that church, I am happy to hear stories about worship that are positive."

"Actually, in one sense, this situation really was fairly positive to begin with. The church had both so-called contemporary and traditional worship services—one at nine o'clock and the other at ten thirty. People generally were quite satisfied. The fact that the services were so different from each other, however, made me consider intervening. I will spare you the full story because it is really long—it extended over more than a year. It was not just long; it was intensive. In the process, most everyone explored in depth what constituted a positive worship experience for them. It was also a very hard process; some are not so sure they would want to go through it again. But the final outcome was embraced by the large majority. It is a blended form of service that incorporates elements of both prior orientations, as well as other new aspects. The former contemporary service was not really contemporary—it was stuff from thirty years back at least. And the traditional service was stale as well. The congregation learned a lot about worship and there was another benefit. The same approach is used in both the nine o'clock and ten thirty services and now people are not so locked into one particular worship time. What time people attend is more fluid."

"Your story sounds great," said Kevin, "but I'm curious how you brought about all these changes."

"I want to be cautious about how I respond because the way you asked the question makes me wonder if you are thinking that somehow we came up with a plan for a blended service and found a way to put it in place. That emphatically is not what happened. The changes emerged from within as a result of the process. It was not a plan initiated from the outside. In other words, this complex congregational system operated in an adaptive way. Nobody was thinking it was what every church should do, but it was what they wanted to do."

"That's helpful. It gives me more of a sense of what you mean by a complex adaptive system."

"Maybe it is time for me to move on to my third mode of intervention then," Swen said.

"Yeah, go for it."

As Swen began to talk, his pen went to the paper again and wrote: EMERGENT INTERCONNECTIONS. "I am looking for interconnections—which, in this case, mainly means relationships between people—which are in the process of changing, or possibly have the potential of changing. One obvious example today is the rapidly increasing use of social media—Facebook, Twitter and such. But obviously the interconnections between people in a congregation are much greater than social media. So, I am taking into account lots of different ways in which people relate. There are things such as letters, e-mails, memos and written reports, of course, but there oodles of contexts in which people have face-to-face interactions—both formal and informal. There are also phone conversations."

"So, you are looking at ways in which people exchange information, right?"

"Yes, but more than that. There is a strong affective component to most interactions. Some is affirmation and obviously there is criticism as well."

"How about interconnections that aren't such a matter of human relationships?" Kevin asked.

"Materials of various kinds are exchanged, such as lesson plans for a class, but one that gets lots of attention would be financial transfers. Finances seldom are totally under the radar and often they generate considerable emotion. Financial procedures in a congregation generally are fairly fixed and stable, but they still are candidates for being emergent."

"You gave congregational examples of the other two modes of intervention. How about one for emergent interconnections."

"Sure," Swen responded. After thinking for a moment he said, "I'll describe a church board I worked with. They worked through their business very thoroughly and carefully with little rancor, but most members were not enthusiastic about their service on the board. In fact, when most finished their term on the board they did not want to sign on for another term. As is true for most new board members, they began their terms with expectations that it would be a positive spiritual experience. Before long, they began to think there was nothing much spiritual about it and that it was basically a series of tedious meetings. I zeroed in on the interconnections within the board as having emergent possibilities."

"You're not going to tell me that serving on the board was turned into an uplifting spiritual experience, are you?" Kevin asked with a little laugh laced with a touch of cynicism.

"Yes, I am," Swen asserted. "Now people are most happy to sign on for another term and they talk about it as a positive spiritual experience"

"Okay, I guess I have to accept that, but I am wondering what happened. On second thought, I imagine you will tell me it was a long process and it emerges from a process. Aren't you impressed that I'm catching on? But at least give me a brief description of what it means to serve on the board now."

"Sure, and let me give you a hint of how it came about. The senior pastor was the key in this one. Under their church polity, he was the leader of the board. Through the coaching process with him, I encouraged him to experiment with some changes. At the end of this period of time the board operated in a different manner. No reports were given orally; they had to be in writing. They were not discussed unless there was a specific need. They had a consent agenda which included everything that did not need a decision. He placed many items on the consent agenda and they were never discussed unless someone specifically requested it be moved off of the consent agenda. Otherwise, it was just entered into the minutes. A few changes like this and the business of the board was handled in a different manner that was more expeditious."

"Are you telling me," Kevin asked, "that such changes in how business was handled dramatically changed members' attitudes toward being on the board? It is a little hard to believe."

"You haven't let me finish the story. Less time was spent on board business now but they actually spent more time together as a board. The most important change was that the pastor now led substantial sessions of Bible study and prayer with the board. In addition, he regularly brought up ministry topics that related to the board and the ministry of the church. They were not matters that needed a decision of any kind—at least not in the immediate future—but they were fundamental issues that related to the ministry of any church."

"That's fascinating."

"The point of my story, of course, is that the changes emerged from a somewhat extended process in which the pastor engaged the board in discussion of what he was doing and got their agreement on trying various ideas over a period of time. He did not suddenly introduce a master plan of how the board was going to operate."

"I think I'm getting it," Kevin said. "Making change as you see it, is a fundamentally different process than making change from the top down."

"For sure. Modes of intervention are not of interest as means of finding ways to manipulate or control the system. They are of interest for finding ways to influence the system—to encourage adaptive change, much of which can't be predicted in advance. Of course, to influence such change, one often has to let go a bit and give up some control."

At this point, Kevin took the pen and as he wrote, said, "Although I am not totally sold on it, I think one of your key messages is that this kind of leadership means you will be losing control of what happens." As he talked he wrote on the paper: LOSING CONTROL.

With a chuckle, Swen said, "Not quite. It is not so much a matter of losing control, but giving up some control." With that, Swen took the pen from Kevin's hand and made a little change to what Kevin had written. He placed a caret next to the O in losing and above the little inverted v wrote another O. The edited phrase now said: LOOSING CONTROL. "It is not a matter of losing control, but affecting the system somewhat differently by loosening up control. And it is not just a matter of loosening up control and doing nothing else. It is a matter of leading by influencing the system to adapt itself in positive ways." As he said this, he added another item to the paper: BECOME A PASTOR-LEADER WITH INFLUENCE.

Kevin got a pensive look on his face, hesitated, and then said quietly, "As I recall, our original conversation started with some of my puzzlement about top-down and bottom-up change. I think I now understand more about bottom-up change and how it can be promoted by influencing the system. Influencing our congregational system is something I do to some extent, but I am a long way from mastering the art, and I have lots of questions about how to influence it. One of the points you made that has stuck with me is the need for a pastor to cast vision, but that means I need to have a sharp vision of where I think the church should be going."

"I think you have put your finger on it. What vision do you have and how will you help the congregation and its leaders develop a vision that is authentically biblical and guided by the Holy Spirit?"

Both of them paused at this point, seeming to sense that their lunch-time conversation was coming to a close. Kevin broke the brief silence by saying, "I really appreciate having the chance to talk about all of this. Your input has been very helpful and I have a lot to think about."

Swen was quick to respond. "This conversation has been a pleasure for me as well. I don't often have a chance to sit and talk about what I do with someone who isn't a client. This was more of a friend-to-friend conversation."

"I'm glad you used the word 'friend' because it has felt the same way to me. Sometime before long, I hope we have a chance to get together again, maybe in a setting that isn't so focused on business."

"Yes, if you see a good opportunity for us to get together, give me a call."

chapter 4

Goals Are Determinant

Waypoints

Reflecting upon the goals of the church is important. A fundamental goal of the church is disciplining people, i.e., aiding God's work of forming followers of Jesus. A disciple:

- is a believer;
- is obedient to God in all things;
- sees discipleship as an essential aspect of being a believer;
- is a person for whom Jesus is their model;
- has faith in the love of God and his purposes;
- has love for other people;
- serves other people;
- follows his or her gifting and calling;
- has a special concern for the down and out—the outcasts of society;
- lives by particular norms and commitments—different from society as a whole;
- disciples other people in partnership with others in the church.

Pastors are pulled in many directions, for example, needing to provide both pastoral care and leadership for the congregation. In all of this tension from multiple goals, however, the primary goal must remain primary.

THE WEDNESDAY LUNCH WITH Swen had come in the midst of what, for Kevin, was a rather ordinary week. Sermon preparation, a committee meeting, dinner out one evening with Susan, attending to some church members wanting individual time, a late afternoon soccer game at the nearby school and other typical activities finished out the time prior to the usual full day on Sunday. Monday was his Sabbath, a day to play and pray, as he often told others he understood the biblical expectation to be.

In the days following the lunch with Swen, Kevin had thought often about various parts of their conversation. It was not a concentrated time of reflection, but snatches here and there between the week's events. On Monday, his mind drifted back to it again. He usually tried to avoid concentrated thinking about church matters on Mondays, but somehow this was a bit different. It was not dwelling on the nuts and bolts of his responsibilities, but more a matter of reflection about church generally and the biblical picture of it.

After a leisurely hike—including some "praying while walking"— through the nearby open-space area, he stopped at a favorite reflection spot. It was a small rise that had as much of a vista as was available in the area. It was a good spot since the log he usually sat on had a tree next to it that served as a back rest and he could sit in the sun—a good thing at this time of year.

The various reflections of the past few days seemed to come together as he settled on the log—a bit like waking from a lengthy sleep and finding that many thoughts and events of the previous day had coalesced into a coherent perspective. At least that was how it struck him at first, but as he continued his reflection he realized that what had coalesced consisted of questions as much as answers.

His mental processes of the last few days kept coming back to the differences between top-down and bottom-up attempts at changing a congregation. The conversation with Swen had expanded his understanding of both, including more appreciation of how they were different from each other. Even though Swen clearly was most interested in bottom-up changes, he appreciated both and asserted both were appropriate and necessary at some point in a congregation. Kevin realized in the past he had not given much thought to personally leading change in a congregation other than in a top-down manner. He may have been engaged in more attempts to influence change from the bottom-up than he realized; he just had not thought of what he was doing as being an attempt to make change in the church. Swen had opened up new vistas for him but he was not sure they were internalized enough to be the basis for his leadership of a congregation.

The truly intriguing part of the conversation with Swen was about complex adaptive systems. That label spoke more to Kevin than the other one Swen used, self-organizing systems, because he had no need to be convinced of the complexity of a congregation. The adaptive part was what was so intriguing, the idea that change just happens without outside intervention; it's natural and it can be positive. On second thought, maybe the idea of calling it self-organizing was good; adaptive and self-organizing were labels for the same phenomenon.

As he relaxed in the sun and gazed out over the nearby tree tops, his thoughts turned more to the nature of the church, not as a system, but more from a theological perspective. There had always been a tension for him between the biblical metaphor of the church as the body of Christ and the contemporary conception of the church as a social institution. He didn't have any hesitation about the biblical metaphor, it fact it was exciting to him and a motivation for his work as a pastor. It wasn't just that seminary had convinced him of it, his experience as a pastor reinforced it. The institutional aspects, however, came crowding in from many directions. It was the reality of much of what he had to deal with daily.

Kevin had a couple of pastor friends who seemed to thrive on the institutional aspects. They seemed to do their preaching and other pastoral duties well enough, but what really got their juices flowing was being the leader of an organization. Budgets, committees, growth plans, schedules and such seemed to be part of their DNA. Kevin dealt with such matters adequately, but there was often a nagging concern that they were getting in the way of his ministering to Christ's people. The conversation with Swen had brought some of these latent concerns to the surface in a renewed way.

Somehow these concerns seemed to be related to his questions about how to be the leader of a congregation which he was coming to understand as being a complex adaptive system. These questions had been stirring in his mind more than anything else these last few days. He had some glimmering thoughts about the similarities between being pastor to a group of people and being a leader of change in a self-organizing congregation. There were some connections here and he hoped that over time he would get some clarity about what they were, as well as the role all of this would play in his job as a minister.

The emphasis that Swen repeatedly placed on establishing a vision for a congregation—as well as keeping it continually before them—had stayed with Kevin. He agreed that the pastor should be the primary person to do so, but was not so sure establishing the vision for a congregation was as simple as it might seem. He had been down this road before and the experiences he recalled in several congregations were not as uniformly positive as he would have hoped. He was aware of a number of processes used to reach collective visions, but he was not so sure of the end product.

In trying to sort through his uncertainly about this matter of vision, he thought of discussions among some of his fellow pastors about a proper vision for their congregation. It was clear that most congregations have done a shoddy job of reaching closure on even a rudimentary statement about where they are headed. He concluded that a fair number of congregations have formulated a concise and simple statement of purpose—what a lot of people call a mission statement—but few have a vision statement that would meet Swen's criteria. Given his emphasis on clarity as to specific outcomes, Kevin was doubtful that he had ever been party to creating the kind of vision statement Swen had in mind. Vague generalities seemed to be the order of the day.

Kevin also was very much aware that the Christian church in the developed world—and specifically the U.S.—is in flux. He realized most mainline denominations are in rather steep numerical decline and are conflicted over some divisive issues. He wasn't so clear about what the issues are in the evangelical denominations—they seemed more ambiguous—but he sensed concerns about cultural conformity, differences over the role of women, ambivalence toward the pursuit of growth measured quantitatively, and an unease about being captive to consumerism. When he talked to fellow pastors of various persuasions, he didn't get the sense of commitment to clear goals for the church, at least as far as he could see. This matter of church goals had nagged him for a long time and the discussion with Swen about vision had only served to heighten his concerns about a lack of clarity.

For a moment, he thought of the possibility that an outsider such as Swen, in his position as a consultant, could help him and his congregation in this regard but quickly realized that was not Swen's role—even though such people were skilled in helping a congregation clarify what they themselves perceived their goals to be. In his experience, however, the understandings of individuals in a congregation varied considerably

and consensus did not come quickly. His fleeting thought about the possibility that a consultant could help achieve a clear and unambiguous
sense of direction reminded him of a quip he had heard attributed to
former president, Harry Truman. He was said to have claimed he would
like to gain the services of a one-armed economist. He was tired of being
advised by economists who were constantly saying, "On the one hand
such and such, but on the other hand . . ." Kevin smiled to himself as he
recalled this anecdote, but also craved some of the goal clarity it brought
to mind. He wondered what Swen would be saying about these reflections
if he were present to engage with Kevin's internal dialog. He speculated
Swen would say something like, "Things are as they are. Deal with it."

The ambiguity over goals brought to mind a recent discussion he
had seen in an article in a denominational publication regarding whether
it was best for a pastor to self-identify as a leader or a chaplain. Apparently, some of the people interested in church growth and revitalizing
churches in decline were strong advocates of pastors seeing themselves
as leaders. The conviction was that if growth and revitalization are to
occur, the pastor must self-identify as a leader, gain leadership skills and
devote substantial time and effort to moving the church forward. Many
of these same people were prone to label pastors without this leadership
focus as chaplains, i.e., pastors whose primary focus was caring for the
people in their congregation. This characterization tended to be used
in a pejorative manner. It seemed such pastors just focused on caring
for those already in their congregation and gave insufficient attention to
reaching out to others not yet in the fold. Their outlook was a failure
of courage and goals.

Although Kevin could see where the author of the article was coming from, he was not totally comfortable with this characterization. Being
a leader and caring for the people were not mutually exclusive. How could
a pastor lead his people without also providing a lot of caring as well?

He thought again of the two pastor friends who seemed to thrive
on the institutional or organizational aspects of their work. They also
seemed to be of the leader type lionized in the article. He wasn't sure
that the two—an organizational focus and this idea of leadership—were
synonymous, but there certainly was some sort of correlation, at least
among the pastors he knew. What was their goal, building the institution
or caring for the people in it? Life would be easier if he could focus; it was
sort of like the wish for a one-armed economist. Life would be easier if it
weren't so complex—if one didn't have to do two things at the same time.

His ruminating about goals brought to mind the focus of the two challenges often brought before the church as goals—the Great Commandment and the Great Commission. He was among those who used the first label to enjoin two components, "Love the Lord your God with all your heart, soul, and mind," and "Love your neighbor as yourself." This expression of the Great Commandment was often cited by George, a pastor acquaintance from across town, as the goal of the church and thus the goal of his ministry. For George, this expression of a goal was the basis for a strong focus on service to other people in need—expressing Christ's love for others through such projects as the local homeless shelter, mentoring for struggling youth, Habitat for Humanity, and various disaster relief projects. Kevin admired what was being done through George's church.

The Great Commission was often prominent in any conversation with Brice, another colleague whose church was in the same neighborhood as his own. Brice's shorthand version of it, "Go into all the world and make disciples," was usually connected with his focus on evangelism. His church was big on the Alpha program, had a booth at the county fair each year for evangelism, and financially supported missions having this focus.

In Kevin's mind, both of these imperatives were part of the goal orientation of a biblical congregation. He didn't have a need for a one-armed advisor, but this did not alleviate all of his dilemma. Without a focus, it seemed that he and his congregation were trying to do more than was possible. His goal dilemma was real because his goals seemed so diffuse and seemed to pull first in one direction and then in another.

As he sat on the log in the sun, he had two realizations almost simultaneously. First, in spite of the leisure of his Sabbath, he felt as if he wanted to continue on his way down the trail; his reflections could continue as he walked. Second, he recalled a book he had started to read a couple months ago that probably was related to where his mind had been wandering. As so often happened for him, he had gotten a chapter or two into the book, but then other aspects of his life took over and the book was left aside. As he recalled the book, however, he realized there was a strong connection between it and the dilemma with which he was wrestling. He resolved to pick it up again as soon as possible.

* * * * *

Shortly after the time on the log in the sunshine—but before locating the partially read book—Kevin sat down to do some journaling, a practice he engaged in sporadically. He found himself preparing an organized compilation of the issues on his mind—basically a list with a few sentences of explanation for each item. Some fans of journaling probably would have thought his writing not free-form enough to be of their liking, but it suited him. It was his way of sorting out his thinking, i.e., identifying issues for which he had largely reached closure, those with some degree of progress, and others that were still in a fog.

The first item he listed was top-down versus bottom-up change. It was the issue that started all of this thinking and remained with him still. His early conclusion was both had been confirmed repeatedly, and now he was thinking more about how to make change, especially of the bottom-up variety. The top-down type seemed to be what most people were thinking about when change was the topic, and he realized that making change from the bottom-up was a fuzzy matter for him.

The unpredictability of self-organizing change was second on his list. The introduction of complex adaptive systems into his thinking had been an abrupt shift in his understanding of congregations. It actually was exciting to begin to grasp this perspective, but the unpredictability of it was a bit unsettling. Actually promoting change while not knowing for sure what will happen was not in his comfort zone.

Next on the list was whether to view the church as an institution or as the Body of Christ. This issue seemed to have been around forever but it took on new significance in the midst of this discussion of change. Somehow it seemed that viewing change as self-organizing connected more with the biblical metaphor than it did with the institutional perspective but he wasn't sure. He was aware from his conversations with Swen that many contemporary organizations were treating change from a self-organizing perspective so it could apply to either conception of the church, but somehow intuitively he saw a compatibility between self-organizing and the biblical metaphor. This question was unresolved.

His fourth issue was how to establish vision for a congregation. While at first he had thought of this matter in how-to-do-it terms, rather independently of the prior issues, he was beginning to get a sense of a connection of some sort between establishing vision and one's understanding of the nature of the church and the process of change. Casting vision was more fundamental than that. It seemed especially so after accepting Swen's notion that vision had to have specificity—not just generalities.

The fifth item was the extent to which a pastor should be a chaplain or a leader. Obviously it was both, but the matter still was somewhat unsettling. As he reflected on it, he began to think that his uncertainty was not so much about which emphasis, but what it meant to be either a chaplain or a leader. This realization was not totally pleasant for obvious reasons and he began to wonder how this matter may relate to other items on his list. He decided this issue was not the place to focus his attention for now but certainly he would be coming back to it.

The Great Commandment and Great Commission appeared on his list as a pair. His first inclination had been to list them as alternative perspectives—probably as a result of his experience with fellow pastors, George and Brice, who leaned so heavily one direction or the other—but immediately set that notion aside. He began to think that he needed to explore more deeply what each of them demanded of a follower of Jesus—possibly as a result of considering the vision question. Specificity about vision drove one back to attending to such fundamental matters.

The seventh and final item on his list was the point on which his lunch with Swen had ended—control versus influence. Swen obviously was persuaded that the way to understand leadership was in terms of influence rather than control. He made a persuasive case but freely giving up control was not comfortable. He had come to accept that this matter was related to all of the other issues on his list—especially the unpredictability of self-organizing change—but this realization did not increase his comfort level.

As Kevin leaned back and reflected on his journaling, he realized his work had both a logical and emotional component. The logical aspect was clearly noted in his writing. The emotional aspects were not very apparent. He smiled slightly as he thought about how Helen—a big fan of journaling in his congregation—would react to his journaling. She would be saying something like, "Get out of your head and write what you feel." Looking back over his writing, he recognized the places where his anxieties were present. Not surprisingly, they were related to his role in the congregation. Was he a chaplain or a leader, how did he cast vision, and what about this unpredictability stuff?

This ruminating brought his mind back to thinking about congregations as emotional systems, which in turn drew his attention to anxieties. When considering such anxieties, he generally thought about anxieties among people in the congregation rather than his own anxieties. His personal anxieties, however, certainly were apparent now. Then he had a sudden insight. Thinking through the logical aspects of issues contributes greatly to alleviating anxieties, and he certainly was doing such thinking now. Maybe he was getting closer to his feelings than it first appeared.

* * * * *

A few days later, Kevin finally had occasion to uncover from among some magazines by his living room recliner the book he had remembered. The book, *Traveling Together*, by Jeffrey D. Jones, had a subtitle which indicated why he found it of interest. It referred to *disciple-forming congregations*. As he glanced over the first two chapters—the ones he had read a couple months ago—he was reminded of both why he found the book intriguing when he first started into it and why it came to mind again while he was sitting on the log in the sun. It attended to his desire to clarify in his mind the goals of the church.

The writer was a mainline Baptist pastor but the foreword indicated the book was directed to people in both mainline and evangelical circles, which so far at least, it was easy for him to accept. An aspect that engaged Kevin deeply was a discussion of the Great Commission. He recalled specifically Jones pointed out the word disciple, as used in Matthew 28:19, was a verb not a noun in the original Greek, thus the common translation that said to "make disciples" really was a bit off the mark. As he leafed through the early part of the book he saw where he had highlighted the author's translation of the Greek, which included, "As you are going into the world, disciple all people." Somehow this translation expanded Kevin's horizons. In Kevin's mind, it did not reduce the text to the classic focus on evangelism that most saw in this text, but expanded the charge Jesus gave to his disciples. They were to be engaged in discipling people, baptizing them and teaching them to obey everything Jesus had commanded. They were not just to bring people into the fold but disciple them.

Somehow this perspective helped Kevin with the wrestling he had been doing about how to put together the Great Commandment and the Great Commission as determiners of the goals of the church. The bottom line is discipling people, with discipleship being the foundation for both an emphasis on evangelism and an emphasis on serving and loving other people. If George and Brice were present, he thought he would try to convince both of them to make adjustments in the missions they had for their churches. It would not be a matter of changing their missions, but placing them on a more solid foundation—a foundation of discipleship.

With this foundation, Kevin sensed he would have more confidence in both of their visions.

As he leafed through the pages he had read, he got the urge to return to his journal—again with an inclination to writing out some of his thoughts about the issues floating around in his mind. As with his last stint of journaling a few days before, he sensed it would be heavy on the logical side of his mental activity. He started to list characteristics of a disciple, thinking that such a listing would help clarify what his vision for Trinity Community Church should be. If being a disciple was the foundation for fulfilling both the Great Commandment and the Great Commission, he'd best have a firm handle on what it meant to be a disciple. This topic obviously was not a new one for him, but he didn't recall ever attempting to put on paper any comprehensive picture of it. As he wrote, he wasn't sure how much of it came from the book he was reading and how much came from his life experience, and prior reading and study. But that was of no consequence to him; he wanted to clarify where he was at the moment.

As he puts his fingers to the keyboard, he smiled, thinking again of Helen, the true practitioner of journaling in his congregation. For her, writing by hand in a notebook was the only way to go and here he was using his computer and entering into a rather dispassionate endeavor she probably would call a "head trip." In defense of calling it journaling, he could point out it was in a folder in his word processing program labeled "journal" and it required a security code to open, unlike others in his computer. He would have to ask Helen about this someday and see if she thought this qualified as journaling.

He put a heading on the page, Characteristics of Disciples, and started in. For number one, he wrote, "God and his work are the highest priority in the life of a disciple." Obviously, a disciple must first of all be a believer, but a disciple is more than a believer in some abstract sense of that word. A disciple has a commitment to following Jesus, a commitment so deep that God and his work are the highest priority in life. As he thought about his congregation, several questions floated through his mind. "How many of us, including myself, have this level of commitment? How many of us even have it as our goal? To what extent do I set this goal in front of us on a continuing basis?"

Second, he wrote, "A disciple is obedient to God in all things." In some ways, it seemed to be a restatement of number one, but he saw it as having a somewhat different slant. It requires not only commitment, but discernment. To obey requires knowing what God is expecting. He thought about the phrase in the Great Commission that says, "teaching them to obey everything I have commanded." As he thought about his congregation, he realized that they did a fairly good job of providing such teaching, at least on a theoretical level. The nagging question concerned the extent to which they helped each other put this obedience into practice. Standard classroom teaching can only go so far in this regard and he began to think about his long standing concern about complacency in the congregation. Was there some connection here?

His third entry was "Being a disciple is for all believers." Again he wondered if this item was really all that different from what he had already written, but he felt a need to list it because some people in the congregation seemed to hold back, as if discipleship is only for the elite, or specially gifted, or for those blessed with a strong desire to engage at a special level. Kevin's desire was to see a congregation emerge where being a true disciple, in all the senses he had just listed, was the norm, something contagious that was hard to avoid if you participated in this community of faith. If a real vision, in the sense Swen described one, were formulated, he wanted to see this desire come through as an integral part of the vision.

"Disciples pray," was his fourth entry. Jesus is the model here. The Gospels record a number of prayers of Jesus, sometimes in the presence of the twelve and sometimes in more public settings. In addition, however, there are the references to Jesus heading off by himself to pray in private. Certainly there was prayer in the various services and meetings of his congregation, but Kevin wondered about the extent to which his congregation prayed in private. Prayer had to be a part of his personal vision for the congregation, but it was not clear how to incorporate it into a formal vision that would be specific at the individual level and expressed in such a way that one would know to what extent it was realized in practice. On second thought, he wasn't so sure knowing how much it happened was necessary for it to be included in his vision for the church. Can't you have something as a goal even when measuring it in an objective way is not feasible?

For his fifth entry, he wrote, "A disciple has faith." In particular, Kevin was thinking of faith in the love of God and faith in the realization of his purposes for the world. This faith includes one's personal life—a faith that God has a purpose for me and this purpose will be reflected in the life I live. Kevin's mind drifted to the many times he met with someone in private conversation and the matter of faith came to the fore. Again, as he thought about a vision for his congregation, he wondered how it could be addressed with the specificity Swen had as his standard. It is a critical matter, but putting it in operational terms seemed hard to realize.

Thus far, Kevin had listed matters that seemed to have an individual focus. They largely were considerations pertaining to the life of an individual without much attention to other people, whether inside or outside the community of faith. His sixth entry pertained to a disciple's love for other people. This love grows out of the love of God; the love of God and the love between a disciple and others is intimately tied together. Discipleship is about a growing relationship with God that includes a healthy concern for self and for other children of God.

In keeping with these loving relationships, he next noted that a disciple serves others. In Kevin's mind this is what the Great Commandment led to in its full flowering. Everything listed so far is a foundation for this aspect of a disciple's life. Without it, acts of service have the potential of being something of a lesser nature, such as conformity to the social practices of others or a seeking for recognition. Certainly these acts of service are good regardless of motivation, but service that grows out of discipleship has more potential of being helpful to the recipient in many dimensions—physical, emotional and spiritual. It is holistic.

Kevin then noted the service of disciples is tied to their gifting and calling. All disciples have not been given the same gifts and all have not been called to the same forms of service. He thought of evangelism as he wrote this item. Some people have a gift for evangelism and calling to engage in it. The Great Commission is clear that all believers are commissioned to disciple others, but various people may be called to different aspects of discipling. Thus, evangelism may be a particular focus for some, just as other aspects of discipling may be a focus for others. Saying that evangelism is a special focus for some disciples, however, does not mean others should avoid it. All disciples, in fact, have a responsibility to be transparent about their identity as a disciple and ready to explain why they have the perspective that guides their life. Kevin's mind again moved to a vision for their congregation. This vision probably needed specific attention to helping people identify their giftedness and discerning their personal call to ministry.

As Kevin made his next entry, he realized he was up to number nine; the list was getting longer than he had expected. He noted here since a disciple is living a life patterned after Jesus himself, this life needs to exhibit a special concern for those who are down and out, the outcasts of society. This concern for the less privileged, of course, was not just displayed in the life of Jesus; it is seen throughout the Bible. He thought of one of his pastor friends who was fond of saying that God had a preference for the poor. However expressed, it was clear that his vision for the congregation must take account of this characteristic of a disciple.

As he prepared to add number ten to his list, he noticed that his thinking had started with a focus on the individual and then moved to the church and beyond it to the larger community. He noted in this entry, "A disciple does not live by the same rules as society as a whole; it is a different set of norms, commitments, and expectations." As a result, a disciple does not look like all the neighbors, and sometimes suffers as a result. As he reflected on this entry he realized it was hard for some people in the congregation. They wanted to be liked and as a result it was hard to be different.

His entry numbered eleven noted the mandate in the final chapter of the Gospel of Matthew—to disciple people—was given to the eleven disciples and thus by implication to the entire church. As a result, this charge must be seen as something that takes place in the faith community. As he made his notation, however, he recalled the accounts of Philip in the book of Acts that Swen had made a big point of and understood that while it is the role of the faith community, its realization extends out beyond the boundaries of this community as well. It is an important responsibility of his congregation, but he better not restrict it to what happens with the walls of the church.

His final entry sounded a bit like the previous one, but he was persuaded that he needed to add that discipling people must be a primary focus of the church. It is not just one of many things they do; it is a dominating purpose. If people are to have a relationship with God that reflects his previous eleven points, he would have to make it a central element of his vision for the congregation. He sighed as he thought of Ray, the last person to join their fellowship. Immediately after he became a member, someone asked him to be on a committee, the education committee to be precise. He wasn't aware of any other involvements that were pressed on Ray so quickly, but it made him wonder how close the congregation's priorities were to discipling people. They had work to do and he now thought that clarifying their vision probably was a good place to start.

chapter 5

Essential Principles

Waypoints

Twelve candidates for the essential principles of an authentic church are considered as follows.

1. *Discipleship focus*. An authentic church is focused on developing disciples of Jesus Christ. "Comprehensive" programs are not sought at the expense of this central spiritual purpose.

2. *Simple goals*. The church's goal should be that each believer develop the spiritual gifts needed to reach out beyond him- or herself to further the Kingdom in accordance with the direction of the Spirit.

3. *Personalization*. Teaching and various aspects of spiritual formation should be personalized to the maximum extent possible. One-on-one formation and small group interaction should predominate

4. *Believer-as-kingdom-seeker*. The governing metaphor of the church should be believer-as-kingdom-seeker rather than the more traditional metaphor of teacher or pastor-as-deliverer-of-spiritual sustenance.

5. *Church-as-community*. The church as a community of believers should be the guiding image rather than the church as an institution.

6. *Tone*. Within the context of the community's basic statement of faith, the tone of the church should be explicitly and self-consciously

one of accepting diversity in the way the Spirit directs the lives of the community's believers.

7. *Measures of success.* The measure of success of the church should be growth in discipleship.

8. *Unbounded by a building.* The church is located wherever its people are found, including their homes, work places and "third places."

9. *Staff.* All members of the community (not just paid staff) should see themselves as ministers and in a role of ministering to others, both inside and outside the community.

10. *Budget.* At the most, one-half of the tithes and offerings of this Christian community should be directed to supporting the community itself, that is, to fostering their own spiritual growth. The majority of their money should be directed outward.

11. *Worship.* The worship done in community is focused on telling the story of God, celebrating it, and responding to it.

12. *Missional.* The community, individually and collectively, reaches out in love to others as an outgrowth of their relationship with Jesus Christ. Their *doing* is an outgrowth of their *being*.

ELROY BANOVER WAS A professor at a seminary located within the same metropolitan area as Kevin's church. Elroy was a New Testament scholar with a long-term interest in the nature of the church. For a long time he had extended his New Testament studies to include close attention to the contemporary church in America. The denominational affiliation of Elroy and his seminary were not the same as Kevin's but they had enough in common that professors from the seminary occasionally provided pulpit supply for churches like Kevin's. The two were acquainted and had had a few brief conversations over the years, but did not know each other well.

The local ministerial association to which Kevin belonged had a monthly lunch gathering with a fairly low-key agenda—often just some announcements and lots of social time. Occasionally they had a more formal program and this month was one of those times. Because of ongoing discussions about the nature of the church in the current social context, someone suggested bringing in Elroy to give a presentation on the current state of the church and his assessment of its future. When Kevin saw the announcement of Elroy's upcoming presentation, he resolved not to miss this meeting.

After the lunch, Kevin thought that Elroy had made a good presentation although he didn't find much new in it. He was already quite familiar with the statistics on church size, rates of growth, demographics of church members, and such. Of more interest was the cultural information and the degree of compatibility between the typical church culture and the broader culture of society. A lot of the time was taken up with questions and answers and Kevin was struck by how so many of his colleagues were caught up with anxiety about the future of their congregations. His unspoken assessment was that most of them were fearful about the future, but unsure of what to do about it. Although he did not have an opportunity to get into it very deeply, it was clear Elroy had some concrete ideas about what churches should be doing in the way of forward-moving change. He made the point that these ideas varied depending upon the context, and given the limited time, as well as the varied church situations represented in the group, they didn't get to a lot of specifics.

When the meeting broke up, Kevin went up to chat with Elroy. After thanking him for coming to meet with the group, Kevin started to describe his recent odyssey, including his focus on top-down and bottom-up change, his time with Swen, the examination of self-organizing in congregations, and his recent attention to vision including discipleship. It was quickly clear they shared some mutual interests and Kevin asked if it would be possible to get together to talk about them.

Elroy's response was immediate, "I'd love to get together. This week I'm finishing up the grading of the last of the final exams for this term, but next week the schedule opens up and the campus should be quiet. How about coming over to the seminary sometime next week and we can have a conversation without much interruption?"

"Sounds good. Would sometime on Wednesday work; that's a good day for me."

Elroy pulled out his calendar, looked at it briefly and said, "Okay, how about ten in the morning?"

"That's good. I'm tempted to launch into some these ideas now, but I guess we better save it for next week and then really get into it."

"I'm in room 228 of the main building. See you there."

With that Elroy turned his attention to another person with a question and Kevin started toward the door with anticipation of a good conversation next week.

* * * * *

Since this was break time between terms, Kevin had no problem finding a parking space close to Elroy's office and soon was in front of his open office door. After the typical pleasantries, Elroy said, "When I saw you last week you indicated you have been on what you called an odyssey. I would like to hear more about it."

"I'm not sure when I first thought of it as being an odyssey—probably not that long ago—but for quite some time I have been uneasy about an apparent state of complacency in our church. This unease was magnified when I started to reflect on how one goes about making change. At about the same time, I saw a grassroots, spontaneous initiative meet resistance from the board—not vociferous objection—just a somehow inflexible expectation that any bottom-up initiative had to have formal approval from the top before it could proceed. If the board and I had some initiatives of our own underway that were in competition with the new initiative, that would have been a different matter, but I saw our situation as one in which not much new was happening and when something did pop up, it was met with hesitation and even suspicion."

"I don't think it unreasonable," Elroy interjected, "to expect that significant initiatives get some sort of approval at the top—at least a rubber stamp approval—because it keeps the lines of communication open and helps avoid the kind of trouble that on rare occasions jumps out to surprise you. What I sense you are objecting to is a climate of commitment to the status quo."

"That's it exactly," Kevin said. "It reflects a resistance to change and my concern about our church is that there isn't much new happening, either from the top-down or the bottom-up."

"When I saw you at the lunch meeting last week, I recall you making a passing reference to spending some time with Swen Quesoda about self-organizing systems."

"Yeah," Kevin replied. "Do you know him?"

"Well, I know of him. I can't really say I know him. And I can say something similar about self-organizing systems. I think I know what they are, but I have not given them much thought—certainly not in a church context."

"Okay, you at least have a sense of where I have been on my journey in this regard. The part I was most interested in talking to you about is our goals as a church or, as Swen is fond of talking about, my vision as pastor for the congregation."

"Now you are in my ballpark," Elroy responded.

"Just recently, I have zeroed in on discipleship as sort of the bottom line purpose for the church. In fact, as the result of some reading and reflection on the matter, I wrote out a list of a dozen characteristics of a disciple-forming congregation."

"I like that label—disciple-forming congregation."

"Yeah, it's a good one," Kevin acknowledged, "and I think it captures much of my vision for our congregation. If we were truly the disciples Jesus is seeking, I wouldn't have reason to be concerned about our congregation being committed to the status quo and resistant to change."

"That's for sure."

"What I'm wrestling with at the moment is this business of having a vision for our congregation that is focused on discipleship and is something I have some possibility of putting into practice. As I understand it, my vision has to have specifics if there is hope of implementing it and I am struggling with that."

"Okay, I think I see your issue," Elroy said, "and it is one I have thought about a lot. Most churches do not have a well-defined vision and that is problematic. Sometimes it seems they are locked into the status quo, or on the other hand, latching on to various fads that come along and thus wandering about without focus and going nowhere in a different sense."

"My concern at the moment, obviously, is about being locked into the status quo, but on the other hand I want to be sure any direction I set us off on is focused on our core mission and is not one of those fads you mentioned."

"I sometimes think that any change a status quo church makes is good just to get them moving, but in my more coherent moments, I realize possible changes should be considered very carefully. Looking before you leap doesn't mean you stay still forever. As I think I already hinted, I'm convinced focusing on discipleship as you intend is ideal."

"We are agreed on that," Kevin replied, "but I have come to realize that I am still at the level of generalities and don't have the specifics needed for a vision that can be the basis for action."

Elroy paused to reflect for a bit and finally responded. "I'm not sure how helpful I can be on the specifics. They are something you and others will have to formulate so they are in keeping with who you are as a congregation. I may have something more to offer, however, in terms of some general principles."

"I guess I should have realized," Kevin said with a chuckle, "that anything I got from a seminary prof would be long on generalities and short on things useful in the real world."

Elroy smiled and seemed to appreciate the attempt at humor. "Some generalities can turn out to be very useful in the real world. What I have in mind are some principles—what I call essential principles—that are the basis for making positive change in a congregation. They can help keep focus and avoid wandering off after fads. They can provide a foundation for choosing the specifics that make up your vision. They can be truly useful for the person who is open-minded enough to consider them."

Kevin smiled at the little jab and charged ahead. "Okay, my mind is open; put something in."

"I do have a set of essential principles that I think should guide a congregation that seriously wants to make fundamental and significant change and I would be happy to share them with you." With that, he stood and went to the modest-sized whiteboard on the side wall of his office, erased what was there, and wrote and underlined a heading at the top: ESSENTIAL PRINCIPLES. He then started a numbered list but paused after writing the number one. "Before writing them here, maybe I should indicate where they come from."

"Yeah, that would be good."

"As you probably suspect, one key source is the New Testament, which shouldn't be surprising given my job. But in addition to study of the New Testament, my list is shaped by my deep involvement with contemporary churches. The basic nature of the church I find in the New Testament. The church in its institutional form is shaped by various societal norms, values and beliefs. Since my essential principles pertain to organized churches, they to some extent, have their origins in both the New Testament and our general culture."

"That makes sense," Kevin said. "Let's see what you have."

As he wrote on the board: 1. SPIRITUAL FOCUS, Elroy elaborated on what he meant. "The church should focus on helping believers develop the spiritual dimension of their lives. It should not attempt to have a comprehensive set of programs at the expense of its central spiritual purpose. I want to emphasize, however, that I don't mean spiritual as something divorced from the physical realities of life. My point is that even programs of mission and evangelism must have a spiritual foundation or they miss the mark."

"I mentioned that I have come to think of discipleship as the central purpose of the church. How is your item number one different from my notion?"

"I don't see an essential difference. I think we are in the same place. I would be happy to cross out the word spiritual and replace it with discipleship. I think we are agreed that the core commitment of the church shouldn't be diluted by a lack of focus."

While engaged in conversation, Kevin also was busily writing on a sheet of a sheet of paper. In addition to the simple listing from the whiteboard, he was writing his personal elaboration of the point as he understood it so he would have it for future reference. "Okay. I sensed we were pretty much on the same page."

Elroy wrote on the board: 2. SIMPLE GOALS and continued, "The church's goals should be simple. I often think of them as helping each believer master the spiritual disciplines most central to that individual and reach out beyond himself or herself to further the Kingdom in accordance with the direction of the Spirit. These goals should apply to all believers, although the means to reach the goals will vary as those believers themselves vary."

"Those goals sound so individualistic. It seems to me there is a strong community dimension to the church."

"There certainly is a strong community dimension to the church and that shows up later in the list, but the strength of the community depends on the strength of the individuals. Does that make sense?"

"I guess so," Kevin responded, "but I have another question. I'm wondering about your strong focus on the spiritual disciplines. I don't usually think about spiritual maturity in terms of mastering some disciplines, although there are a lot of spiritual disciplines I think are important."

"Well, if you don't like this way of expressing it, why not say your simple goals are focused on discipleship. I suspect we are on much the same page even though the semantics are different."

"Probably so," Kevin acknowledged. "Why don't you continue since I get the impression some of this may come up again further on in your list."

"Okay," Elroy said as he wrote the next item: 3. PERSONALIZATION. "Teaching and various aspects of spiritual formation should be personalized to the maximum extent possible. To that end, a significant portion of teaching should take place in small groups with peer leadership, and spiritual formation on an individual level should be common. Decisions about programs, use of time, teaching approaches and modes of spiritual formation should rest with the people engaged in these activities rather than a governing group not engaged directly in the ministries themselves."

"It is hard to argue with any of that," Kevin said after a long pause, "but it sounds like an approach that will demand lots of resources."

"Yes, but note that I mentioned peer leadership of some activities and putting decisions of how to do things in the hands of the participants. In the final analysis, it is not so much the amount of resources devoted to teaching as it is in the manner in which it is conducted and facilitated."

After another long pause, Kevin responded again, "That probably is true, but I doubt that I or anyone else in our congregation is well-prepared for putting this into practice."

"That may well be true but it doesn't negate the principle and such skills can be learned. Right?"

"I can't argue against your point, so I guess we should move on to the next one on your list."

Elroy wrote on the board 4. BELIEVER-AS-KINGDOM-SEEKER and chuckled a bit as he said, "You may find this one an awkward phrase but I think it is firmly grounded in the New Testament. Jesus mentions the Kingdom all the time. Note the focus on the believer. The more traditional metaphor for the church focuses on the teacher or pastor as deliverer of spiritual sustenance. Coaching and spiritual direction should be prominent, to help believers learn how to examine their own lives and foster their own spiritual development in the context of Christian community."

"I'm glad you included that last phrase, 'in the context of Christian community.' Again, you are zeroing in on the individuals and this seems to be a departure from so much of current practice."

"Yes, I am committed to the focus on community, but the apparent emphasis on individuals and personalization is a correction, in my view, for a situation where churches go about running programs with insufficient attention to their impact on the people in them. What I am talking about is so similar to your attention to discipleship."

Kevin paused again before responding. "I think you are right; we are headed in the same direction. I think what I am hearing from you that is different from what I have been expecting may be an emphasis on results. Your expression of these ideas keeps pushing me to focus on the effects on people and not be satisfied with just having operated a program."

"Okay, moving right along," said Elroy as he wrote: 5. CHURCH-AS-COMMUNITY. "I think you should be happy with this one, based on what you have said already. I'm saying that the church as a community of believers should be the guiding image rather than the church as an institution. Church is the stuff of relationships, prayer, and worship rather than programs, budgets, and management. This community, with its focus on relationships, prayer, and worship, should not be constrained by, or dependent upon, an unresponsive institution."

"Yes, I do like this one, although church as an institution is not coming off very well here. Remember, my job in some sense is running an institution," Kevin said with feigned indignation.

Elroy smiled as he replied, "I realize that, but you have to grant that the church we see in the New Testament doesn't have a lot of the institutional characteristics you and I have to deal with. Due to our societal context, our churches are more institutional and that is all the more reason to work real hard to make sure we are not compromising the authentic church."

"Okay, I'll grant your point."

"Then on to number six," Elroy said as he wrote: 6. TONE. "Within the context of the community's basic statement of faith, the tone of the church should be explicitly and self-consciously one of accepting diversity in the way the Spirit directs the lives of the community's believers. This is a New Testament theme. For example, in Romans, chapter 12, it says, 'Just as each of us has one body with many members, and these members do not all have the same function, so in Christ we who are many form one body, and each member belongs to all the others. We have different gifts, according to the grace given us.'"

Kevin caught himself thinking that Elroy must have a lot of Scripture memorized, but that wasn't too surprising for a New Testament scholar. He listened as Elroy continued, "I'm afraid that sometimes the church promotes, often unconsciously, a deadening uniformity and conformity. Given the fundamental importance of this direction of the Spirit in individuals' lives, the community as a whole should avoid collective actions that do not have full community support. On the other hand, as a true community of believers, it should have open communication about fundamental matters of faith and practice in a manner that provides both mutual support and encouragement of individuals' prayerful examination of themselves and give subgroups within the congregation the freedom to follow the direction of the Spirit for them."

"For once I don't have any comment other than 'right on.'"

"Okay, then. Here is number seven," and with this comment, Elroy wrote: 7. MEASURES OF SUCCESS. "The measure of success of the
church should be spiritual growth, or to use your favored term, growth
in discipleship. It can be assessed by individuals in the context of community interaction. The primary focus should be on what is often called
being, that is, who we are as person, not on *doing*, that is, the work we
accomplish. Our doing should be an outgrowth of our being. Numerical
growth in the size of the congregation should not be basis for measuring
the spiritual growth of the congregation."

"I'm sure you have been told that growth in the number of people in
the congregation is an indicator of successful evangelism and increased
commitment to the cause of Christ and thus is a valid measure of success.
How do you respond to that argument?"

Elroy responded rather eagerly to the question, "Of course, we all
like to see an increase in numbers, but if you use that as your measure
of success, you are very likely to be led astray in your thinking. There
are lots of ways to attract people to a group setting, and if we lose sight
of our basic goals, it is so easy to fall into doing things for the wrong
reason. Focusing on the true bottom line is so important. Do you have a
quarrel with that?

"I guess not, but I have a hard time imagining going to our local pastors' meeting some time and saying 'Our numbers are down 20 percent
over the past year, but spiritual commitment is up 40 percent so we think
we have had a good year." Kevin said it with a straight face but internally
knew he was trying to provoke some kind of reaction.

Elroy smiled and said, "Some things are hard to put in numbers and
I would want to see how you came up with 40 percent as your increase in
spiritual commitment."

"Okay, it was a facetious comment. I'll let you go to your next item."

With that Elroy wrote the next item: 8. UNBOUNDED BY A
BUILDING. "I once gave a sermon in a small church where I began by
reading a list of addresses. They were the street addresses of the members of the congregation. I went on to say that these addresses were
the location of the church, not the address of the building where the
congregation gathered. Even those sites together didn't define the location of the church, of course, because the church is located wherever its
people are found, such as at their places of employment, the local coffee
shop, or the place where their hobby group meets. The point is that the
church is not a set of activities located in a building, it is what goes on

in the lives of the members of the congregation, all week long, wherever they find themselves."

"I think people like me have no quarrel at all with what you are saying, at least in theory, but we are not good at operationalizing this conception of the church. We don't think deeply enough about it to put it into practice. We are captured by a culture that defines church in terms of what goes on in a special building designated as the place where church happens."

"Unfortunately, I think you are right. We have the theory right but we haven't given enough thought to how we can practice our theory. This principle is in my list because I'm convinced that a congregation that wants to become all it was meant to be must engage this issue in depth. It requires concentrated and continuous effort over the long haul."

"I imagine you could describe some examples of congregations which did operationalize this point, rare though they may be," Kevin said, "but I'm betting you are ready to move on to the next one."

"Okay, here is the next one," Elroy said as he wrote: 9. STAFF. "In one sense, the staff includes every member of the church. All members of the community should see themselves as ministers and in a role of ministering to others, both inside and outside the community. Although paid staff members devote more of their time to serving the community itself than the non-professionals, and may have more education related to these roles than most of the non-professionals, there is no qualitative difference in the roles played."

"I hear where you are coming from, but I think there are a few qualitative differences and I have a New Testament basis for saying so. In the fourth chapter of Ephesians, reference is made to pastors and teachers who 'prepare God's people for works of service.' I think pastors and teachers are preparing others to do ministry, rather than doing this ministry themselves."

"Okay, I'll grant your point that there are some qualitative differences, but at the same time you were making my main point which is that everyone in the congregation is to be a minister."

"In seems then," said Kevin, "that we are essentially in agreement."

"In that case, let's go to my next essential principle," Elroy said as he wrote on the whiteboard: 10. BUDGET. "At the most, one-half of the tithes and offerings of this Christian community should be directed to supporting the community itself, that is, to fostering their own spiritual growth. The majority of their giving should be directed outward, with much of this money ideally directed through ministries in which these believers themselves are actively involved. Inevitably, this approach will require the reduction of some programs now provided in many churches."

"Well, professor," Kevin said with a smile, "in the words of an old saw, you have now gone from preaching to meddling. You have enough connection with lots of congregations that you have to know there are very few places where this principle has any chance of seeing the light of day."

"That may be, but I don't think that is because I'm wrong; I think it is because most churches have some of their priorities seriously out of whack. How can a congregation justify spending most of its money on itself when there is a world around them that needs to hear the Good News and have someone respond to their needs in the name of Jesus?"

"But all the money spent on the church building, for example, is not just for the benefit of the members," Kevin said a bit heatedly. "That building is a place where you can bring friends and neighbors to hear the Gospel."

"I'm not sure about the past, say fifty years ago, but certainly today, not much of that is happening. When the unchurched today hear about Jesus, it usually is not because they have decided to try going to church, it is because someone has left the building and gone out to where they are to engage them. Think about your church. In the last year, how many unchurched people, and don't count churched people transferring from another congregation, have come to your church?"

Kevin paused for a long time and finally said, "If you limit it to the last year, I would have to say none. I wanted to say there was one, but to be honest I have to admit it was because a member of our congregation developed a relationship with him over a period of many months and after a long period of dialog about Jesus, brought him to a Sunday service."

"That illustrates my point, and I could say something similar about people who are hurting. How many unchurched people in our community who are going through a divorce, or experiencing the death of someone close to them, or facing foreclosure on their home, or having life-threatening medical issues, or have lost their job, turn to the church for help? Some do, of course, but in the great majority of cases, we have to go to them in some way or another."

"I have to admit that, based on the experience of our church, I can't make much of an argument against your position."

"What I am arguing here," Elroy said, "also supports a couple of my prior essential principles, the one about not being bounded by a building and the one about everyone, not just the paid staff, being the ministers of the church."

"Okay, I think you have made your point, but you have to admit that half of the budget being for some form of outreach sets an awfully high bar, one that is outside of reality in many, if not most, cases."

"Maybe not in the next year or two or three, but over the long haul, it may not be as far out of reach as it seems. In general, we tend to overestimate what we can accomplish in a year but underestimate what we can accomplish over a period of years. So I am reluctant to back off from this idea as a goal."

"I understand you argument," Kevin admitted, "but you said yourself that your argument also related to who was doing the ministering and where it was being done. Why the drastic stance on the budget?"

"One reason is that this one is really tangible. In addition, unless progress is made on this principle, I doubt that much will happen on the other two."

"I'm not so sure. I would be inclined to say it would best to tackle all three of these ideas simultaneously."

"Sure," Elroy responded. "You want to keep the big picture in mind all the time, but I am not ready to let go of my budget ideal, although I have to admit I've not convinced many people to sign on for it. Let me go to another one of my essential principles."

Elroy wrote 11. WORSHIP on the board as he continued, "Several of the items we have just been talking about concern the way in which the congregation reaches out beyond its boundaries to other people, but we have to be concerned about the nature of what happens within the congregation as well, and an important one is worship."

"I agree, but it also seems to be a difficult area for some churches, probably because for many people it is so much about music and the fact that people have such varied tastes in music."

"Yes, it does seem to be caught up with people's musical preferences," Elroy responded, "but if it does, it may be an indication that people are not focused on the central issue. To me, worship is telling the story of God, celebrating it and responding to it. The focus needs to be on celebrating God's purposes and being open to God, including repenting of our brokenness and allowing God to redirect our lives. We are gathering as broken, repentant sinners preparing to be sent out into the world as disciples."

"I like that way of putting it. When a congregation is conflicted about style and musical taste, it may be because they have lost focus on why they are gathering together."

"Yes, a key reason for gathering together is to be open to what God wants to do in our lives and then going out as disciples who are open to being transformed," Elroy noted, "which leads to my final essential principle about outreach." As he talked, he wrote on the board. 12. MISSIONAL.

"This word is used in varied ways today," Elroy continued, "but what I'm wanting to emphasize is related to the previous principle and several of the others. What people do as their mission should be an outgrowth of their relationship with Jesus Christ. One of my favorite ways of expressing it is that our *doing* is an outgrowth of our *being*."

"I'm with you on this one, Kevin said. "We should have a sense of mission that includes consideration of all dimensions of human life, including physical, psychological, and spiritual. What mission we pursue, however, should come from what we have become as a disciple."

Seeming to want to move on, Elroy said, "At any rate, there you have my list of essential principles. Do you have any overall reactions to the list?"

"Overall, I like what's here," Kevin was quick to reply. "As you see, I have been taking notes about each item on the list. I want to reflect on them as I wrestle with this vision thing. I think it will be helpful. It usually takes a while for things to crystalize in my thinking."

"That's to be expected. Now that I've dished out my load of ideas, let's go back to this odyssey you are on. I'd like to hear some more—at least about some key parts."

"Well," Kevin continued, "earlier I think I made quick reference to top-down versus bottom-up change and the self-organizing systems ideas Swen was talking about. It's a big topic, but here is one related idea that may be worth pursuing. When he described complex adaptive systems, he included the Holy Spirit as one of the elements in it, and the influence of the Spirit permeates the system. This caught me a bit off guard at first, but it quickly was apparent that we have to think of our systems this way. When I think about it, I get caught up in the top-down versus bottom-up issue. There seems to be a potential tension here between the direction leaders at the top think they are providing and what people at the grass roots level sense is the direction they are receiving. I imagine a New Testament scholar would have some thoughts on this."

"I better have," Elroy responded with a smile, "given the way you have framed it. I think the key is for both those at the top and those at the bottom, so to speak, to recognize, in their discernment, that change comes from both directions. Everyone needs to be open to listening to what others—whether at the top or the bottom—sense the Spirit is directing them to do. What they are hearing from these other people needs to be taken into account in their discernment process. The typical negative examples one hears about involve a leadership group making top-down decisions without staying in touch with the people in their charge."

"I guess a good way to put it is that making a decision, or a choice of direction, or any change for that matter, must be listening both to the Spirit and other people who are part of the system they are in."

"I couldn't agree more," Elroy said. "And the way you expressed that, is a reminder that we are rather constantly considering change in our lives—maybe small changes, but change nevertheless. One needs to remember that change is a New Testament imperative. The expectation is that we will be growing, which obviously is a form of change."

"I imagine you could cite a bunch of verses that describe this biblical imperative."

"Sure, how about Romans 12:2? 'Do not conform any longer to the pattern of this world, but be transformed by the renewing of your mind. Then you will be able to test and approve what God's will is—his good, pleasing and perfect will.' This one is not just talking about minor changes; it is talking about big change—being transformed. Change is happening in our lives all the time. The imperative here is to have those changes be positive changes, and big ones at that."

"I'm with you on that one. How about other insights you may have."

Elroy paused for a long time as he gazed up and to the side. Kevin was tempted to break the silence but resisted and waited. Finally Elroy said, "A big word these days is missional, a word we were just using. Given what I hear you wrestling with, I think it will be helpful to distinguish between missional congregations and missional people. They are both important and they probably relate to this top-down, bottom-up stuff."

"How so?"

"It is easy to imagine the leaders of a congregation initiating a variety of top-down missional activities or programs. It is also easy to imagine a collection of people who are truly missional-minded doing a lot that is bottom-up. Since you seem to like the word influence better than control, I would say that the people at the top—the leaders—need to be influencing the people to be missional-minded and support the bottom-up expression of this missional-mindedness. Ideally, I would like to see a lot of spontaneous missional behaviors among individuals, various spontaneous missional actions within clusters of people, and some top-down initiatives from the leaders which take account of the spontaneous missional action among the people."

"This fits with the discipleship emphasis that has emerged in my odyssey. By definition, a real disciple is missional."

Kevin and Elroy's conversation soon drifted off into a variety of other matters—what was happening at the seminary, the ethos of Kevin's ministerial association that Elroy had just addressed, soccer matches, and more. When Kevin left, it was with his thanks for Elroy's time and Elroy's expression of appreciation for an opportunity to discuss the world for which he was preparing his students.

Kevin left with his notes on the list of essential principles, satisfaction with some new insights, and comfort in knowing there were knowledgeable people available who could discuss his personal world of work with sympathy and appreciation.

chapter 6

Discipling—the Central Goal

Waypoints

Discipling people should be the central goal of a congregation. Churches need to focus on their central goal or risk diminishing their impact.

To be authentic, an institutional church must adopt a focus that reflects biblical principles, as well as resonates with the societal context in which it finds itself.

AFTER ANOTHER SUNDAY WITH many responsibilities—and his usual Sabbath day immediately following it—Kevin decided to give Swen a call. He got him on the first try and indicated he thought it was time to schedule the lunch they had planned. They settled on Wednesday the next week and as before, it would be eleven thirty at Goolsby's.

As the previous time, when Kevin arrived at Goolsby's, Swen was already there seated at a booth on the right side. After the usual pleas-antries, including an update on the latest soccer events, and getting their orders placed, Kevin zeroed in on what was on his mind. "As I indicated on the phone, I've found myself engaged in a couple of recent ventures related to understanding change in a congregation and I wanted to run them by you."

"I've been looking forward to our conversation," Swen responded. "I've been wanting to hear what you've come up with."

"I've actually got two items in writing that I brought with me, both generated since we last talked, and both popping up rather unexpectedly." As he said this, Kevin produced two items, one a two pager with the list of characteristics of disciples he had generated and the second, a listing of Elroy's essential principles for a congregation.

"All this stuff written out—you obviously have taken this seriously."

"Yes, I have. This first one is a list of characteristics of true followers of Christ that I wrote out after reading a book about disciple-forming congregations by Jeffrey Jones. What prompted me to make this list was a need I felt to clarify what the goals of a congregation should be. The more I thought about it, the more I was convinced that forming disciples was at the heart of what the church is all about. So I put together this list. It is a list of twelve, but with my brief explanations for each one it extends onto a second page. I would really like to have your reactions to it, so I would be happy to sit here quietly while you read it."

"Sure, let me look at it," Swen said as he took the two stapled sheets of paper and began to read. While Swen was reading, Kevin glanced around at the people nearby, wondering what brought them here at this time and what was going on in their lives. His speculation ended when Swen laid the papers on the table and said, "I like your list. If I were doing it, I might change a couple items a little, but in the main, I am in the same place. What is of interest to me, is not so much the specifics of your list, but the fact that you are thinking of this as the central goal of a congregation."

"That's really what I wanted to talk about. There are so many goals we are pursuing as a congregation—like other congregations I know— that it seems we sometimes lose focus. The author of that book is saying we need to concentrate on the central purpose of the church and I am thinking he is right."

"Absolutely," Swen responded. "In my work with congregations, I see the problem of lack of focus in so many churches. Without focus, so many congregations seem to drift along, doing business as usual and never developing a vision for becoming all they were meant to be. I'm guessing you intend to do something about this at your church."

"Yes, but I am not all that sure just how to go about it. I have been thinking I might try to engage some people in the congregation in some discussion of the Jones book—possibly in some small group settings."

"Sounds good. I'm sure there are lots of other books and materials of this general type you could use for this purpose, but you have found this one resonates with you, so I would say, 'go for it.' I have one suggestion to offer. How about starting with your board? Do a study of the book with them, possibly extending over three or four of your regular meetings along with the other board business. That should give you a sense of how others in the congregation may respond to it later and it may get your leadership to start developing focus."

"I like that," Kevin said. "It probably will take a bit of convincing on my part to get the board to agree, but I think we are at a point where I can do that. But let me ask you a question about how this sort of thing fits into your work as a consultant. Do you tend to zero in on this matter of focus?"

"Definitely, but how I do it varies from one setting to another. Before I get into that, however, I probably should say a bit about my orientation as a consultant."

"Sure, I'd love to hear about it."

"Well, as a consultant coming into an organization, in this case a congregation, and helping them to develop focus and goals, you enter into a process where they—not you the consultant—develop their own goals. Some church consultants take this approach to the point that they don't zero in on those matters that are explicitly Christian. I think that is a mistake. I work with a wide range of congregations—both mainline and evangelical—but all ones that claim to be Christian. So I am not hesitant to challenge them as to whether their purposes are consistent with their stated Christian commitment."

With a smile, Kevin said, "I guess you don't want them wandering in the wilderness."

"You could put it that way. If you don't confront the underlying question of who you are and why you exist, you can spend a lot of time wandering. It is not my job to tell them what their specific goals should be, but I would be derelict in my duty if I didn't challenge them to focus on what it means for them to be followers of Christ."

"Given what you have just said, I think you may like the other list I brought with me." Kevin placed his second list in front of Swen, another two-page typed list which, in this case, had been distilled from the notes he took while Elroy was making his list on the whiteboard in his office.

"Okay. Let's see what you have."

Kevin continued. "Do you know Elroy Banover, a New Testament prof over at the seminary?"

"Well, I know there is such a person over there, but I don't think we have ever met."

"He is the one who came up with this list of twelve essential principles for churches. I was in his office when he told me about them. He put the list on the whiteboard in his office and explained them one by one. He just put a heading for each one on the board, but I was taking notes and afterward wrote out this more detailed description."

"Looks intriguing," Swen said. "When he set out these principles for the church, was he talking about the Body of Christ as we would understand it from the New Testament? That is what I would suspect since he is a New Testament scholar, but there are items here that look to me that they pertain to the institutional churches as we find them in our society."

"He says both, but he also acknowledges that he put them together mainly with the contemporary church in mind."

"That makes sense," Swen continued, "and as I said, they look intriguing. Give me a minute and let me read the entire list."

As Swen perused the list, Kevin went back to his people-watching but found himself mostly watching Swen and his facial expressions as he studied the list with its brief description of each of the twelve principles. It seemed apparent that Swen was giving the page some deep thought.

After what seemed a long time, Swen said with a smile, "Are you sure a seminary prof came up with this list? It seems to have a real world orientation."

"Yeah, it surprised me a bit too. I agree; it is not just an academic piece."

"As you might guess, there are some places I probably would modify it a little, but overall I would be happy to work with a church that was ready to go down this road."

"How about being a bit more specific," Kevin responded. "What is it about this list that brings such a positive response?"

"Well, for starters, I think it does a good job of taking account of both our biblical understanding of the church and the institutional character imposed by the societal context in which we find ourselves. Both are essential and both are here."

"What are some of the specifics related to both of these dimensions of the church?"

"Okay," Swen replied. "Let's start with the biblical nature of the church. This is where the list starts, that is, with its insistence on a spiritual focus."

"I had a strong positive response to that one as well, and it ties in with my characteristics of a disciple. As I told Elroy, I could see my list being an expression of his spiritual focus."

"Right on. The list starts with a focus on being followers of Christ, not on operating an institution. And you probably noticed as well that you see this focus continuing in the very next items, the ones about keeping the goals simple, emphasizing personalization, and I love that next one—the metaphor of believer-as-kingdom seeker."

"Yes," Kevin continued, "and the fifth one—church-as-community—certainly is a biblical idea as well."

"Actually, you see the idea of the church as the body of Christ in most of the rest of them, for example, the ideas of the measures of success being growth in discipleship and not being bounded by a building. You know," Swen continued after a long drawn out pause and a chuckle, "maybe it isn't such a surprise that this came from a New Testament scholar after all. Maybe the surprise is that it also attends to the institutional aspects of a church."

"I've generally thought of church consultants as paying a lot of attention to the institutional aspects, so maybe you are the person to offer a critique of what you see of the institutional dimensions in the list of essential principles."

"Well, as we have already seen, both the biblical and institutional dimensions show up in some way in most of the items on the list, but the institutional aspects seem to be particularly present in the ones pertaining to measures of success, buildings, staff, and budget. I find lots of congregational leaders thinking about these four. And in contrast to how I hear many people talking at times, these four are framed here in valid biblical terms."

"I responded the same way," Kevin said. "I hear many of my fellow pastors talking about those four fairly often, and unfortunately, I have to agree that at times it is in a way that does not seem to be biblically grounded. Say, there is one we haven't mentioned, the one about tone. What did you think about it?"

Swen paused to read over item six about tone again and then said, "This is another one that takes account of both the biblical and institutional aspects. It's about having a tone that is affirming and welcoming of diversity within a congregation in terms of how the Spirit directs the lives of the members and the diversity in their giftedness and the roles they play. It is solidly biblical and in addition it is really important to me from the organizational perspective. It brings me back to thinking about the systems ideas we have talked about and this matter of top-down and bottom-up change."

"Hey," Kevin said with an enthusiastic tone, "I've been wanting to talk about those things, so I'm ready to hear more."

"Okay. In some congregations there seems to be built-in pressure for uniformity and even conformity. Unfortunately, this pressure restrains change, especially of the bottom-up type. So I am delighted to endorse this principle in Elroy's list. The greater the diversity in a system, the greater the potential for self-organizing change. And don't forget, self-organizing change and bottom-up change are related."

"So this one is a big deal for you as a church consultant."

"Yes, it certainly is. I am ready to work with a congregation whether there is a lot of diversity or not, but the ones where the tone values this kind of diversity are more fun for me and I generally see more positive change."

"This must mean," Kevin said, "that you encourage congregations to focus on helping the members to identify their spiritual gifts and engage each other in discerning how these gifts can be employed."

"Absolutely, and it ties in so tightly with your focus on having a congregation be disciple-forming as you were putting it."

"This focus would also seem to fit well with another of the ideas on the list that we were talking about, church-as-community."

"You were just talking about people helping each other discern how to put their gifts into practice," Swen said, "and that is part of being a community together."

"Hey, there is one here you haven't said anything specific about, the one about at least half the budget being directed outward rather than spent on themselves. I bet like me, you think that one is unrealistic."

After a long pause, Swen replied, "I'd have to think about it some more, but at first blush, I'm not sure I'm as skeptical about it as you are. It is hard to sort out what part of the budget is directed inward and what is outward. It reminds me of the earlier one about measures of success. Both of them are quantitative in nature and are related to things that are difficult to sort out and neatly categorize. The key measure of success is spiritual growth, or growth in discipleship, but that is tough to measure. It is much easier to measure butts and bucks—the number of butts in the pews and bucks in the plate—than something as amorphous as spiritual growth. In the same way it is hard to determine what part of the budget is inward and what part is outward. I'm sure you can point out lots of things in your budget where this is the case."

"Oh, yeah. How about the budget item for our youth mission trip?"

"Yes, that is a good example. Is the main outcome the spiritual growth of the youth of your church families or the service they provide to others. And there is also the matter of possible evangelism of youth. Does your youth group bring unchurched youth into such endeavors or is it only youth from your church families? All this is tough to sort out."

Kevin chuckled as he said, "I can imagine one of the accounting types in our church—I'm thinking of a guy named Fred—setting up an accounting system to analyze all this. It would have different categories for the number of kids who are outsiders and how many are from church families and you would have columns where you break down the relative impact on the youth and the value to the recipients of the mission."

There was levity in Swen's response also. "Sure, and you have it all computerized and you have a committee of people to decide what values you put in each column. But seriously, the absurdity of such a pseudo-sophisticated approach does not negate the value of thinking about these matters. You may not be able to measure them precisely, but you certainly need to be thinking about these matters on an ongoing basis. They are serious stuff."

"So you think it is realistic to have half of the church budget devoted outward rather than inward?"

"Like I said, I would have to think about it awhile, but right off, I don't see why it couldn't be a realistic goal for the budget-building process. For starters, I think everyone in the church—not just the board and the staff—needs to think about things like this. People need to be thinking about who they are and what they are about. Far too often, the process of building the budget is a matter of perpetuating the status quo rather than thinking deeply about how it relates to the earlier items on your list of essential principles."

"Okay," Kevin said, "you have at least convinced me it is worth serious consideration."

"So much of this is tied to your goals and purposes. Remember in our earlier conversation about systems, when I said one of the three components of any system is its purpose. This is basic stuff for someone thinking about positive change, whether top-down or bottom-up, whether self-organizing or imposed from the outside."

Kevin leaned back, started to speak, and then paused for a long time. Finally he said, "I'm getting the impression that this idea of self-organizing change is favorably connected in your mind with both the church as we understand it in a biblical sense and in an institutional sense as well. Am I right?"

"Yes, you are on target."

"Well then," Kevin continued, "I guess I find myself wondering about what you do as a church consultant that takes account of all of this. How is your work as a church consultant influenced by your understanding of congregations as complex adaptive systems and how do you go about influencing self-organizing in a congregation. I know you put the emphasis on influencing what happens rather than controlling it, but this is still somewhat ambiguous to me."

At this point, Swen paused for a long time before responding. "Well, that is a big topic. I suppose I could give you some brief examples here, but it is a bigger topic than we can handle very satisfactorily over this one lunch."

After another long pause, Swen continued. "Something just occurred to me. I don't know if you would want to devote this much time to it, but I am doing a series of sessions on this topic for a group of pastors on the other side of the metro area. Maybe you would like to be part of it?"

"That's certainly a possibility. Tell me more."

"Well, all the pastors from this one denomination in the greater metro area are having a series of weekly gatherings at one of their churches over in the Belmont area. They are meeting on Wednesdays. I don't know their full schedule for the day, or even how much of the day they are meeting, but I do know they are having lunch there and I am on the schedule at one thirty for an hour and a half. They are meeting for seven weeks starting three weeks from today."

"Really? These pastors are meeting every week for seven weeks?" Kevin exclaimed. "I wonder what kind of attendance they will have."

"I wondered about that too. And it is amazing that it fit my schedule. My travel takes me away on weekends more than the middle of the week, but even so, it is surprising it worked out. And it is not a very efficient use of my time. It is a half hour drive over there and the same time back. Besides it takes time to get started each time and fully under way again. I probably could accomplish all most as much in one long full-day session. But I long ago gave up figuring out why certain people do certain things in a certain way."

"Say," Kevin said, "I think this event really does fit that description of a consultant I gave you last time. You know, that one about a consultant being someone who blows in, blows off and blows out."

"Careful my friend. This looks a lot more like what you do—a weekly meeting to blow off. Only I talk for an hour and a half—enough to give them their money's worth."

Their easy laughter was an indication that they really did enjoy each other's company. "You know," Swen continued, "if you were interested, you could ride over with me. We both live over here in the same part of town and we can talk on the way. Especially on the way back, we can talk about the stuff I have presented and maybe we can get more into the top-down, bottom-up stuff you are interested in and, of course, the self-organizing systems aspect of it."

"Are you sure they will welcome a pastor from a different tribe in their midst?"

"How can they object? I am bringing you with me, so in their eyes you can just be my assistant, gopher, or something."

"That makes me think of the tee-shirt one of the kids in our youth group has that says on it, 'I'm with the band.' Maybe I could get a tee-shirt made to wear each week that says, 'I'm with the consultant.'" Kevin was in a jovial mood.

"Sure," Swen responded, "but I think you will need to wear a clerical collar with it to show you have some status and are not just my gopher."

"Before this gets totally out of hand, I want to say I am intrigued with the idea. I will have to check my calendar for sure, but, in general, Wednesdays don't have a lot of scheduled events for me and I probably could do it. There are the unpredictable emergencies that hit a pastor's life that make it unlikely I could do it every week, but you never know. At any rate, I appreciate your invitation and would like to do it."

"Good, I look forward to having you with me on the drive back and forth to Belmont."

With that the conversation moved off onto a miscellaneous collection of topics. Knowing that they would be spending a lot of time together in the upcoming weeks seemed to take the pressure off the need to talk about serious matters. They were just enjoying each other's company.

chapter 7

Systemic Thinkers

- Small changes may produce big results.
- Static systems are not healthy.
- Shifts in purpose may bring big changes.
- It is important to seek the right goals.

Three of the twelve essential principles of effective churches are developed more fully in this chapter.

- Effective churches have a discipleship focus.
- Their goals are kept simple.
- They highly value personalization.

SWEN'S TOYOTA CAMRY WAS obvious in the far southwest corner of the Walmart parking lot where they had agreed to meet at twelve thirty. He still had feelings of disappointment about missing the first week of Swen's series of seminars but was glad that he would be at this one. Last week's seminar was blown out of his calendar by a mid-morning phone call informing him of the death of Ruth—a member of the congregation—that morning in a tragic car accident. Her family was in deep distress and obviously their pastor was not going to a seminar that day. Swen had been understanding, of course, and said it would be the same plan for next week except the time would be twelve thirty.

Memories of the previous Wednesday were fresh in mind as he climbed into the passenger seat of the Camry. Swen wanted an update on what had happened in the events that followed the accidental death and Kevin was glad to have a place to talk about what he had experienced in the wrenching time of dealing with the aftermath of the tragedy. It had not been an easy week.

The talk finally shifted to the upcoming seminar and Swen was quick to reassure Kevin that he would not suffer from having missed the first week. Most of what he had presented had been part of their two lunchtime conversations in weeks gone by. It had centered on systems ideas, with an emphasis on complex adaptive systems, and how they apply to congregations.

"Am I right in guessing," Kevin asked, "that you gave your summary of the actions of Philip from the book of Acts early on?"

"You are perceptive, my friend," Swen responded. "I wanted to establish early on that I was coming to them as a fellow member of the community of faith as well as a person with some additional specialized expertise. And, of course, the New Testament basis for all of this is truly important."

Swen continued with thanks for the permission Kevin had given him to use the list of essential principles he had compiled from his conversation with Elroy. Kevin had called Elroy to get his permission to use the list. He had assured Elroy that he would not be saying the specific description he had compiled was from Elroy, but he did want to give credit where credit was due. They were on the same page in treating the list as a work in progress for people to discuss and shape for their own purposes.

Swen had the same view of the list and said that was how he wanted to use it in his seminar. Everybody present probably would not agree with each principle as presented, but it did enable everyone to zero in on the key dimensions of an authentic congregation and ground other discussion in the realities of church life. Swen had not used any of the items on the list during the first week, but he intended to present two or three each week from this point on.

Kevin was pleased that he was making a contribution to the seminar series and said, "I guess I am not just here as your gopher now, so I won't have to be totally invisible."

"That's right, but I think you should have followed through on your idea for a t-shirt that said, 'I'm with the consultant,'" Swen responded, "and you should have worn it with a clerical collar. They would look good on you. Can't you see that clerical collar floating around over a t-shirt?"

Kevin smiled as he thought about their joke about the t-shirt at their last lunch. The conversation in the Camry continued on in a jovial manner as they completed the trip on the cross-town freeway. They were ready for the seminar itself.

As they entered the meeting room of the church where they were gathering, Kevin noted that tables were set up in the shape of a large U with chairs behind the tables for the participants. The presentation equipment Swen would be using was already set up at the top of the U. It appeared that someone had done a good job of getting the room ready. From what he had come to know about Swen, he was quite sure the room had been set up according to his specifications.

When the seminar got underway, Swen began with a quick review of the concepts they had discussed the previous week. During this three or four minute review, Kevin recognized the ideas he and Swen had discussed over lunch.

Swen then drew a line across the whiteboard at the front of the room and wrote three headings on it: STATIC on the left end, DYNAMIC in the middle and CHAOTIC on the right end. He said the line represented types of systems with the extremes on each end. His elaboration of the left end included words such as planned, controlled, organized, and predictable. His elaboration of the right end included words such as random and unpredictable. Before talking more about the middle—the part he had labeled dynamic—he asked the group for examples of churches that they thought fell on either end of the continuum. Although there were some joking references to chaos in churches, everyone seemed to agree that they were not familiar with any church that, as a system, would fall on the unorganized, random end of the line. On the other hand, they came up with descriptions of many congregations that appeared to fit the organized, controlled end of the line. The most extreme example was a tiny rural church known to one participant which included only a few older people, allowed the use of only the King James 1611 Bible, and scheduled Sunday morning worship, a Sunday evening service, and a Wednesday night Bible study and prayer meeting, and nothing else. The other examples were not that extreme, but even so, the group did not have difficulty coming up with lots of examples of churches which seemed to fit easily on the left end of the line. The programs were fixed and unvarying, the same people tended to be present at given events, and things did not change much over the months.

Swen then turned their attention to the middle of the line—the part he had labeled dynamic. His elaboration here included descriptions like organic, shifting over time, and a degree of uncertainty. He also talked about self-organizing, a concept he had introduced the previous week. Again he asked for specific examples with explanations of why they belonged at this point on the continuum. The examples the participants came up with tended to be their own congregations; they obviously thought of their congregations as not static, a characterization that had taken on a negative cast in the discussion a few moments before.

Swen pressed them to elaborate on why they thought their examples were actually dynamic and other participants joined in by raising questions that seemed to reflect doubts about the degree of adaptability existing in the examples that had been described. It was clear from the discussion a lot of the participants were not fully accepting of the portrayal of some of the examples as being obviously adaptive. One gained the sense that some of the examples looked fairly static and those deserving the label of dynamic were a lot closer to the static end of the line than the end called chaotic. One of the sentiments expressed by a few participants—without a lot of response from the others—was that the existence of so many churches that are plateaued or in decline was related to them being toward the static end of Swen's continuum.

Swen then moved on to talk about systemic thinking. He obviously was persuaded that people generally do not think enough about what they observe around them—including congregations—in a systemic way. He thought there is a tendency to look at the world in a linear manner rather than as systems with interactions that have patterns of behavior that include repetitions of these patterns. He was out to persuade them to become more fully what he called *systemic thinkers*.

He proceeded to give them two different lists of characteristics of systemic thinkers, the first list pertaining to how such people think about systems generally and the second about how they think about *changing* a system. In the process of introducing his two lists he mentioned the many resources available on this topic including internet sites. In particular he mentioned the site of a group that provides assistance to schools, www.watersfoundation.org, as the inspiration for the two lists he had developed and was presenting. He began with his general list of characteristics of systemic thinkers.

Characteristics of Systemic Thinkers

1. *Think holistically.* A systemic thinker thinks *holistically*, that is, attends to the many interconnections between the elements and the overall dynamics of the total system. A systemic thinker wants to see the big picture and how the parts fit together and interact. A systemic thinker looking at a church does not just see a collection of programs or a group of leaders, but also sees how the various programs are related and contribute to a common purpose and how the leaders interact with each other and the various programs.

2. *Recognize circular connections.* A systemic thinker understands internal relationships are *circular* rather than linear. A common example is the thermostat in a house that controls the heating and cooling system. It is set at a particular temperature and when the thermometer detects that the temperature in the room has deviated from the established setting, a signal is sent activating the unit to

raise or lower the temperature in the room. Once the designated temperature is reached, the unit shuts off. This balancing feedback process is circular in nature, not linear. Not all feedback loops are directed at such balance. There are, among others, reinforcing feedback loops where change stimulates more change in the same direction. Growth in a population of an organism produces more members who in turn yield more offspring and the population keeps increasing until some limit is reached. For example, people in a small group within a congregation may be pleased with the group's intimacy, sharing, and support and, as a result, encourage others to join the group. Eventually, however, the group may become so large that it loses some of its intimacy and positive benefits, which then curtails the growth of the group or even results in its demise. There are many different kinds of feedback loops. The key point is that they are circular relationships, not linear.

3. *Focus internally.* A systemic thinker realizes that the totality of *internal* elements, interconnections, and functions of a system yield the particular outcomes of the system, rather than external factors. A particular group or organization within a church, for example, may flourish because of the leaders, the makeup of the group, the manner in which they relate to each other, the purpose of the group, or a host of other factors. Similarly, another group may flounder for the same reasons. The point is internal factors determine the behavior of this system, not external factors.

4. *Attend to change over time.* A systemic thinker observes how the system changes over time, including how the elements change over time, the interconnections change, and the functions or purposes shift. This person expects to see such changes, looks for them and acts accordingly. Proceeding on the assumption that a situation is constant can lead to being blindsided. A worship leader, for example, who is committed to including music that reflects the current stylistic taste of the church's youth must be committed to rather constant change. Even though other types of change in a church and/or the surrounding culture may not be as rapid or obvious, change is constant.

5. *Seek many perspectives.* A systemic thinker looks at the system from as many different perspectives as possible with an open mind about various interpretations. A systemic thinker will carefully and

thoroughly examine both assumptions and interpretations underlying their understanding of a system *and* how it may be evolving. Systems are typified by complexity and it is rarely easy to understand social systems. There are multiple perspectives on a given system and the careful thinker will examine the assumptions underlying a given perspective and hold the current interpretation loosely. A church considering, for example, moving its nursery facility to a location next to the sanctuary, and in the process displacing worship preparation activities formerly held there, potentially will send ripples of change through the system. The changes may be many and the perspectives on them will be multiple and diverse.

Swen presented his list of five characteristics of systemic thinkers projected on a screen from his computer. They proceeded through the list one by one with at least some discussion about each of them. Then Swen moved on to his characteristics of what he called systemic change thinkers. What he had presented thus far was about systems and he now wanted to move on to how one thinks about introducing change into a system. Again he projected his list on the screen and encouraged the group to talk about each one.

Characteristics of Systemic Change Thinkers

1. *Be patient.* A systemic thinker is patient and does not jump to conclusions about the functioning of a system and how it can be influenced. It takes time to ascertain how a system operates, but even more time to make plausible inferences about how it can be changed in a desired direction. Quick solutions can easily lead to unexpected and undesirable consequences. For example, a congregation with two ministerial staff members, a senior pastor and an assistant pastor, suddenly had a position to fill when the assistant pastor resigned. A decision was made to redefine the vacant position to that of youth pastor because it was felt a focus on youth was the key to the future of their church. The experience of making this change, and later analysis, caused them to judge that, in this particular instance, the change led to diminished attention to children and young families in a way that hindered the development of the

total congregational system. Systemic thought needs to be deep and thorough.

2. *Model the system.* A systemic thinker creates mental models of a given system that aid understanding of it, and how it can be influenced. Consideration is given to how the various parts of the system interconnect and operate together. In the example just given of a redefined position, assumptions had been made about youth being the future of the church and the value of youth programs for bringing youth into the adult portion of the congregation over time. More careful modeling of the system and its future would have given appropriate attention to the place of children's programs and provision for young families. Careful attention to the full sweep of this complex system may well have led to a different proposal for changing it.

3. *Find leverage points.* A systemic thinker wishing to influence a system looks for leverage points where even a small change may have a substantial and long-lasting effect. A seemingly inexhaustible number of possible interventions present themselves in most systems, but, obviously, some have far more potential impact than others. Available resources generally limit actions to a small number and the ones with greatest impact are first choice, thus a search is mounted for those whose impact stands out. One of the intervention points with the most leverage in a system pertains to its purpose and, in a church context, the matter of establishing a vision for the congregation has big potential. Establishing this vision deserves to be high on the list of a pastor seeking to make change.

4. *Consider timing.* A systemic thinker is mindful of both long- and short-term outcomes of any actions undertaken to influence the system. Some outcomes are rather immediate, while others may only be apparent over the long-term; the latter generally are of most consequence. Impact delays are not unusual and must be taken into account when attempting to change the system. Research on church congregations has shown that disciple-forming programs can have significant results and the most substantial and fastest changes take place among individuals who already are at more advanced stage of discipleship. It is yet another example of a key leverage point as identified above. In addition, it may well be a medium-term

intervention—not short-term, but also not limited to results that will be seen years into the future.

5. *Proceed deliberatively.* A systemic thinker takes account of possible unintended consequences of any actions undertaken to influence the system. With these unintended possibilities in mind, a systemic thinker attempting to influence a system does so iteratively, that is, checking the results of any change and taking account of these results in making the next change in a process of fine-tuning the system. For example, a new staff member initiating a renewed focus on children and young families did not announce a detailed master plan with numerous components to be established over the next year. Instead, one by one, with deliberate consideration of the initial results of each step, actions were taken. On the monthly communion Sunday, the children were brought into the worship service instead of being in the usual children's church, and given a visible presence. Shortly thereafter, a periodic evening gathering for families with young children was initiated with a strong social component. In each case, attention was given to results and decisions made about its continuance. As these steps, and numerous others, were taken, a new and effective focus emerged.

As with the first list, Swen engaged the group in lots of interaction about what had been presented. While much of what had been presented could be applied to a static system as well as a dynamic one, the discussion was mainly about dynamic systems, ones with flexibility and significant potential for change to occur.

The discussion continued with Swen focusing on additional characteristics of dynamic systems. One characteristic is that anyone who connects with a dynamic system in any way (even observing) influences it. This idea was counterintuitive to some participants, but most quickly recognized the human tendency for people to change their behavior if they know they are being watched. Swen was making the point that as an outsider coming into a congregation simply to observe what was happening, he was aware that the system was behaving differently than if he had not been there. To emphasize this idea, he wrote on the whiteboard: OBSERVING IT CHANGES IT. Just looking around and consciously reflecting on what was happening—and what could be changed—was a useful beginning point for a pastor in what was hopefully a dynamic system.

Swen also went out of his way to note that any person doing something to transform a system is, in turn, being transformed in the process. He added to the whiteboard: THE SYSTEM CHANGES YOU. Kevin got the impression that Swen was pushing the participants to accept that they personally needed to embrace change if they were trying to make change in their congregational setting. He seemed to be pushing back against the common notion that "nobody likes change" and was saying change can also be both productive and fun.

His next point was: OVERALL OUTCOME MAY NOT BE THE SAME AS THE GOALS OF ANY SUBUNIT. He said the outcome of a larger system may not be the goal of any subunit within it. He was talking about a church congregation as a total system, of course, and pointing out that various subunits such as a youth group, children's Sunday school, a women's circle and a men's group could all have goals that may or may not be consistent with the eventual outcomes of the church as a whole. Swen appeared to be emphasizing both that goals and outcomes are not necessarily the same—for either the total system or its subunits—and that what happens in the various subunits may or may not be in concert with the system as a whole. The ensuing discussion went in many directions.

As Swen wrote yet another phrase on the board, it occurred to Kevin that what he was seeing Swen do on the board resembled in many ways what he had been doing with a pen on a napkin when they had gotten together for lunch. He seemed to want to have some sort of tag to attach to ideas he was elaborating. Kevin smiled a bit as he thought about how what was written on the board seemed to be forming a list. Was the discussion of ideas about dynamic systems simply an extemporaneous spillover from the formal presentation from his computer or did Swen have a well thought-out list of points he was presenting? An answer was not obvious.

The next phrase on the board was: NEW ELEMENTS MAY NOT BRING CHANGE. Swen emphasized that if new elements are substituted in a system without changing the interconnections and function, the system often remains constant. He noted churches are often a good illustration of this idea. Many churches have considerable turnover in people while the church seems to stay the same. The church is somewhat dynamic in the sense that some of the people (people being among the elements) keep changing, but the system does not change much because the way people interconnect is quite constant and the overall purpose of the system does not vary. This discussion connected back to the earlier

discourse about static and dynamic congregations and Swen noted that it
also was a precursor to conversation coming up next week about making
change in a church.

Swen then launched into the assertion that sometimes little changes
produce big results as he wrote: LITTLE CHANGES MAY PRODUCE
BIG RESULTS. Kevin thought that Swen was pushing people to think
not just about big changes but to recognize that small changes to a system
sometimes result in large effects. He seemingly wanted pastors to be on
the alert for little things they could do to move the agenda of the church
forward. It seemed to be about having a vision for where they wanted
their church to go and making the effort to take small steps whenever
they presented themselves.

Swen got some pushback when he asserted that dynamic systems are
most healthy when they are not in equilibrium. He had written: STATIC
NOT HEALTHY. His point was the best situation is one where at least
some amount of change is constantly present. When a couple of the pastors protested that they wanted some stability in a situation that was often
uncomfortable, Swen said they seemed to be arguing for having a static
system, something they earlier had been arguing against. He was quick
to agree that there are some dynamic situations which are dysfunctional,
but it seemed he would prefer that to one that was totally static.

It was becoming clear that the purpose or function of a system was
key in Swen's thinking about a system. As he wrote, PURPOSE SHIFTS
MAY BRING BIG CHANGES, he said a change in purpose generally
results in big changes in a system even though the elements and interconnections have not changed much. As some of the participants latched
onto this idea and expressed their interest in using some shifts in purpose
as a means of changing a congregation which was too static for their taste,
Swen introduced a somewhat different tone by noting that this did *not*
mean they could predict what those changes would be. The lively discussion which ensued ended when Swen pointed out again that even though
their main focus next week would be making change, he wanted to make
a final point now along the same line.

As he wrote, SEEK THE RIGHT GOALS, he said systems are very
sensitive to the goals addressed in their feedback loops. It is easy for systems to become responsive to goals that are not wanted or were never
intended. The solution is to be very thorough and careful in specifying
goals and be especially careful not to confuse effort and results. He said
it was very easy for a system to end up pursuing the wrong goals. The

ensuing discussion was on the somber side as the ideas pertaining to goals, purpose and function were emerging as major considerations in changing a church system.

After what had become an extended time talking about systems and change, Swen said he wanted to take some time to talk about the nature of the church and where it should be headed in our current society. With this introduction, he put forward the essential principles for a church that had originated with Elroy—not all twelve, but simply the first three. He said he had a longer list but wanted to get the first three on the table this week. He said what he had was a "work in process" which was subject to modification, but he was serious about these items because he believed they directed attention to what the authentic church was intended to be—something that was not just a product of our culture. He put the first one on the screen and Kevin was pleased to see the language about discipleship—the terminology he had substituted for Elroy's original words.

Essential Principles

1. *Discipleship focus.* The church should focus on developing disciples of Jesus Christ. It should not attempt to have "comprehensive" programs at the expense of this central spiritual purpose.

Kevin was surprised at the amount of resistance to this first principle, most of it seemingly due to the perception that a church needed a comprehensive program that responded to people of all types. The discussion was the most intense it had been at any point. The arguments for comprehensiveness seemed to reflect a need to address people's social, personal, economic and other needs in addition to the spiritual. The picture was complicated by the perceived differences among children, students, young adults, families and senior citizens. The counter arguments centered on discipleship—rightly understood—as pertaining to all the other dimensions of life and being applicable to people of all ages. As the discussion on this point wound down, Kevin sensed that the initial resistance to it had lessened considerably but had not disappeared.

When the second principle appeared on the screen, Kevin sensed less resistance, although, in his mind it had some common elements with the first principle.

2. *Simple goals.* The church's goals should be simple: each believer should master the spiritual disciplines most central to that individual and develop the spiritual gifts needed to reach out beyond him- or herself to further the Kingdom in accordance with the direction of the Spirit. These goals should apply to all believers, although the means to the goals will vary as these believers themselves vary.

The intent here was for focus. If efforts are too diffuse, the results are scattered as well as unpredictable. Kevin was pleased to see the commitment among the pastors to the goal being rooted in the presence of the Spirit in the lives of their people.

While the next principle was well regarded, Kevin picked up some resistance simply on the basis of practicality. It reflected a mode of operation that was not the norm in all of the congregations represented in the group.

3. *Personalization.* Teaching and various aspects of spiritual formation should be personalized to the maximum extent possible. To that end, a significant portion of teaching should take place in small groups with peer leadership, and spiritual formation on an individual level should be common. Decisions about programs, use of time, teaching approaches and modes of spiritual formation should rest with the people engaged in these activities rather than a governing group not engaged directly in the ministries themselves.

It was clear to Kevin that not all of the pastors were comfortable with an approach as decentralized as reflected in this statement. The phrase, "control freak" came to mind in listening to a couple of the more vocal participants. By and large, however, most of the pastors liked this principle, at least in theory.

By this point, the hour and a half time period was about up and Swen brought the session to a close with a brief preview of what was coming up next week. After some informal conversation following the closing of the seminar, Swen and Kevin headed for the parking lot and the trip back across town.

The conversation on the trip home was relaxed and congenial; eventually it turned to the reluctance of many pastors to pursue significant change in their congregation.

"I didn't see a lot of it in the discussion at the seminar today," Kevin said, "but I know many pastors really are afraid to make meaningful changes in how they are leading their congregation."

"You have no difficulty convincing me of your point," Swen responded. "In my work I see this fear a lot, in spite of the fact that I am working with churches considering changes. If there were no openness to change, they never would have brought me in from the outside as a consultant. Even so, I see a lot of hesitation about taking significant steps toward change."

"I imagine you have some insight into that reluctance as a result of your experience working with churches."

"Oh sure, but its roots vary from one person to another."

"Let me hear about some of them," Kevin responded.

"Well, some pastors, like a lot of other people, have a high level of fear and apprehension about all kinds of things. With some pastors I can hear it creeping out all over the place. I am usually aware of it rather quickly and I try to do something about it."

"Like what?"

"I'm certainly no counselor," Swen replied, "but within my coaching role I try to be sensitive to such fears. More substantively, I sometimes redesign what I would otherwise do with a given congregation. I may scale back the actions I am proposing, generally not for the long-term end point, but in terms of steps along the way. I may begin with smaller steps at the beginning of the vision that is emerging. Or I may suggest limiting initial efforts to a smaller group of people. And it is always easier to sell something as an experiment than as a permanent change. In all of this, of course, I have to be sure the pastor is on board with me because this leader will have a key role in making things move forward. In fact, it typically is the pastor who really is putting plans into action, not me."

"It sounds to me as though you are talking about dealing with someone who has a fearful personality. This can't be the only source of reluctance."

"Of course not. Some very healthy people are simply averse to taking risks—often for very plausible reasons. A pastor in a fairly stable situation, for example, may simply conclude that he probably will only be there for a few more years so why should he risk creating conflict by making changes that probably will not have major benefits for him personally. When dealing with such risk aversion, I work hard at clarifying and articulating the important differences between the old and the proposed new status. I then try to identify the potential implications of the alternatives to remove as much of the ambiguity as possible. This clarity does not remove all risk aversion, but it does help reduce it."

"How about cultural differences?" Kevin asked. "Aren't they at the root of some resistance to change?"

"Certainly, and where such differences exist within a congregation they must be addressed. In fact, such differences often are the basis of important changes. In the process of understanding differences between groups, the groups have the potential of working out plans that are the foundation for important changes within the congregation."

"There is another source of resistance I am aware of—lack of time. I often feel this one myself," Kevin noted. "How do you deal with this common problem of too much to do and not enough time to do it?"

"This situation calls for refocusing on the most important matters and setting priorities as to where time will be expended. It calls for careful analysis and discernment."

"I imagine there are still other sources of resistance—not just from pastors but from everyone else."

"Certainly," Swen responded, "and generally the major source of resistance is not the pastor. Resistance is something I find myself dealing with on a continuing basis. It goes with the territory. In all of these situations, however, the pastor is the key person and I go out of my way to ascertain how ready this person is to really engage."

"So, what sort of things are you looking for?"

"As much as anything, it really is a matter of helping the pastor self-assess the situation. Is the pastor able to see things from many different perspectives and recognize whether the congregation is ready for change and what is likely to happen when change is made? Is the pastor capable of handling the relationships involved, that is, make the needed investment in key relationships, focus on problem solving with people and develop trusting relationships with them? Does the pastor have the energy needed for a new initiative, the readiness for acting when needed and the ability to deal with the unexpected?"

"I can see that initiating change is a serious undertaking and I would like to talk about it some more," Kevin said, "but I can see my car over there and I guess we have to bring this conversation to a close for today."

Their trip down the expressway was about to end and as they prepared to part ways, Kevin offered his thanks for being invited along. Swen, in turn, expressed his appreciation for having someone join in with him and his pleasure at being able to expect Kevin in the car with him again next week.

chapter 8

Leverage Points

Waypoints

Key leverage points for change (in reverse order of importance) include:

- managing inflows and outflows;
- changing structures;
- providing information flows;
- encouraging self-organization;
- clarifying and prioritizing goals, purpose and functions;
- influencing the paradigms or mindset.

More on control versus influence. The distinction between control and influence is elaborated, including influencing mindset.

Ways to influence self-organizing are central to leadership.

Three additional essential principles of effective churches are developed in this chapter:

- Believer-as-kingdom-seeker
- Church-as-community
- Tone of acceptance for diverse callings

THE TRIP ACROSS TOWN in the Camry the next Wednesday was a pleasant interlude. The quick but good lunch he had had before meeting Swen, sunny weather, light mid-day traffic and relaxed conversation all contributed to Kevin's sense of tranquility. As they entered the meeting room for the seminar, he noticed that again the room was all set up in the style Swen wanted. While enjoying a cup of coffee, he watched the interaction of the people gathering in the room. In particular he was watching Swen as he greeted people and engaged in light conversation; Kevin began speculating about the scene he was observing. Given that this was the third week, Swen had minimal logistical matters to handle and he now seemed to know the names of the participants and a bit about their connections. He appeared to be checking in with people and catching up on what was going on with them at this point, somewhat like what is done in a more formal way in some small groups when they gather. He smiled to himself as he realized that this was the sort of thing that he as a pastor would recognize.

When the seminar got underway, the first topic Swen introduced was continued consideration of the church "essential principles" he had introduced the previous week. Last week, they had considered the first three of a list he said had a total of twelve. This week, he wanted to look at three more.

Swen saw this list as an aid to dealing with the tension between the church as an institution and as being organic, specifically the Body of Christ. The intent was to shift thinking to being less about it as an organization and more about it as organic. He noted that both were systems in the sense that they had been talking about, but they were different kinds of systems. He saw a tension between the two conceptions of the church and, more significantly, a tendency for the organization focus to dominate in most considerations of church in our society. He thought the list did not remove the organizational dimension but put the two orientations more in balance. With that introduction, he put one of the principles on the screen.

Essential Principles

4. *Believer-as-kingdom-seeker.* The governing metaphor of the church should be believer-as-kingdom-seeker rather than the more traditional metaphor of teacher or pastor-as-deliverer-of-spiritual sustenance. Coaching and spiritual direction should be prominent to help believers learn how to examine their own lives and foster their own spiritual development in the context of Christian community.

Swen launched into his rationale for the importance of this principle. He was persuaded that when people think about church they think about it as a place where they get spiritually charged by the pastors and teachers who are delivering spiritual sustenance to them. They go there to have something given to them and enjoy a positive experience. He didn't see this picture of a Christian as the one found in the New Testament. The church was about forming disciples and the most significant aspects of their life were outside the church building as they went about being disciples in all facets of their lives. It was about following the biblical mandate to be out seeking the Kingdom in all dimensions of life. The gathering together should be for the purpose of facilitating this way of living.

The ensuing discussion seemed to head the group in the direction Swen intended. While some addressed the difficulties of changing the orientation of an organization that seemed to have a life of its own, the main hesitation was about getting the people in the church to change their expectations of what church should be and especially getting them to change their orientation to life in general. Swen ended this part of the discussion by noting that this matter of making change would be discussed later. It was time to put the next principle on the screen.

5. *Church-as-community.* The church as a community of believers should be the guiding image rather than the church as an institution. Church is the stuff of relationships, prayer, and worship rather than programs, budgets, and management. This community, with its focus on relationships, prayer, and worship, should not be constrained by, or dependent upon, an unresponsive institution.

Swen did not provide much of an elaboration of this one. The discussion which ensued, however, was protracted. Weekly worship was not a big point of discussion; seminar participants seemed satisfied with their worship and Swen didn't protest their satisfaction. The struggle most of them experienced centered on community life outside the weekly worship service. Widespread and deep relationships centered on prayer and being a disciple did not seem to be the norm in their congregations. Again the discussion turned to how to change from the status quo to the ideal and Swen again turned to the next principle with a reminder that they would be returning to this topic of change before long.

6. *Tone of acceptance for diverse callings.* Within the context of the community's basic statement of faith, the tone of the church should be

explicitly and self-consciously one of accepting diversity in the way the Spirit directs the lives of the community's believers. Given the fundamental importance of this direction of the Spirit in individuals' lives, the community as a whole should avoid collective actions that do not have full community support. On the other hand, as a true community of believers, it should have open communication about fundamental matters of faith and practice in a manner that provides both mutual support and encouragement of individuals' prayerful examination of themselves and should give subgroups within the congregation the freedom to follow the direction of the Spirit.

Although this principle did not provoke much debate, it was clear the people in attendance had differing ideals for community life. Some had a preference for lots of diversity in the modes of living among individuals and subgroups of the congregation, while others were somewhat nervous about it. Some seemed to fear that too much diversity could lead to a loss of common focus and even a loss of orthodox commitment. More basically, however, it seemed that few were ready to commit much to changing current reality in their setting.

When Swen indicated he wanted to move on, one gained the sense that he was getting to a matter of high importance for him. He was ready to address change from a systems perspective and this matter was at the heart of how he thought about congregations. He wanted to start with something he called *leverage points*.

Swen's transition included making sure everyone understood that he considered *both* the church as an *organism* and the church as an *organization* to be systems. While they might be quite different systems, they were in fact both systems. As he introduced ideas about making change in systems, it would be about change in systems of both sorts. He intended to address system changes in a general sense and along the way he would differentiate between how various approaches to change can be applied to churches as understood in both ways.

While announcing that the new topic was *leverage points*, Swen noted that a 2008 book by Donella H. Meadows, *Thinking in Systems,* was the source of a list of twelve leverage points in systems, i.e., points in a system where one can intervene with a reasonable expectation of bringing about change. Only six of the twelve would be described in the seminar, ones Swen thought were particularly applicable to church systems of various kinds. As in the book by Meadows, the leverage points would be presented in the seminar in reverse order, i.e., from the least effective to the most effective. Swen explained that Meadows was a true expert, someone who had studied systems for decades and was a leading thinker in this arena. In addition to crediting her as the source, he emphasized her overall outlook on the list. "It is a tentative list and its order is slithery" (p. 165). In addition to saying he loved that word, slithery, he said he found great insight in the list. He also noted that the descriptions of the selected leverage points he would be presenting on the screen were his own.

Leverage Points

6. *Inflows and outflows.* A system can be changed by adjusting the inflows and outflows. For example, spiritual sustenance flowing into people, and disciples flowing out of the church building to be part of the community may be key parts of a system. Making a direct attempt to manage either of these flows, however, probably will be less effective than using other leverage points. Increasing the length of teaching sessions in various church programs from fifty minutes to seventy-five minutes, for example, may not have a notable increase in outputs from the system.

In his comments, Swen noted that this kind of leverage is among the first kind that many people think of when wanting to influence a system. This common sense approach of adjusting inflows and outflows, however, rarely has the assumed degree of influence. A system—made up of elements, interconnections and functions—is subject to influence in many ways and an intervener had best consider a number of other alternatives before acting. Thus, he proceeded rather quickly to the next leverage point.

"Are you suggesting that we shouldn't waste our time on these matters?" asked one of the pastors on the left side of the room.

"Not really," responded Swen. "There obviously are matters of this type that often need attention and it would be a mistake to ignore them. What I am saying, however, is that when I am thinking about ways to make positive change in my church, I would not begin with any of these. The time and energy available to make change is limited and I don't want to waste any resources on the less influential actions. I would start with other leverage points, so let's continue with the others."

5. *Structures.* Both physical facilities and programs are structures within a congregational system. Both are common leverage points for those wishing to make change in a church. In reality, however, they are relatively low on the list of influential leverage points. Church examples include building new and/or additional buildings and initiating a new program such as Alpha, mission trips, or a welcoming and assimilation program.

Swen was not coming out against any of the examples of structural changes he had used as examples, but he cautioned against expecting too much from them, or letting them deter someone from considering alternatives that possibly would be more influential. When earlier he had asked the participants to identify ways they thought of as means for making change, many of the suggestions had been of this type—structural changes. He had positive opinions about many of these structural changes and said some were included in plans he had helped churches develop in his role as a consultant. He cautioned them, however, to move beyond such changes and not expect the desired outcomes from such changes independent of additional interventions.

"One of your examples here," noted Albert, one of the pastors, "was the Alpha program. We starting using it a couple years ago and I thought it functioned very well and the participants liked it. But over time I can't see that it had much of an impact on our congregation. You are making me think all the time and energy we point into it was a bad decision."

"No, no, not necessarily. Alpha, in many cases, is used with great effect. I don't know much about your situation, but I think you may have been expecting too much of it by itself. Note I emphasized *by itself*. It may be very effective in a context created by some of the other more influential leverage points we are coming to. So let's come back to this point later. On to the next one."

4. *Information flows.* Not having information is one of the most common sources of malfunctions in a system. People often tend to avoid information because they don't want to be accountable for their decisions. Providing new information feedback loops can be an effective intervention. Leaders often want to curtail such information flow and the "masses" want it because it tends to empower the followers. A church example could be financial or participation

numbers, especially if this information can be closely tied to goals and purposes.

In Swen's extensive experience working with churches and other organizations, he had never encountered even one where inadequate communication was not cited as a problem. Seemingly, there always is a need for more information. He went on, however, to say he was addressing something else here—direct changes in information flow for the purpose of introducing specific changes. Appropriate information flow, for example, could be essential for successfully initiating a given structural change. It also could be an essential ingredient for developing a sense of vision in a congregation. Influential leaders pay close attention to information flow.

At this point, Swen announced that he was about to make a big transition. As if to emphasize the point he wrote on the board: CHANGE FOR DYNAMIC SYSTEMS, but then found he had to explain himself. His point was that the three leverage points he had presented thus far pertained to both static systems and dynamic systems as he had described them the previous week. He was now moving on to a leverage point that only pertained to dynamic systems. He acknowledged that any church systems they were considering were really dynamic systems even though they were very status quo situations. It was just the nature of most any human system. So what he was about to introduce potentially applied to any church context.

His major point was people in churches—including their leaders—tend to think of their congregations as static systems even though, in reality, they are dynamic, with a resulting failure to consider ways of making change that can be powerful in a dynamic setting. He was about to introduce a leverage point that was at the heart of how he advocated making congregational change. He had used a term the first week—self-organizing—that he now wanted to put it front and center as the key way to think about change. With that claim, he put the next leverage point on the screen.

3. *Self-organization.* The self-organizing character of complex adaptive systems can be capitalized upon to foster change in the system. Among the ways to encourage self-organizing are fostering diversity in the system, promoting experimentation, and encouraging new interconnections or relationships. Encouraging diversity and

experimentation means "losing control" and depending on influence. A church example would be promoting diverse, experimental
mission groups.

Kevin sensed that Swen's energy level had risen and he was onto a
matter about which he was really passionate. He emphasized again that
self-organizing is a characteristic of dynamic systems—something he had
introduced the first week—but he now wanted to go beyond that fact and
capitalize on its presence as a vehicle for intervening in a congregational
system to help a congregation reach its potential. He made the connection back to the week one discussion of control versus influence and then
said the topic was much bigger than what had been apparent thus far. The
concept of self-organizing as a leverage point for intervening in a church
system would be prominent in the rest of his series of seminars. After taking a couple of questions, he rather abruptly said he wanted to complete
the list of leverage points and they would be returning to self-organizing
later. With that statement the next leverage point appeared on the screen.

2. *Goals, purpose, and functions.* The goals and purposes of a congregation often are not recognized or articulated and bringing them
   to the fore can be the beginning of major changes. Identifying current goals, clarifying them and then redefining them can be the
   avenue to major change. A given congregation, for example, may
   have a diverse collection of goals including discipleship, friendships
   and social status that are in need of being clarified, redefined and
   prioritized.

Swen said the power of this major leverage point within a church
system generally is not recognized. In most cases, the purposes of the
congregation are assumed without being carefully analyzed or articulated, and the assumed purposes may vary considerable from one person to another, even among some of the leadership, such as members
of the board. In addition, what some people express as the goals of the
church may not in fact be those they value most. When the actual goals
of its members differ from "official" ones—or differ from those of the
leadership—a sense of ambiguity and uncertainty about the direction of
the church tends to emerge.

As a means of intervening in the system and introducing change,
this leverage point is powerful. The lead pastor of a congregation can
exert great influence by articulating a clear vision for the congregation.

The more thoroughly this vision has been "massaged" and accepted by the leadership of the congregation—including the staff, board, and informal leaders—the more influential the vision will be. The pastor, in the role of congregational leader, exerts great influence by articulating this vision in sermons, committee meetings, ministry team gatherings, and informal discussions. Pastors who excel in using this leverage point are consciously engaged in doing so in some manner essentially every day.

When asked if this leverage point pertained just to self-organizing systems, Swen was quick to say it was *not* limited to such systems; it pertained to all systems, both dynamic and static. He dropped back to discussing the basic nature of a system, i.e., that any system consists of elements, interconnections, and purpose or function. What was being discussed at the moment was the purpose or function of the system and a change in this aspect of a system often had rather dramatic results. He noted that even for a top-down change in a rather "stuck" church, addressing the goals was a major leverage point.

The final leverage point appeared to have some resemblance to the previous one in that it dealt with the purpose or function aspect of the system.

1. *Paradigms or mindset.* A major change can be attained by continued focus on the mind-set (the deepest set of beliefs and assumptions) of the system. It means examining the totality of the system and looking for ways to influence this mindset. It may mean transcending the prevailing paradigm—stepping beyond it, recognizing it for what it is and realizing that there may be other possibilities.

When pressed for an example, Swen described a congregation that engaged in an extended season of prayer and related study of the Christian life in which they challenged themselves to a close examination of their deepest beliefs about what it meant to be a follower of Jesus. Their prayer focused on the unknown and asking the Holy Spirit to bring new insights about the potential of congregational life. This process extended into all areas of the church. He mentioned a men's group in the church, for example, that took a portion of Romans 12:2 as its guiding principle for this process and posted it in a prominent place for all their meetings: *Do not conform any longer to the pattern of this world, but be transformed by the renewing of your mind.* The group—individually and collectively—was explicitly opening itself up to being transformed and acquiring a new mind-set.

When asked if this leverage point was a self-organizing principle or something that pertained to other approaches to change, Swen did not hesitate to tie it to self-organizing. In his view, it would be expected to foster self-organizing and the outcomes were not predictable. He thought of it as self-organizing at its best and with the potential of important results over the long haul. Given where Meadows, the systems expert, had placed paradigm in her list of leverage points, he claimed they needed to take very seriously its potential for positively shaping a congregation.

In response to a question, Swen tied this leverage point back to the first essential principle he had introduced the previous week—the one about the central goal of a congregation being to form disciples. Having this goal be so central would require a change in mind-set for many congregations. It would require deep change and self-organizing would be central within the process.

"You said earlier," interrupted Albert, "that you would come back to our Alpha program that I brought up."

"Oh, yes. What I want to say now is that the impact of a program, such as Alpha, probably depends greatly on the purposes the congregation holds, and even more importantly, their mindset, their deepest set of assumptions and beliefs. In the context of a congregation with an invigorating mindset, the program could be powerful, yet in another context, it seemingly would not accomplish much. So, my basic point is start with these two key leverage points and let other actions grow out of them."

As he concluded the discussion of leverage points, Swen noted—in response to yet another question—that someone could introduce a change in a system in a very directive manner with no intent of having any self-organizing occur and yet self-organizing probably would happen anyway. The reason, of course is that self-organizing is a characteristic of any dynamic system. A leader simply cannot avoid having self-organizing occur. The wise leader, however, can utilize leverage points to influence the self-organizing that occurs. It cannot be controlled, but it can be influenced.

As Kevin observed, he concluded that Swen was getting to one of his most fundamental points. He thought back to that lunch were Swen had been writing on a sheet of paper and emphasizing the key to being an effective leader was "loosing *control*" and focusing instead on exercising *influence*. *Influence, not control,* seemed to be his mantra. As he reminisced he also realized the essence of Swen's perspective was beginning to come through to him. Sufficient examples and elaboration of this view had come his way and it was becoming a part of how he viewed change in a church setting.

In the midst of his reminiscing, Kevin realized that Swen had been asked a question that caused a longer hesitation than usual, "Making change is awfully hard, isn't it?" The response began with, "It all depends." Swen then began to describe his experience years before in doing some research studies of change in portions of the U.S. educational system. He referred to the many attempts to reform education with which his audience was quite familiar; after all, the news media had been carrying reports of reform attempts by the federal government, state education agencies and local school boards for decades. He said one emphatic conclusion he had drawn was, in that context, *change is hard*. To emphasis this point he cited the title of a book by a leading researcher named Sarason, *The Predictable Failure of Educational Reform*. He then went on to emphasize essentially all these educational reforms were initiated from the top-down, using leverage points that were not high in effectiveness on Meadows list. He asserted that not only did these attempts at reform not depend upon self-organizing, but, in fact, in many cases, they provoked resistance from educators and actually inhibited self-organizing. Swen did not go into a lot of detail, but everyone was familiar enough with the decades-long attempts at educational reform that they got his point. That kind of change is hard and, in addition, it may not be lasting.

Swen then went on to claim that self-organizing change is easy, which brought some startled reactions from the participants. His point was that self-organizing happens naturally and, in a dynamic system, you cannot stop it from happening. The wise leader will do just the opposite—promote self-organizing and influence it.

Then it seemed to some participants that the other shoe dropped when he emphasized again that it happens but you cannot control how it turns out. You get change, but you don't know what it will be. One of the participants expressed a lot of nervousness about this point and Kevin thought he probably was deserving of the label of control freak. A lot of discussion resulted, including some bantering back and forth that included someone calling across the group to the person with control issues, "Hey Nolan, can't you trust the Holy Spirit?"

Swen then pressed on to explore what self-organizing looked like—or potentially could look like—in the context of the example congregations they had discussed. He did not go far with this line of thought before raising a couple of questions, the first of which was: To what extent do congregations allow (or even encourage) themselves to be self-organizing?

He went on to restate this question in several ways: Do congregations suppress and stifle their natural self-organizing tendencies? Do they even recognize that these tendencies exist? Do they attempt to capitalize on their existence? A fairly lengthy discussion ensued and Swen wound up this part of the discussion by saying he was not aware of any significant studies that would provide definitive answers to these questions, but he doubted that many careful observers of our churches would argue with his judgment that the great majority of churches (with a few notable exceptions) have a strong tendency toward stifling new self-organizing patterns and instead press toward maintaining the status quo. Often, he asserted, they suppress even small conflicts without recognizing in the process they are stifling transforming exchanges growing out of significant differences. A fear of conflict restricts creativity and new orientations. He said, in his experience, a culture that attends to the needs of the current members crowds out ideas about reaching out to the unchurched and commitment to an established set of ongoing programs limits attention to new programmatic endeavors growing out of ideas about new forms of outreach, new senses of purpose, or new links to their community. He thought the press toward the status quo and the press toward restricting self-organizing go hand in hand. He obviously was persuaded while thoughts to the contrary may be espoused, resistance to change is the reality.

Swen did not seem to get a lot of push-back to his opinion on this point and he moved on to his second question: To what extent *should* congregations encourage and foster their natural self-organizing tendencies? On this question there seemed to be rather strong agreement with Swen's opinion that congregations *should* encourage and foster their natural self-organizing tendencies, although Kevin also sensed that some of the participants again were displaying nervousness about it which brought to mind his minister friend who was fond of saying that the sheep don't tell the shepherd what to do.

In support of his position, Swen started with a biblical rationale and referred back to the reference he had made a couple weeks before to the experience of Philip in the book of Acts. He noted that Philip clearly lived a portion of his life within the structures and direction of the church, i.e., the established body of believers in Jerusalem, but a portion of his life also was lived under the direction of the Spirit in a context that for a time was absent direct connection with the physical community of faith. Local churches need to foster both, i.e., ministry within the programs of the congregation as well as living out life under the Spirit in contexts not directly established by the congregation. But then Swen went on to emphasis that what he was pushing was not just matters outside the congregation, he was talking about self-organizing within the congregation and the adaptive emergence of actions within the congregation that were bottom-up, not top-down.

At this point, a lot of discussion ensued that reflected differences of opinion on how much of this self-organizing was optimum and how it could be fostered. Swen encouraged a bit of this discussion and added that the topic would get more concentrated attention in the coming weeks. Before moving on, however, he did launch into talking about the big topic Kevin had been thinking needed more attention: control vs. influence. This topic had been a new perspective when Swen introduced it at their lunch meeting and he was waiting for it to be addressed here with more than tangential comments. Swen had the participant's attention when they started to focus on what was entailed in exerting influence rather than control and—not surprisingly to Kevin—he again turned to the topic of *vision* for a congregation and how it is acquired.

Swen claimed although it was far from the full story, discussion of how to influence a complex adaptive system should begin with vision. Noting again the prominent ranking of the item about goals, purpose, and functions in the list of leverage points, he turned to some of the traditional forms of goal setting and strategic planning used in organizations. Such approaches often are used in a manner that assumes that once goals have been established they will be implemented in a rather top-down manner. He asserted that such assumptions about implementation were not inherent in many of the goal setting and planning processes themselves and they could be used—with caution—for developing plans that would be initiated in a manner that encouraged self-organizing.

He set out one of his favorites—appreciative inquiry—as an example of a good approach to goal setting. With this approach, a large number of people are involved in examining their personal history in the congregation and using it as a springboard for identifying what they wish the congregation to become in the future. The resultant goals usually are tied to the realities of people's lives and the experiences that have proven to be spiritually powerful for them. The focus is on the *positive, not problems*. When someone asked for more detail as to what the process looked like, Swen hesitated and then said he would first say some more about its underlying assumption. In addition to the assumptions that there are always some positive happenings in any group or organization and that the process needed to be based on the many realities present there, it also assumes that asking questions of people in the group influences them in some way. Furthermore, it assumes that the best of our past is what should be carried forward to the future. Swen then acknowledged that a couple of the assumptions underlying this approach were especially important to him because they were so consistent with his desire to foster self-organizing, namely the assumption—just mentioned—that asking questions of people influences them in some way, and the assumption that it is important to value differences among the people. He said when they addressed ways to foster self-organizing next week, this connection would be more obvious.

Swen then described the basic steps in a typical use of appreciative inquiry, while acknowledging the numerous variations in how it commonly is applied. The first step is careful selection of a topic to be addressed, a matter that takes extended time. Positive questions regarding this topic are then developed such as, "Describe a time when you were most excited about the spiritual life of our congregation?" These questions are the basis for interviews—typically conducted by the people in the group who generated the topic and questions—of a large number of people in the congregation. In addition to questions about the past, there are questions about the future, such as, "What is one wish you would have for the future of our congregation?" After conducting their interviews, the group moves on to generating "provocative propositions," which grow out of their reflections on the many wishes heard in the interviews. These propositions become the basis for moving into the future.

Swen concluded his brief summary by repeating his earlier assertion that one of the powers of the process is it focuses on the positive, not problem-solving. He liked it not only because it has the potential of yielding realistic and valuable goals, but because the process itself stimulates valuable self-organizing within the congregation, including stimulating new interconnections and causing some rethinking of purposes and functions in the congregational system. He cited positive experiences with this form of goal setting in contexts where he had wanted to foster self-organizing. The potential for self-organizing appeared to be a key part of his enthusiasm for appreciative inquiry.

At this point a participant cited an example of appreciative inquiry which apparently did not accomplish much; it was said by people in the congregation a year or two later to have been a waste of time. The obvious inference was that this approach—like others—may work well sometimes, but most often will not bring dramatic change.

Swen appeared to welcome the challenge. Quick to note that he knew nothing of this particular instance and the thousand-and-one things that could have influenced the outcome, he suggested two possible constraints on the process in some situations. One was a lack of vision within the congregation and on the part of leaders who were in a position to promote it. He noted, in most cases, there is a past that includes excitement about significant matters, but also granted that there may be congregations whose past excitement was grounded more in dimensions other than the spiritual and were in need of exposure to other possibilities. A second possible constraint was a failure to recognize the self-organizing potential of the approach and treat the outcomes of the process as directives to be imposed, rather than the beginning of a long-term process.

Influence, rather than control, returned to the conversation at this point. Swen claimed that appreciative inquiry is a tool which an effective leader could utilize—along with casting vision in many ways—to move forward in a manner consistent with the character of a dynamic organization. He went on to refer to strategic planning, in its many forms, as having potential as well, but again there was the caution about doing it in a way that allows maintaining conditions conducive to self-organizing.

Time had now run out and Swen had to close the seminar at a point where there seemed to be both some anticipation and frustration. Both Swen and his audience were anxious to get into the specifics of influencing self-organizing in the various facets of a church's ministry, yet it was time to close. The session ended with an explicit promise that next week would be the start of examining self-organizing in the areas of leadership, spiritual formation, worship, and outreach.

The drive back across town was relaxed and filled with wandering conversation, although in response to Kevin's questions, a portion of it ventured into Swen's work as consultant. Kevin asked, "Do you go into a church with a clear plan of what you will be doing?"

"Human systems are unpredictable," Swen responded, "so I find my work as an agent of change requires me to be a careful observer and to adapt to what I find. I go into any situation with an overall plan in mind, but the details, and occasional sharp turns along the way, come from what I find. I need to be responsive, thus the attention to careful observation and questioning."

"After you have gotten to that point of understanding, do you make real firm plans to put in place?"

"Well, first of all, I'm not making the plans as much as they are being made by the leaders and others in the congregation. But as to the plans themselves, they may not be as firm and fixed as you suggest. The changes being promoted are not all mapped out in advance. They come about from many influences from various directions at different points in time within the congregational system."

"It sounds as if the plans emerge over time rather than all at once," Kevin said.

"Yes, and what emerges may be patterns within various parts of the congregation that have not been mapped out in advance. It is part of that self-organizing process we will discussing more in the seminar next week."

"It is sounding like you don't have a big plan of a lot of things that you want to do. It seems to happen in bits and pieces that are not highly coordinated"

"I'm not really ready to accept that characterization," Swen responded. "Certainly there are times when something like that happens, but we always have to keep the big picture in mind. Simultaneous small interventions can push the system toward change and I am always mindful of the opportunities to give such a push."

At that point, the drive was coming to a close and Kevin realized that he was looking forward with anticipation to considering self-organizing change again next week. There was always that hesitation about the possibility of some congregational emergency, but he expected to be with Swen again next week.

chapter 9

Everyone a Minister

Waypoints

A case study of local church leadership is utilized in this chapter.

An additional essential principle of an effective church is elaborated in the context of this case study:

- The staff prepares others to do ministry.

As THEY ENTERED THE seminar room the next week, Kevin immediately noticed that the room was set up in a different style than the usual U-shaped arrangement of tables with chairs on the outside of the U. The room instead had round tables with chairs around each one.

"Hey, Swen," he said. "They forgot to get your room ready. This setup must be left from a different meeting."

"Oh, no," Swen responded. "This is what I told them I wanted and like usual they followed my request quite carefully and have everything all set."

As the session began, Swen was pressed by the participants to explain what was going on. The new arrangement meant that nobody could find their usual "pew" and they were hesitating as they figured out where they were going to sit. Kevin chuckled to himself as the scene reminded him that change always seems to create at least a little bit of disequilibrium. But it also can create some degree of excitement as evidenced by his anticipation over what Swen would be doing today.

Swen explained that the new arrangement reflected a new mode of operation for today and the following three seminars. They would be engaged in more small group discussion than previous weeks and would be using some case studies as the basis for their dialog. In a joking reference to a couple of expressions of dismay at the change, he made a dramatic pledge to not change the format again. He would keep it this way from now on.

Swen also explained that each of the final four seminars would focus on a specific facet of church life, a different one each week. The topic for today was leadership in the church with attention to both the staff and lay leaders. He rather quickly moved to the case study he had promised them would be a focus of attention. A copy was distributed to each person and he asked them to read it carefully and reflect on the issues it raised in their minds. He encouraged them to read and then reread it with the intent of identifying the most important issues. The case was as follows.

CASE STUDY
Emmanuel Church

JORGES VELEN JUST COMPLETED his first year as pastor of Emmanuel Church, an established congregation with multiple staff and an average weekend attendance of about 650. The first year at this church was an invigorating experience for Jorges. It was more than three times as large as his previous congregation, his ministry was well received, and the church seemed to be maintaining the relatively level path it had been on with the previous pastor. In contrast to what often happens in such situations, the ministerial staff who had been at the church before he came stayed on. Jorges was pleased with how this turned out, since they were competent people, were well liked by the congregation and meshed well with Jorges' philosophy of ministry. Most were relatively young, but they had the potential to grow; they were competent and committed. He was convinced that the staff stability had contributed to the relatively smooth transition from the former pastor to his leadership of the congregation.

An area of uncertainty for Jorges was his leadership of the board and the staff. He did not think that the board collectively had a unified sense of direction and a commitment to the church becoming something beyond what it currently was. He was comfortable providing spiritual leadership for the members of the staff, but there were areas of needed interpersonal and professional growth he was not sure how to foster. In addition, as staff members they performed their responsibilities quite well, but they were not a team in the sense he had observed in the large church where he was an intern while in seminary.

In different ways, he was looking for both the board and the staff to exercise leadership in the church, yet he was uncertain how to help them do so. In addition, he felt responsibility for helping each of them—especially the staff—to grow individually in their roles. His uncertainly was reflected in how he worked with the staff—at times being quite directive and other times being quite hands-off when issues came to the surface. Thus far in his tenure at the church, his uncertainties in this regard did not seem to have posed big problems, but he sensed going forward that significant progress toward the congregation becoming what it should be was limited by how he was playing his role. He was questioning how to move forward.

After a suitable period of silence, Swen asked each group to discuss the case at their table and see if they could reach consensus on the key issues raised in the situation. Rather intense discussion followed and finally Swen brought it to a close and said he would like to hear their key issues and he would list them on the whiteboard at the front of the room.

The first group to report in prompted Swen to write on the board: PLATEAUED CHURCH.

At this notation, a couple of strong reactions came from elsewhere in the room. "How can you say this church is plateaued? It has a stable staff and apparently is operating in a very positive manner. It says right here in the case study that with this new pastor the church is 'maintaining the relatively level path it had been on with the previous pastor.' This sounds like the kind of place where I would like to be the pastor."

A person from the first table was quick to reply. "That word 'level' you just read sounds like the top of a plateau to me." Considerable discussion ensued about what constituted a plateaued church. A perspective about plateaued churches emerged that was decidedly hesitant about their long-term prospects. The contention was that a church not moving forward is at high risk of sliding into decline.

A clear consensus did not seem to emerge and Swen finally terminated this topic with his perspective. "I'm on the side of those of you who contend that this church is plateaued and at risk of sliding into decline. I saw nothing in the description of this church to indicate any new endeavors were on the horizon. In fact, it said explicitly that the pastor did not see any commitment by the congregation to becoming something beyond what they currently were. It is very difficult for a church or other group to stay just as it is. If you are not moving forward, you probably are sliding back. I think this generalization is true whether you measure moving forward in terms of increased numbers of people, growth in spiritual maturity, greater outreach in ministry, or some other indicator."

Swen proceeded to expand the list of issues on the whiteboard by soliciting additional input from the people at the tables. Ideas were numerous and the list on the board got long, although it included ideas that were largely alternative expressions of topics already on the list. He concluded the discussion of the case study by picking out four ideas he wanted to give explicit attention. They appeared on the whiteboard as:

- Plateaued church
- Role of the pastor
- Role of the staff
- Role of the church board

He wanted to tackle them one by one.

Swen said he wanted to address the matter of a plateaued church by looking at it from a self-organizing perspective and examining ways a leader might influence this church system. He began by reviewing three modes of intervention (or points of attack) for influencing a system that he had introduced at an earlier seminar: 1) points of influence, 2) significant differences, and 3) emergent interconnections. After briefly defining them again, he assigned each table one of the three to address. He set them to work with the goals of identifying possible examples of their assigned category. Since the description in the case study was quite sketchy, he gave them license to imagine the church to be whatever was convenient for their discussion. Once started, the subsequent discussion was lively and ended only when Swen cut it off.

He then asked the people working on *points of influence* to report to the total seminar how they had defined their arena and what they had come up with. One person spoke up immediately and said they had decided most anything in a system could be a point of influence; it could be one or more of the elements in the system, any of innumerable interconnections, or the functions of the system. Neither Swen nor any of the other participants wanted to argue this definition and Swen went on to elicit their specific examples.

As various people spoke, Swen listed items on the board:

- Budget
- Mission activities
- Staffing and job descriptions (paid and volunteer)
- Worship schedule
- Types of small groups
- Mission or vision of the congregation
- Community/social connections of the congregation

As Kevin listened, he also reflected back on the initial conversation he had on this topic with Swen when they first met for lunch at Goolsby's. In that conversation, Swen had given some concrete examples that resembled some of the examples the group was producing, such as the configuration of physical space in an office or classroom, but he had also included such matters as people's sense of identity and the culture of a congregation, that is, the values and various beliefs they hold. Kevin was reminded that most anything was a potential candidate as a point of influence. There obviously was an art, however, to figuring out which ones had the greatest potential.

As the discussion continued, Swen reminded them of the essential principles they had been considering, saying that such principles certainly would affect what points of influence they would choose to give their attention.

The group selected one of the points of influence (staffing and job descriptions) to develop more fully and as the conversation continued, Swen reminded them that they shouldn't go into this expecting predetermined outcomes from addressing a particular point of influence. They could be reasonably sure that a certain point was truly an influential one—such as how money in the budget is allocated or the sense of identity people develop—but as self-organizing proceeds, the outcomes may be quite different than what was anticipated by the leader who chose a given point of influence.

Swen moved them on to the second mode of intervention, *significant differences*. There was agreement that most congregations had differences of many kinds; the only question was identifying those of consequence, i.e., those related in some substantial way to the interconnections and functions of the system.

Again the people who had addressed this topic started listing off the ones they had identified and Swen began listing differences on the board:

- Worship styles
- Ethnic
- Socio-economic
- Theological
- Age
- Gender
- Cultural
- Clergy/laity

As Kevin listened to the discussion of these differences, his mind returned to that first lunch with Swen at Goolsby's. A difference Swen had talked about then was power differences, something Kevin could see reflected in several of the items on the board that had come from the group. He could see power differences as being foundational to such differences as age, gender, and socio-economic level, and also to the one that Swen chose to pick up on for more extended discussion in the seminar.

Swen chose to direct the seminar toward consideration of the clergy and laity difference, apparently because it was related in some way to several of the essential principles they had begun to consider, such as a discipleship focus and believer-as-kingdom-seeker. It was apparent even in the discussion within this group of mostly ministers that there were differences in their understanding of their role with respect to lay persons. Clericalism was alive and well within some of them, yet others were suspicious of such differences and wanted to reduce them.

Discussion ensued about how these differences were a fruitful target of intervention. Suggestions for using differences as an entry point included having discussions about the topic within the congregation, addressing it in job descriptions, considering it in selecting new staff members, and others. Again, Swen ended attention to this topic by emphasizing that attending to these differences could have unpredicted outcomes, which is what you would expect in a self-organizing or complex adaptive system.

The individuals addressing the third mode of intervention, *emergent interconnections*, seemed especially enthused about their topic, possibly because many of then saw it as a matter of new relationships, and relationships were central to their understanding of their role. Swen again listed their ideas on the board and came up with the following:

- Youth and Adults together in new contexts
- Mentors and mentees together in new contexts, e.g., non-work
- Social media
- Online learning
- Community connections—social, missional and/or artistic
- Hobby groups
- Other congregations

By now it was almost automatic for Kevin to compare the list with what he remembered from that early conversation at Goolsby's. The only thing that came to mind was a recollection of more attention to interconnections with inanimate items such as lesson plans and financial transfers. It was a reminder that interactions were not just personal relationships and needed to be conceptualized broadly.

Swen chose to develop several items in some detail, possibly because they seemed to be especially relevant to the topic of today's seminar: leadership. A wide-ranging discussion ensued, but Kevin took note especially of Swen's commentary on two of the items.

"The essential principles we have been considering imply or require a substantial connection between a congregation and the community in which it is located, yet many churches are relatively separate from the broader community. This gap represents opportunity. The effective leader will be looking for many opportunities for new and stronger interconnections. The champion of self-organizing will not be attempting to impose new interconnections but fostering opportunities for them to emerge."

The second item they discussed produced a bit more response. "I see a lot of potential for more interconnections between congregations, especially between ones with similar visions of what a congregation should be."

Resistance came rather quickly from one participant who said, "Other than with an occasional special project such as a youth mission trip, in my experience, trying to coordinate activities across two congregations is more trouble than it is worth. I just don't see the mileage in it."

"I am not pushing for forced engagement. The collaborative activities you experienced may not have been ideal, for whatever reason. I am talking about a relationship which may or may not result in collaborative activities. Much like accountability between individuals in a covenant group, I think congregations can help each other in appraising where they are and where they are going. For example, the leaders of several congregations could use a common appraisal instrument and then meet to compare the individual congregational appraisals. They could help each other assess whether they are staying focused on their mission and following through on their commitments. Here are examples of some of the questions I have in mind."

With that comment, Swen projected the following questions:

- How has your congregation reached out to your community in the last year to serve those in need and fulfill the Great Commission?

- How is your congregation enabling everyone (all genders, ages and ethnicities) to become more fully disciples of Jesus?

- What evidences have you seen in your congregation of the transforming work of the Holy Spirit in the lives of people?

"An opportunity to share appraisals and hold each other accountable is important for congregational leaders," Swen concluded. "It is a very different activity from the typical pastor-gathering where everyone is trying to put the best face on things back home and not expose all the issues that are being faced."

Swen ended this discussion of plateaued churches with three concluding comments. He first related creativity and self-organizing, claiming they had a lot in common. He referred to artistry and inventiveness as human characteristics, saying that people with such gifts often flower in self-organizing systems resulting in new ways of moving forward. One hope for plateaued churches is openness to creativity, developing a receptiveness to new and novel approaches.

He went on to argue that plateaued churches need to encourage variability rather than uniformity and engage as much as possible in experimentation. Try new approaches with the expectation that many of these new initiatives will not continue for long, but will be the fertile ground from which even newer ideas will blossom and grow.

Finally, Swen noted that all of this openness to change meant that the leaders needed to give up control and instead be satisfied to influence what was emerging. It was all tied to the nature of complex adaptive systems.

As he heard this last comment, Kevin thought again how it seemed to be Swen's mantra, but the more Kevin wrestled with these ideas, the more it seemed that it really was a linchpin for an effective leader in this context, which was where Swen was poised to go in the next phase of the seminar.

Pointing to the second issue on the board, ROLE OF THE PASTOR, Swen said everyone in the room probably would agree with him that the pastor is the key person in this situation. With the right pastor, there is hope that this church not only will avoid drifting into decline but will begin to gain momentum and become a more vibrant and vital community. The issue at hand was how the pastor can exercise leadership in a manner consistent with the nature of a self-organizing system.

As Kevin suspected, Swen started by addressing the "vision thing," but then moved beyond it to talk about the pastor helping the congregation develop a new mindset about the nature of their community of faith. He reminded them that the most potent leverage point in the list he had introduced last week was this very one—focusing on their deepest beliefs and assumptions and finding ways to influence this mindset. He went on to emphasize that this point was the reason during the seminars he had been introducing "essential principles" of a thriving church. These principles constitute central matters that everyone needs to address in shaping their mindset. If the church in their case study was to move beyond its complacency, a new mindset probably was needed.

In response to a question about how a pastor could help a congregation develop a new mindset, Swen introduced two additional characteristics of system thinkers that went beyond what he had mentioned earlier. He said a systemic thinker creates mental models of the system at hand that help in understanding the system and how it can be shaped. This is an art, of course, and requires some reflection. What motivates people in this system to take the actions they do, foster the attitudes they hold, and pursue their particular interests? The effective leader spends a lot of time listening to "what makes people tick," tests tentative conclusions in additional dialog, and uses these insights to form mental models of both what is and what could be.

His second point was that in looking for leverage points the effective leader should consider those where even a small change may be possible. Given the nature of complex adaptive systems, even a small change occasionally may result in a substantial and long-lasting result. In other words, don't look for the one "silver bullet" but look for a combination of leverage points and stay in it for the "long haul."

Another participant, reflecting a bit of self-doubt, said, "Somehow, what you are describing makes leadership seem like a complicated job and I am wondering if I am cut out for it. What is it going to take for me to be not only a pastor to my people but someone who influences change in this complex setting?"

Swen responded by complimenting the person for raising the question and saying self-assessment is a valued characteristic. He described three clusters of skills he thought were important for a pastor-leader, starting with relationships. This leader must develop caring and trusting relationships with people in the congregation and help these people develop their own capabilities. The pastor's goal should be to help them learn and act rather than to solve problems for them.

The second cluster of skills had to do with seeing and understanding the system they were working in; Swen compared it to a quarterback "reading the defense" in a football game. The pastor-leader needs to see what is going on from various perspectives and have a sense of what may happen as a result of various actions.

Finally, the effective pastor-leader must be ready and willing to act when needed to move things forward. There must be a willingness to act even though the outcomes are uncertain and mid-course corrections may be needed. A willingness to cope with ambiguity is needed, along with not being unduly risk-averse. He concluded his response to the question by saying these clusters of skills can be developed and he encouraged the pastors in the seminar to recognize them and work on developing them.

The discussion of the pastor's role concluded with Swen's reminder that pastors needed to focus on the three previously mentioned modes of intervention in influencing a complex adaptive system, namely addressing 1) points of influence, 2) significant differences, and 3) emergent interconnections. He urged his audience of pastors to champion variation rather than uniformity in their congregations and engage in experimentation wherever possible.

Then Swen pointed to the third issue on the board, ROLE OF THE STAFF, and said, "Here is another major responsibility of the pastor, helping the church staff develop into what they were meant to be. In our case study, the lead pastor, Jorges, seemed to be uncertain about this responsibility, yet he was in a relatively large, multiple-staff church where this aspect of his role is crucial. A major component of being a leader in such a setting is development of the staff."

At this point, Swen said he wanted to take a bit of a detour and introduce yet another of the essential principles of a vital church that he had been inserting along the way in recent weeks. Kevin again felt a sense of satisfaction, and a bit of pride, about his contribution to the seminars. The principles that had originated in his discussion with Elroy had been useful in previous weeks and as the next one appeared on the screen he expected similar benefits.

Essential Principles

9. *Staff.* All members of the community should see themselves as ministers and in a role of ministering to others, both inside and outside the community. Although paid staff members devote more of their time to serving the community itself and preparing others to minister, ministry itself is done by all.

Swen gave the participants time to read the item, reflect on it silently for a moment and then invited them to discuss it at their tables. After giving a brief opportunity for discussion with the total group—which seemed mainly to be sure the meaning was clear—he moved on. In doing so, he made an emphatic point. He was firmly convinced of this principle, thinking it scripturally grounded and foundational for a church that expects to reach out to the community beyond their walls.

A question, however, interrupted his attempt to move on. "You previously cited significant differences as an important source of self-organizing and thus valuable, yet here you seem to be pressing for uniformity. Aren't you being inconsistent?"

"Aw, an important consideration," Swen acknowledged. "We need to talk about this one. If, in fact, there are differences on this point among the staff, it certainly needs to be explored and examined in depth, in which case it may be the source of some new ways of viewing the situation and new ways of operating. I suspect, however, that this issue may be so central to the purpose of this overall system—that is, this particular local congregation—that substantial agreement on this matter may be important for the full functioning of this system. I am not ready to say it is as crucial as a system claiming to be Christian being totally committed to the lordship of Jesus Christ, but it is fairly basic. This matter of the role of the staff is one of those matters which the church board needs to address in depth and declare what the philosophy of this particular church is. We can come back to this matter later when we consider the role of the board, but for now, let's just say this is a fairly basic matter."

"Are you saying," continued the questioner, "that you are open to alternative versions of this principle, but the board needs to declare just what version the church is operating on?"

"Yes," Swen responded. "I think that's a good way to put it. Some matters are so basic to the functioning of a system that some agreement is needed on the part of all the key actors. The secret is identifying which are primary and which are secondary matters. Unfortunately, it is easy to find churches that fall off the log on both sides. Some impose a rigid uniformity on lots of matters and others seem to be adrift on fundamental philosophical and operational matters."

With this comment, Swen moved on in his agenda. Given this essential principle, he set out three aspects of a staff that he would seek. He declared that he would want a staff to be 1) a team, 2) united on goals, and 3) prepared to equip members of the church to minster to others.

Swen's call for a church staff to be a team appeared to be an easy sell. Nobody wanted to argue with his desire for a staff made up of people with distinctly different roles, but united in support for each other and their commitment to the goals of the church. While the participants agreed on the importance of unity on goals they wondered about how a church can expect to attain this unity of purpose and Swen assured them they would address the matter when they got to the role of the board.

One participant referred to his experience on a staff that was "a dysfunctional collection of fiefdoms" and wanted to know how Swen would develop such a staff into a team.

"Well," Swen said with hesitation, "that may be a big task, but in most cases it is doable. There are ways of working with a staff to build a true team. It generally is best pursued in a concentrated time together, maybe in a retreat setting, specifically devoted to this goal. This is a bigger topic than we should address here, but let me note, from my perspective, the team should become a self-organizing unit. Rather than being a source of dysfunction, the differences between members of the team should be become the source of productive ideas and enhancing enrichments of ongoing work. Positive relationships between team members should result in new initiatives and mutually supportive actions. I haven't answered your question of how to make it happen, other than to say it is doable, but what I want to emphasize is that building an effective team does not mean building a predictable unit in which each person is a pre-designed cog in a machine."

"From a systems perspective," asked a participant, "is it a commitment to the function or purpose of the system that is most important for this team to become what it should be?"

"While commitment to the basic purposes of the team is essential," Swen replied, "I tend to zero in on trust within a team. Recall that along with function, interconnections are an essential aspect of a system. In a human system, these interconnections are the relationships between people and, without trust, these relationships don't amount to much. So if I were trying to work with the dysfunctional collection of fiefdoms mentioned a moment ago, I probably would start with trust. One starting point for doing so is the differences between people. The long-term intent is to build a team in which these differences are the source of positive self-organizing rather than dysfunction."

"If you have a dysfunctional staff like you have been talking about," said another person rather heatedly, "my hunch is that a person or two needs to be canned. Firing a person or two probably would straighten out the mess."

"Certainly there are times when a person must be removed from a team. There are occasional individuals who just don't play well with others, as we sometimes say. In a sizeable number of cases, however, the overall situation will not change that much by replacing a person. If the team is a collection of fiefdoms, replacing the key person in one of them with a different person is not likely to change a collection of fiefdoms into something else. To put it in systems terminology, changing some of the elements in a system may not do much to change the modes of interaction or their goals. The only exception I would make to my generalization," Swen continued, "is with the person at the top. The leader of a team, the senior pastor in the situation we are addressing, is in a position to shape the goals of the team and the modes of interaction. Changing this person may have a dramatic effect in some instances."

With this comment, Swen moved on to his third aspect—the staff's role in preparing church members to minister to others—and declared that this was a place where the principles of self-organizing really came into play. If the staff truly was a team, and they were united on goals—such as they had a primary responsibility of preparing others for ministry—there was room for lots of variation in how individual staff members would contribute.

"Are you saying," one participant asked, "that there would be no church-wide programs of preparation for ministry?"

"No, no; not at all. There may or may not be. My point is that if this essential principle is really of central importance for this congregation, the work of preparing others for ministry will permeate the work of the various staff members in this church. You will see it showing up in lots of places."

"You have been making a big point of self-organizing," commented another participant. "Where does it come into this picture?"

"Aw, now we are getting down to the central matter," Swen responded. "There is great potential for self-organizing to contribute to reaching this goal and it may give us an opportunity to take our case study to a deeper level. Earlier, the various tables here were trying to identify examples of potential 1) points of influence, 2) significant differences, and 3) emergent interconnections. If we had time, I would ask each table to return to the one of these three you had been discussing and address it again with respect to this very specific matter of equipping everyone for ministry. If you had points of influence, for example, you could try to identify potential points for enhancing self-organizing with respect to fostering this preparation for ministry. Similarly, with significant differences and emergent interconnections. Since we don't have time, however, I would encourage you to pursue them on your own with respect to preparing everyone for ministry."

Swen made his transition from addressing the role of the staff to the board's role by talking about a characteristic of a system that both needed to cope with. He wanted both staff and board to fully accept in a conscious way that they can't predict the future. They can form a vision of what they want it to be and try in a caring way to bring it into being, but they can't be sure of what they are bringing about. They need to expect surprises and move forward with confidence in spite of not knowing exactly what the future will be. Both staff and board need to learn from the unexpected and profit from what emerges." With this comment, he pointed to ROLE OF THE CHURCH BOARD on the whiteboard and said he was moving on.

Kevin was not surprised that Swen started on his new topic with references to the matter of setting the vision for the church. He noted that it was crucial for the board to operate at the policy level and leave the day-to-day work of the church in the hands of the staff. Micro-managing was out, but dealing with the big picture was their major responsibility. They needed to be deeply involved in establishing the vision for the church—something done in close collaboration with the pastor—and, of course, setting the policies within which these goals are to be pursued.

Swen elaborated. "Think again about the essential principle I was advocating today—the one about the staff equipping the members of the church to do ministry—and the others in earlier seminars. Those are all big picture matters. They reflect a particular vision of what the church should be as well as policies for attaining those goals. That's the stuff boards should be dealing with, not where the youth group will be going on their mission trip next summer, how the men's group will be organized and other such matters. Let the staff deal with such matters. The board needs to deal with the big picture. The essential principles I have been presenting are ones I really believe in, but any board doing its job would not accept some list like that without careful deliberation and discernment. That's their job, deciding on such matters."

One of the more thoughtful participants commented, "What you are talking about—this careful deliberation and discernment—takes a lot of time and effort if it is done right. Are most boards ready to take this on?"

"I'm glad you asked that," Swen responded, "because you are hitting on a crucial matter. Studies show that many church board members finish a term on their church board somewhat disillusioned. The major source of their disillusionment seems to be that they were not dealing with major issues and it was not the spiritual experience they had expected. Spiritual discernment was not a major part of the job. This serious work—setting vision and formulating the polices for realizing this vision—does take a lot of time but it is fulfilling and board members generally are ready to give themselves to it."

"I may be missing something here," noted a younger seminar participant, "but I have not usually thought of the job of a church board being spiritual discernment. Do most board members see that as their role?

"I am not claiming that most boards do see their role that way, but I am saying they should. Many of the problems that occur with boards, such as the disillusionment I just mentioned or conflicts between pastor and board, result from boards failing in this spiritual dimension. I'm convinced that many of these problems occur because of boards not understanding that their role is primarily a spiritual one. I think the key roles of the board are setting policy and supporting the pastor or pastors, but operationally this must be understood as a matter of spiritual discernment."

"I'm convinced what you are saying is the way it ought to be," said another participant, "but I don't think I have really seen it put into practice at a deep level. How can a board become what you are advocating?"

"Well, first of all, the board must become a true spiritual community and this means they have to begin sharing their lives with each other on an ongoing basis. An example of what one board initially did to move in this direction was to have one member at each meeting share their spiritual journey in an unhurried manner. It was the beginning of significant interaction between members about spiritual matters and forming a foundation of a spiritual community. Their meetings became a place where they shared important aspects of their personal lives and provided support for each other. The shared understanding they found in this community became a foundation for spiritual discernment and coming to consensus on important decisions."

"I have a somewhat different concern." interjected another participant. "You have been making a lot of references to self-organizing, which I see as more of a grassroots matter, but boards are at the top. If you have a board that is really strong and influential, won't that squash self-organizing?"

"Most often not," responded Swen. "If a board is operating at the policy level and not micro-managing the staff, they are not squashing self-organizing, but creating an environment in which it can flourish."

At this point, Swen launched into a description of board approaches to gaining input for formulating vision and setting policy. Boards do this in many ways, of course, and generally do not do it in a vacuum absent of congregational input. He went on to describe some of these approaches and identify ways in which they could be managed to retain an atmosphere conducive to self-organizing. The first one he discussed was appreciative inquiry, a visioning and planning process described in an earlier seminar. It is built on storytelling by people in the congregation highlighting positive experiences from the past. His key point here was stories need to be made public as much as possible and not held within closed groups or restricted to documents compiled by a planning group. They need to be known in all their diversity. The congregation needs to know the variety of input, not just a concluding policy or plan.

As he continued, he emphasized that a board can help create a climate in which differences are celebrated and dialog about them fostered. The board can encourage new relationships that result in new insights and initiatives. If a board understands the power of self-organizing, they are in a position to encourage it and expect that it will enhance movement toward attaining the vision of the church as well as influencing what the board does in shaping the vision of the church.

With an eye on the clock, Swen said he wanted to leave time for at least a couple of questions and threw it open for issues broadly, not just the specific topics of the day. The first question was from a pastor who described a somewhat large congregation that seemed to have a flow of rampant rumors and wanted to know what could be done about it. Swen's response was that they probably needed to establish new information systems, not depend on what they had and resign themselves to attempting to stamp out new rumors as they occurred. They should give a flood of new information and in the process real differences (not imagined ones) would be visible and self-organizing enhanced.

The next questioner was concerned about systematic blaming that seemed to persist in his congregation. Swen's response made the point that blaming was to some extent a theological matter but went on to say from a systems perspective it probably called for establishing new forms of accountability throughout and fostering the interconnections between everyone such that the accountability processes worked. With a nod to family systems theory, he emphasized the need to create a culture where triangulation was not respected and where open and positive relationships were valued.

The clock brought the session to a rather abrupt halt and Kevin helped Swen get his materials out to his car. The trip back across town was relaxed with a conversation that roamed over a variety of matters, including a couple pertaining to the seminar topic. Kevin brought up the resistance to change that seems to be mentioned whenever new approaches are discussed. Swen acknowledged that it was real, not imagined, but that someone working in a church context should not just assume it is present. There often is an attraction to new ideas that helps bring about meaningful change. In the right context, change can generate excitement, not just resistance.

Swen also started in on a topic they had discussed before—the tendency in a self-organizing system for similar patterns to emerge in various places in the system. Kevin quickly perceived that this topic had entered the conversation because Swen saw it as related to the topic for next week's seminar—congregational spiritual formation. While not obvious to Kevin at first, he soon realized that Swen saw spiritual formation that reached into large parts of a congregation as being a stimulus for self-organizing. It provoked his interest in what was coming.

chapter 10

Measures of Success

Waypoints

A case study of small groups within a church is explored.

An additional essential principle of an effective church is elaborated:

- An effective church uses appropriate measures of success.

Some additional characteristics of systemic thinkers are developed as applied to influencing or changing a system. They:

- take account of possible unintended consequences of any actions undertaken to influence the system;

- recognize that the various results of any actions taken to influence a system may vary over time and will take account of impact delays in attempting to change the system;

- attempt to influence a system iteratively, that is, by checking the results of any change and taking account of these results in making the next change in a process of fine-tuning the system.

THE NEXT SEMINAR BEGAN with Swen's presentation of another essential principle. A minimum of preliminaries preceded its projection on the screen.

Essential Principles

7. *Measures of success.* The measure of success of the church should be growth in discipleship. It can be assessed by individuals in the context of community interaction. The primary focus should be on *being*, that is, who we are as people, not on *doing*, that is, the work we accomplish. Numerical growth in the size of the congregation should not be basis for measuring the spiritual growth of the congregation.

After a moment for everyone to read it, he said they would start with the people at each table discussing the principle among themselves. Did they agree with it or not?

During the ensuing discussion, Kevin found himself listening rather than participating in the discussion; in fact, he was trying to follow the conversation at the table right behind him, as well as the discussion at his own table. There was a lot of similarity to the talk at the two tables—both were focused on the apparent discounting of growth in the size of a congregation as an indicator of spiritual growth among the people. "What else do you have?" argued one pastor at the table behind him. "There is no way to measure in any practical way, the spiritual growth of someone."

A person at his own table was arguing that an increase in the number of people in a congregation was an indicator of spiritual vitality in the church. "Spiritual excitement is contagious." claimed Segundo, a young pastor. "Spiritual vitality in a congregation will cause it to grow, so I am happy to use growth in the size of our congregation as an indicator of spiritual growth."

At this point, Gail broke her silence and said she had to emphatically disagree. "A lot of research has been done in the US on church growth and it is clear from multiple studies that in many cases what attracts people to a church is that it gives them something they want and it may have little to do with their own spiritual vitality or that of the people in this church. They are captives of the consumerism of our culture and they go to a place where they like the music, or the fellowship, or the preaching, or whatever. Something about the place appeals to them and it probably has nothing to do with the spiritual vitality of the place or its potential for helping this new person grow spiritually."

Segundo took sharp exception to her strong opinion and said, "How can you say that? You don't know what has brought these people to a particular church."

Gail held her ground. "I'm referring to studies done in actual churches. People are sometimes interviewed one by one and given an opportunity to state what has attracted them to a given church. In other cases, church programs have changed in specific ways and people then vote with their feet. The consumerism of our culture has crept into the church and the egos and ambitions of pastors suck them into building their churches on these consumeristic instincts of people."

"Ouch," said Derek. "What you are saying doesn't make pastors look very good. Do you really believe what you just said?"

"It is not a matter of what I believe. I'm just reporting what has been found in some studies of churches. But in terms of what I believe, I suspect all of us are more influenced by the surrounding culture than we realize."

At this point, Swen signaled for their attention and his place at the end of the room became the focal point. As he got their attention, Swen asked if they agreed with the essential principle that he had presented.

The first person to respond said, "I don't think we had any significant quarrel with the principle as such, but we couldn't come to any consensus about how to measure spiritual growth. The statement said spiritual growth couldn't be measured by growth in the size of the congregation, which our table mostly agreed with, but we are not sure how you will measure it."

Swen then began checking with the other groups to see if they had similar reactions, and finding that no group had many clear ideas of how they would measure spiritual growth, he sent them back to work at their tables. "How can you measure spiritual growth in your congregations? It seems like a fairly basic matter. How will you measure success?"

As he observed the participants starting to zero in on this question, Kevin thought they were struggling and became convinced that they probably had not wrestled much with this question before. It appeared that they thought they would just recognize spiritual growth when they saw it and were not sure there was any need to measure it in a manner that was at all as quantifiable as the number of people in a congregation. Swen soon called for their attention again and began to list their ideas on the board at the front of the room. While there were many suggestions, they were not coming up with much of a quantitative nature that could be listed in a church's annual report.

"Note that the statement of the principle says discipleship 'can be assessed by individuals in the context of community interaction.' It can be assessed but it may be really tough to put it in quantitative terms. It must be done individual by individual, and each individual may be in the best place to assess where they are. But this assessment should be done in the context of community interaction. The Christian life is a life in community. This assessment of our being and our doing is best done by the individual with the support and aid of those closest to them in their community."

Swen brought the discussion on this topic to a close with a concluding summary. "Here is my conviction about this matter. First, it is difficult to measure in a quantifiable manner, but this is no reason to avoid giving growth in discipleship a high priority. Give priority to what is important, not to what is easy to measure in objective terms. Second, growth in discipleship is evident in more subjective terms and we need to focus on it, talk about it, give examples of it, and describe the evidences of it seen in the lives of people. It is measurable, just not in the terms usually summarized in reports."

"I don't want to leave this essential principle," he continued, "without highlighting the central point of it, namely that our primary focus should be on who we are becoming, rather than on what we are doing. Doing certainly is important; it will be the focus of our seminar a couple weeks from now. For now I want to emphasize that my understanding of the New Testament is that what we do should be an outgrowth of what we are becoming. With this focus we can expect God to use us to do important things."

At this point, one of the participants raised another matter. "It seems to me that your way of expressing all of this puts a strong focus on the individual, yet much of our doing is done collectively, as an entire congregation, or some subgroup of it. Isn't there a tension here?"

Hearing that comment, Swen wrote on the board, INDIVIDUAL VS. GROUP and proceeded to address the issue. "This is probably a good place to return to this matter of systems."

"Most often," Swen began, "when the leaders of a church start some form of strategic planning or visioning process, they are thinking at the group level. The discussion makes reference to 'the youth,' 'young families,' 'the small group ministry,' 'the women's group,' or uses some other collective language. It's hard to find this sort of language in the New Testament. The Gospels are filled with reports of Jesus's encounters with individuals. The Christian life is lived in community but, within that community, individuals are not reduced to look-alike specimens. They are individuals who potentially are living in a vital relationship with Jesus, not just living in relationship with the group."

"Okay," interrupted someone near the front rather impatiently, "but what does that have to do with systems?"

"Everything," responded Swen. "If the key elements in our system are individuals, we better be thinking about our system in terms of individuals, not just groups. This business of forming disciples takes place at the individual level, which means that the assessment must be focused on growth in discipleship in individuals, not just assessing it in terms of how well a group is functioning, how well people like the group, or other such group indicators."

"Well," continued the questioner in the front, "you have identified the elements in your system. What about interconnections and purpose, the other two parts of your systems?"

Swen seemed pleased with the question and responded quickly, "The main interconnections obviously are the many and diverse relationships between people. The purpose, or function, is really prominent in a system that is focused on forming disciples. In practice it is so easy for the purpose to slip away from the intended function of disciple-making to a wide variety of other interests. The consumerism that pervades our culture creeps in and we begin to assess the results of our system in terms of whether or not people feel like their more superficial wants are being met. A key part of our assessment needs to be at the individual level and needs to be driven by this central purpose of forming disciples."

"Okay, I'm with you so far," continued the questioner, "but you have been talking about systems as if they promised more. Is there more?"

"Yes, patterns develop in systems and we would expect similar patterns to emerge at various places within this system, which I am thinking of as a given faith community. If our system is focused on forming disciples—if that's its purpose and this purpose is being pursued throughout the system—we would expect some similar patterns to emerge in various places. Systems people talk about fractals, but we don't need to get that sophisticated; let's just talk about similar patterns, that is, patterns of behavior or relationships."

"How about some examples?"

"Sure. Some relevant information comes from a study of discipleship done among about 80,000 people in 200 churches of quite varied affiliations and reported in a book titled, *Follow Me: What's Next for You?*, authored by Greg L. Hawkins and Cally Parkinson. It should be noted that they found the spiritual growth among these people to be very individual and it seemed to happen in stages. A fascinating aspect of their results is that while there were some items common to all the movements between stages, for example, study of the Bible, the most influential factors varied for the movement between particular stages. I think we can say that self-organizing resulted in similar patterns in these 200 church settings."

Swen continued, "Most fascinating of all to me was the finding that the most rapid movement in this spiritual growth occurred between the final two stages. It was almost as if spiritual growth was exponential. As this growth occurred, the pace seemed to pick up."

The questioner interrupted, "That sounds counterintuitive. How do you explain it?"

"I agree. Explanations are speculative, of course, but the authors of the study think they have some ideas as to why growth is most rapid as people move into the stage they call Christ-centered. They note that at this point people seem to take more personal responsibility for their growth; they are not just participating in whatever the program of their church is. They also note that people at this point rely less on external factors and function more on internal motivations. Furthermore, they see that these people are putting their passions into action and it seems to feed on itself."

Another question followed. "Are you suggesting that a pattern emerges across these congregations that is similar but was not planned?"

"That is my personal interpretation. Just what such changes will be in any particular situation is hard to predict. What typically happens in systems, however, is that similar events will begin to emerge within the system at quite separated points and they tend to reinforce each other. They take on a life of their own in unexpected ways and with similarities to other places in the system. So to summarize, the changes are unpredictable, similar patterns develop at separated points and collectively they take on a life of their own. In contrast to a random or hierarchical system, in a complex adaptive system, similar patterns tend to repeat themselves at various places in the system."

"You have mentioned some of those ideas before. Why do you make such a point of it with respect to discipleship?"

"Well, for starters, discipleship is grounded so much in individuals and is thus so diverse in how it is exhibited. Also the forming of disciples is so foundational to a vital community of faith. You have a situation where everything is very fluid and not subject to effective micro-managing. Thus, self-organizing is the foundation of effective change. We have here a great example of what potentially could be a very dynamic complex adaptive system."

The persistent questioner pressed ahead. "This brings me back to my role as a pastor. How do I go about making change in my congregation—in this case, increased discipleship?"

"Yes, we certainly are looking again at how one makes change in a system. So I would suggest going back to some of the basics we discussed last week. It includes looking for modes of intervention of the kind we identified, namely points of influence, significant differences, and emerging interconnections. Start with these basics and see if you can influence your congregational system to move toward this goal of an increase in the formation of disciples."

At this point, Swen signaled a change in direction for the seminar by announcing that it was time to look at the case study for this week. He distributed copies and asked each person to read it carefully, taking careful note of the key issues as they saw them in this case before beginning the conversation in their group. He asked them to address the six questions posed in the last paragraph of the case, as well as others posed by members of the group itself.

CASE STUDY
Living Faith Church

LIVING FAITH CHURCH IS committed to evangelistic outreach and has been relatively successful in this regard. They have grown to an average weekend attendance of nearly 1400, becoming the largest church in their city of about 100,000. While a significant part of their growth has been transfer membership, they have been successful as well in bringing in unchurched people. As with essentially all growing large churches, they have a strong commitment to small group ministry. Being part of such a group is the norm in the congregation. The groups are a part of their evangelistic outreach and in a few cases they reach out in compassionate service to the human needs of other people.

The common element in these groups is Bible study and prayer, along with what is usually billed as fellowship. The latter element seems to be the glue that holds most of the groups together. The Bible study and prayer shapes the character of the fellowship but the social aspect itself seems to be the main determiner of people's continued strong commitment to their group.

Both the church staff and the board recently have been examining how to do a better job of fostering people's growth as disciples of Jesus Christ. They have had growing doubts about seeing an increase in the depth of discipleship within the congregation. While they have always viewed the small groups as a key location for such discipleship to be fostered, they have doubts about the reality of such growth.

Among the questions the staff and board are considering are the following. Are small groups the place where this growth in discipleship should be expected to occur or is it somewhere else? If it is in the small groups, what must be done to bring it about? If not in the small groups, where should it be pursued? Aside from the question of locale, what should be done to foster discipleship? Is it a particular program or something more comprehensive? Is discipleship where we should be focusing, or should our central focus be somewhere else?

At his table, Kevin was pleased to find the whole group seemed to agree on an answer to the last question posed in the case study; they were persuaded that discipleship should be the central focus of this congregation. Rather than debating this question, they quickly moved on to the other questions.

His group then zeroed in on the first question about whether small groups should be the place to expect that the church would attend to discipleship. On this question there was more diversity of opinion. One view was that small groups are the ideal setting, since it is where people open themselves up and deal with more intimate matters. Another view was that what happens in small groups is highly variable, not very subject to significant influence by the church leadership, and thus not a setting from which much specific could be expected. As they were debating this question, Swen stopped by their table and listened to the discussion. Given their varied perspectives they were especially interested in his viewpoint. Recognizing that this same issue had been prominent at other tables, he decided to interrupt the table discussions to address the seminar as a whole. He said several groups had been pressing him for his opinion on the question of whether small groups are the place to address discipleship and so would toss out his opinion on the question to go along with the others at the tables.

"'Yes, but' is my response," he began. "I think small groups are a great setting for pursuing this purpose, but you can't just depend on the groups. Remember that we are dealing with a system and we need to look for a wide range of ways we can influence the system. As you probably suspect by now, I would begin with the vision thing. Becoming a disciple-forming congregation should be a prominent feature of sermons on an ongoing basis, as well as in other settings where the pastor can help cast vision. In addition, all the programs in the church should be examined to see where this goal could be pursued within their usual mode of operation. Training should be provided for the leaders of the small groups, and other programs, to aid them in pursuing this goal."

"I'm skeptical about getting existing groups to change," interrupted Evelyn. "Unless a group already has this focus, I think it is hard to move to this orientation. An existing group is what it is and it's hard to get it to change. I think you should start with totally new groups and work hard to establish them as disciple-forming settings."

"I agree with you," Swen responded. "I wouldn't ignore trying to influence existing groups, but I would give much higher priority to establishing new groups with this specific goal. This is the sort of issue where you need to focus on the individual level in an intensive manner and it is really hard to do that on a system-wide level. If you have other ways of getting to the individual level, great, but I suspect your best possibilities are in some sort of small group context."

"It seems we are on the same page regarding this question," Evelyn persisted, "but this still leaves a huge question about how to form such groups or set up other ways to get to the individual level. I sense that you are skeptical about church-wide programs for this purpose but you haven't really told us what to do instead."

"Yes and no," Swen replied. "I find it hard to set up an effective big program for such purposes, yet I think by doing many small things at various places and setting up small experimental activities of varied sorts you can begin to make some inroads and begin to make some headway toward finding activities you can introduce on a larger scale. We don't have time in this one session to lay out many such possibilities, but let me point you to some resources and then talk systemically for just a bit more."

With that comment, he moved to a table at the front of the room where several books were on display and began to talk about them. Kevin recognized some as ones he and Swen had discussed before and others that were new to him. Swen began by pointing out several books by Dallas Willard and commenting, in his judgment, this writer had had more impact on our understanding of spiritual formation than anyone else in recent decades. He noted not just his books, but his impact on other leaders in the area such as Richard Foster and the Renovare organization that Foster founded. Kevin noted two among these several books by Willard that he not only recognized but recalled as being profoundly influential in his own life, *The Spirit of the Disciplines* and *The Divine Conspiracy*.

Swen then proceeded to talk about some studies of spiritual formation in church settings based on survey information and gave important insights about how to proceed in fostering spiritual formation in a church context. Here he singled out the *REVEAL* study and a follow up book titled *Follow Me: What's Next for You?* which he had just discussed earlier in the seminar.

As he finished discussing these and other resources, he noted that time was pressing in on them, but he wanted to finish the day with some additional characteristics of systems thinkers he had not yet addressed. He thought they were particularly important with respect of the topic of the day. He used his computer and projected them on the screen at the front of the room.

Additional Characteristics of Systemic Thinkers

6. A systemic thinker takes account of possible unintended consequences of any actions undertaken to influence the system.

7. A systemic thinker recognizes that the various results of any actions taken to influence a system may vary over time and will take account of impact delays in attempting to change the system.

8. A systemic thinker attempting to influence a system does so iteratively, that is, checking the results of any change and taking account of these results in making the next change in a process of fine-tuning the system.

Swen addressed the three items one by one. He considered the first one about unintended consequences to be particularly relevant in their current discussion because they had been addressing a matter that was highly individualized and the suggested actions to prompt change where quite varied and uncoordinated. They had, in fact, been considering initiating various experimental actions to promote change and also providing training to leaders of small groups which, in reality, would be implemented in quite varied ways. Swen said even a tightly organized program for initiating change in these circumstances could be expected to have unintended consequences, so they should be prepared for the unexpected.

One of the participants displayed some nervousness in saying, "This is why I have been a little apprehensive about where we have been going today. Some of it has seemed too much like stirring things up and then waiting to see what shakes out. I'm not sure that's always wise."

"In some sense," Swen replied, "we never are sure what will happen when we make changes, even carefully planned and implemented ones. What this principle is saying is 'be aware, stay alert for the unexpected and be in a frame of mind that is open to taking new actions on short notice.' I recognize that this is not always easy, but being a systemic thinker in this manner helps you work effectively in the real world."

"The next principle," Swen continued, "is a bit like the previous one in suggesting that you should anticipate the unexpected. The actions you take may have results that vary over time, so don't be lulled into thinking that the results you have just seen over the short term will continue in this same way over the long term. It is also well to realize that some actions have little impact at first, but later on they take hold."

As the discussion continued, Kevin did not sense that Swen was getting much pushback on this principle and they soon moved on to the final principle. One word in this statement seemed to be a favorite of Swen's and he wrote on the board, ITERATIVE. While acknowledging that it was a fancy word for the simple idea of doing something repeatedly, he proceeded to use it often as he advocated for being aware and taking action to keep a system moving toward change. It was assumed that sustaining change in a positive direction required continuing action. He thought of this process of attending to the results of various changes and then making additional small changes as fine-tuning, another phrase he seemed to like. At the prompting of one of the participants, he added to what he had written on the board so it said, ITERATIVE FINE-TUNING.

Acknowledging that time for their session had run out, Swen said he would use the phrase just formed on the board as his motto for the process of discipleship they had just been discussing. Quoting Romans 12:2 (obviously one of his favorites, it had come up before), "Do not conform any longer to the pattern of this world, but be transformed by the renewing of your mind," he said he liked to think of this process of personal transformation as *iterative fine-tuning*, but not so much what individuals did for themselves, but what God was doing in their lives.

chapter 11

Worship

Waypoints

A case study of worship in a church is explored.

An additional essential principle of an effective church is developed:

- Worship is done in community and is focused on telling the story of God, celebrating it, and responding to it.

Four assumptions about change in a complex adaptive system are explained:

- Any dimension of differences has the potential of significantly reshaping an organization.

- Adaptation results from shared values and differences in dynamic tension.

- All environments are different, so best innovations cannot be generalized.

- Cooperation and competition held in healthy tension is most adaptive.

SWEN AND KEVIN DROVE in a steady rain on their way to the next seminar. As they entered their room at the church, they saw several indications that the people already there had come in out of the rain, but everyone seemed to be in a good mood. They were finding their places at the round tables—often where they had sat the previous week—and engaging in friendly conversation.

At the appointed time, Swen got underway, even as a couple of stragglers came in out of the rain. After addressing a couple of procedural matters one of the participants brought up, Swen announced that he would be starting with a case study. As he distributed copies of the case study, he said everyone should read it carefully and then begin to identify for themselves what they thought the major issues are in the case.

CASE STUDY
Bethany Church

BETHANY CHURCH HAS HAD occasional informal discussions over the last couple of years about the nature of their worship service; the format is quite predictable from week to week and has been relatively unchanged for a number of years. The church board has just charged their worship committee with the task of doing a formal review of their worship approach, including the music—the main topic of discussion up to this point—other aspects of worship, and how it connects with other facets of church life. After the worship committee completes their work, the board plans to meet with them to consider the specific changes they want to introduce.

On a typical Sunday about 165 people attend worship, which is one service held in an attractive church building that could easily accommodate 225. Bethany Church can be described aptly as "plateaued." At one point, three or four years ago, the attendance topped 200 for a while and they considered going to two services every Sunday, but attendance soon dipped and has been stable for the last couple of years. The makeup of the congregation is heavily weighted toward what some have called "early empty-nesters." There are many couples whose children have left home for college or employment. A few others still have children in high school, but there is a relative lack of younger children or young adults in the congregation.

The music is led by a praise band consisting of three vocalists and four other people playing two guitars, a keyboard and a drum set. The drums are electronic, which alleviated a past problem of the drum volume being overpowering. The service includes very little liturgy, which is consistent with their denominational heritage. The music itself is what they call "contemporary," although one of the teens recently commented, "The music we sing is the same kind of stuff my mom and dad sang when they were in high school." It is a combination of numerous praise choruses and an occasional hymn, and only very occasionally is a new chorus introduced. The words for congregational singing—including those for hymns—are projected on a screen.

When the praise band plans out their music for the coming Sunday, they rarely have input from the pastor. They select music on the basis of what they think the congregation would like and their personal preferences as musicians. The members of the praise band tend toward middle-aged. Until recently, the band included a high school student, but after he went off to college, a thirty-one year old woman was recruited to take his place and became the band's youngest member.

The worship committee is reviewing worship to come up with recommendations for change. What sort of changes would be good—or even possible in their context? And what could they recommend as ways to introduce desired changes?

When Swen finally turned the groups loose to discuss the case at their tables, Kevin noted that the conversation at his table zeroed in on music and never went anywhere else. It was obvious that different preferences in music style were represented at his table and they were the focus of much of the conversation.

When Swen pulled the total group together, he started by asking them to identify topics or issues the worship committee needs to address in their review of their worship. As various people talked, Swen wrote abbreviated summaries on the whiteboard, occasionally stopping to ask someone if his choice of words captured what they were saying. The comments started to slow down about the time the board was filled with Swen's writing and he paused to look over the collection of statements. After underlining a few items and drawing some lines connecting several of them, he finally said, "There is one issue embedded in a lot of what is here, that I don't think we have yet addressed head on, and that is just what is worship?" With that sentence hanging in the air, he wrote in one of the few spaces left on the board, WHAT IS WORSHIP?

Swen continued with some additional commentary. "One of the essential principles I presented at a previous seminar was titled, 'church-as-community.' It emphasized viewing church as a community rather than an institution. It said the community should focus on relationships, prayer, and worship, but it did not really define what worship is. In other words, it emphasized worship but did not define it; it did not answer our question. I have an additional essential principle to offer today that addresses our question about the nature of worship. When I put it on the screen I would like you to read it carefully and then reflect on it for about sixty seconds. I'll then give a signal and you can discuss it at your table and see if you agree with it."

Essential Principles

11. *Worship.* The worship done in community is focused on telling the story of God, celebrating it, and responding to it. The community is reminded of God's purposes and concerns and celebrates them in a manner where this content takes precedence over style and other matters of taste. Individuals are enabled to acknowledge their brokenness, repent, and open themselves to God's redirection of their lives. The community gathers—as disciples, not consumers—and then is sent out renewed.

Focused discussion ensued at the tables that stretched out over considerable time. Finally Swen pulled everyone together and said it was time to find out what they were thinking about worship.

The first person to speak said, "We noticed that there is nothing in this statement about music."

"So," Swen responded, "is that a problem?"

"Yes and no. We agreed that one can worship without music, but music is so pervasive in the worship of our churches that it can't be ignored."

As Swen responded, Kevin couldn't tell if he was toying with the questioner or not. "The statement does say that 'content takes precedence over style and other matters of taste,' so you can't say it is totally ignored, but clearly content is given priority over the type of music. Will you let me say it puts music in its proper place?"

"Are you saying it doesn't matter if we have music in our worship? Music is everywhere in our society. It is one of our key ways of expressing ourselves. You can't just keep it out of the church."

"Okay," Swen responded, "let me be clear. I am not against music. In fact, it is hard for me to imagine worship without music. My point is simply that the seemingly constant debate in our churches over the *type* or *style* of music, is the wrong issue. The real issue is whether or not we are engaged in worship. If we get this basic matter resolved, it will be relatively easy to take care of our questions about music."

Following that exchange, the discussion moved off of music for a while and on to the prior question, "what is worship?" In the process, Swen found himself defending several aspects of the essential principle statement. It was clear that Swen was committed to the statement and ended up erasing some of what was on the board so he could list his key points. He started by writing WORSHIP IS TELLING GOD'S STORY.

He waxed rather eloquent as he recited a long list of elements in this story, including creation, the exodus, providing the law, his presence in the exile, sending a savior, and the promise of a second coming. His point was that worship is the retelling of this story, celebrating it and opening ourselves up to being transformed by it; it is the story of creation and redemption.

The discussion was now rather lively and seemed to be taking on a pattern of Swen facilitating a discussion among the participants, combined with his presentation of his key points of conviction. The conversation was referencing both the essential principle about worship and the case study they had read. As the discussion flowed back and forth, Kevin took particular note of the places where Swen wrote a phrase on the board to highlight one of his key points.

The second item Swen wrote of the board was IT'S NOT ENTER-TAINMENT. He was now harking back to the part of the case study where it noted the musicians selected the music on the basis of what they thought people would like and what they liked to play. Swen launched into a monolog about the consumerism of our society and how it spilled over into churches such that people often selected the church they would attend based on whether or not it had the kind of music they liked. He obviously was dismayed by this tendency but he got a lot of push back from some people. The counter argument was that people have varied taste in music and there is no reason not to accommodate this desire for what is pleasing for people.

Swen's main points on this issue were simply that worship was grounded in community and if the community truly was worshiping together, the music issues would subside and would not be unduly divisive. In practical terms, the person(s) setting the direction for worship would be selected for their gifts related to worship, not for their musicianship. Swen's promotion of this point provoked the most heated discussion of the day, but Swen wouldn't let go. He said the musicians would have to play second fiddle (yes, he got a couple of groans) to those preparing the sermon, the times of prayer, and any liturgy or other elements of telling God's story. He ended by saying he wanted the best possible music, but he wanted this music to be in support of the rest of the worship, not to be present for its own sake.

The next phrase Swen put on the board was DEEP RESPONSIVE-NESS. While he clearly wanted people to express their thankfulness and praise as part of worship, and felt this was an important part of worship, he didn't want it to end there. While a deep sense of gratitude would often be present in worship, Swen did not want "feeling good" to be the sole measure of success for a worship service. If God's story is being told and people understand how it relates to them, they will often recognize their personal brokenness. One desired outcome of worship is an acknowledgment of our brokenness, resulting in repentance, and opening ourselves up to God's redirection of our lives.

Swen's comment about measures of success for a worship service generated additional discussion. He was not against feeling good as a result of participating in worship, especially feelings of gratitude, but he was looking for more. When pressed for examples, he cited a person who commented to the pastor the *following* Sunday, that he had reflected often during the past week about points raised in last week's sermon about opening up space for God in one's life, and had launched a new initiative in his life as a result.

"It seems to me," said Michelle, one of the youngest members of the group, "that such deep responsiveness demands a focus on repentance."

"Absolutely," Swen was quick to agree. "It is a key part of worship. It is the reason the liturgical churches generally have a portion focused on confession. Worship needs to include a continuing emphasis on repentance."

"It also seems to me," Michelle continued, "that such deep responsiveness has implications for how we use scripture in worship. Churches have many different styles of worship and communal life, but scripture needs to be brought to people's consciousness in ways that promote repentance and lead to changed lives."

Swen expressed full agreement as he moved onto the next point and wrote on the board: GATHERED AND SENT. He said most of the people there probably would recognize these words as a formulation that had been around for lots of years, words that were still in current usage, and, for Swen, were personally very meaningful. He liked the idea of a local group of God's people gathering together for worship and then being sent out into the broader community again to be Jesus' disciples there. These people had not gathered in any sense to be entertained, but to be open to God's influence in their lives, and prepare to be sent out in accordance with God's purposes in their lives.

Up to this point, the discussion had been quite theoretical—philosophical as one participant put it. Swen seemed to sense that people had been caught up in the discussion, but in some cases were anxious to deal with something more practical. He turned to the board and noted that he previously had drawn lines to join several items together that used technology in some manner. With that said he wrote TECHNOLOGY on the board and continued by saying there was a lot to talk about here. He proceeded to list off a number of ways in which technology often is used in the typical church worship service in contemporary America, such as amplifying sound; employing additional amplifying devices for the hearing impaired; projecting outlines, quotes, and images in support of sermons; showing video clips; and balancing the sound of musical groups.

Swen then asked the seminar participants to identify the issues or problems they encountered in their use of technology as an aid for worship. A flood of issues ensued, flavored with amusing anecdotes of activities gone awry. The laughter was a switch from the serious tone of the earlier discussion and everyone seemed to be in a light mode.

Kevin noticed another aspect of the discussion, however, due to his fairly good knowledge of technology and its use in worship. By and large, the participants seemed to assume that they understood the use of technology fairly well, while at the same time displaying a lot of naivete about it. As the stream of comments continued, Kevin was pleased to realize that Swen also seemed to be conscious of this combination of overconfidence and lack of knowledge.

Swen finally terminated his audience's lively portrayal of technology problems and said he would summarize how he saw the issues in three categories: 1) getting the right equipment, 2) learning how to use it, and 3) recognizing what you don't know. He started with number 3—recognizing what you don't know. He then launched into story-telling which described numerous cases of technological missteps and disasters he had encountered in the many churches he had known. In contrast to the earlier collection of stories, Swen's were not particularly humorous, in fact, some were downright painful. He summarized by telling people that they probably don't know as much about technological equipment and its use as they think they do and many of the people they might turn to for help have big inadequacies as well. His point was well illustrated by some of his stories of technology installations that did not work out well and which their users did not realize could have been so much better.

His commentary about a pervasive lack of such technical knowledge in church settings provided the backdrop for his engagement with the first issue on his list—getting the right equipment. Swen's key advice on this matter was GET EXPERT HELP—words he wrote in capital letters on the board. He continued by saying it was usually hard for the uninitiated to tell who was an expert and who wasn't. It was clear that Swen did not think the pool of true experts was as large as the pool of people who thought they were experts. He hammered away hard on what he called the power of three. When looking for a person to help with getting and installing technical equipment, identify at least three potential candidates and then check them out by getting three references for each of these three candidates.

He immediately got some pushback from a couple of people who thought this was overkill for what they needed done. One person said, "We are a small church with a really old system we know needs to be replaced, but getting a replacement system for us should be really simple. We just need two speakers, a couple of microphones and a board."

Swen got some audible expressions of support in the room when he said, "You probably don't know what your possibilities are or how easy it is to go wrong, even in a simple case like this."

Another person said, "A member of our congregation does a lot of work with technology of this sort in the local school system where he works. I see no reason not to depend on him."

Swen's response was low-key but firm. "You may well want to make use of his expertise, but here we are examining very specific applications, so get him some help, or go to great lengths to be sure he really is up to speed on what you need done. I have encountered too many horror stories of the kind I was telling a moment ago."

When he moved on to the next item—learning to use the equipment—he dispensed with it rather quickly, but gave an example of how it needed careful attention. The example was operating a sound board and the need to train people, to limit access to the board, and to have a means of preserving or recording optimum settings.

At this point, Kevin noticed that Swen took a glance at his watch and somewhat abruptly moved on. He commented that when everyone had been discussing the case study earlier in the seminar, most of the talk was about music but he had not really engaged that topic, choosing first to talk about what constituted worship. With a bit of a smile, he said, "Is everyone ready to jump into the music wars?"

Without responding to a couple of cracks from participants about being ready for a good fight, he noted that they were now on a topic that was a great application for all the work they had done earlier on *complex adaptive systems*. They could apply some of what they had been talking about earlier.

A person in the front row interrupted by saying, "You emphasized a couple weeks ago that one of the leverage points in such a system was places of difference, and music would seem to be a prime example."

"I see that a diligent student in the front row is wide awake and remembering what we did before. Yes, music is a place with a lot of potential for self-organizing, if we care to foster it."

With this opening salvo, Swen began to describe the fact that music—and related matters of worship—had for a long time been a source of contention and dispute, but it also was an arena where much fruitful growth was possible. Having earlier explored the nature of complex adaptive systems and then today the nature of worship, Swen said they were at an especially valuable juncture for thinking more deeply about change in a congregational context. He wanted to begin by examining four assumptions about change in a complex adaptive system that were especially relevant regarding music in worship. He addressed them individually as he projected them on the screen.

- Any dimension of differences has the potential of significantly reshaping an organization.

Swen elaborated on a point from an earlier seminar, namely that differences can often be a beginning point for adaptive change. His main point here seemed to be that there was no need to look for just the right difference; any difference was potentially an adaptive entry point. An obvious difference here, of course, was the varied preferences in music. In addition, there may be different understandings about what worship is. He reminded the group that he had spent considerable time just moments ago making his case for what worship is, but he was under no illusions that everyone was in full agreement with his position. In addition, even though there was agreement on how to define worship, there could well be differences in the preferred way of expressing this understanding of worship. If one looked across denominations, there would be obvious differences among the various traditions. Given the varied backgrounds of the people making up a typical congregation, one would expect diversity.

At this point, a woman sitting on the far side asked if conflict resolution methods were useful for resolving some of these differences and getting the adaptive change Swen was seeking. Swen hesitated and then said, "It depends on how conflict resolution is approached. If it is done so it in any way suppresses differences, rather than bringing them out in the open, I don't think it will achieve what I have in mind. If we are wanting to reshape any current practices, we want to get the differences front and center. Conflict resolution sometimes is viewed as a way for people to learn to get along with each other and live together with relative harmony. What I want is to use our differences as a way to find new ways of living together—a launching pad for adaptive change."

At that point, he indicated he shortly would share some specific techniques for addressing differences, but for the moment he wanted to finish the list he had started. With this comment, the second assumption appeared on the screen.

- Adaptation results from shared values and differences in dynamic tension.

Swen said he was assuming because people shared some values, they were then able to address differences in other instances in a manner that brought about the desired adaptive change. In the current context, he said he would hope a congregation would have some shared values as to what constituted worship—along the lines of the essential principle he had presented earlier—and they then could address differences—possibly very major differences—regarding choice of music and other matters of style and taste.

An immediate question tossed to him was, "Are you assuming that people in a congregation will agree on exactly what worship is?"

"No, not necessarily, but I would hope they would have somewhat similar values in this regard—at least a lot closer than the differences in musical taste you find in a typical congregation. One reason I presented my essential principle regarding worship was to see if we could be somewhat on the same page in that regard before going to the matters of taste and style where we know there will be lots of divergence."

He then talked about tension—in particular the tension resulting from differences in taste. He obviously was optimistic about creative new ideas emerging from this interaction. He also was ready to go to his third assumption about complex adaptive change.

- All environments are different so best innovations cannot be generalized.

Swen began his elaboration of the item on the screen. "Just because a particular innovation was wildly successful somewhere else does not mean it will work well in your setting. People have a strong tendency to latch onto an approach that was successful somewhere else and assume that it will work for them. Obviously, every context tends to differ from others in various ways. Effective innovations must reflect the specific context in which they are being utilized."

A participant in the center of the room seemed skeptical. "I think there is great merit in looking for practices that are successful someplace and using them. Why begin using some untested ideas you have invented yourself when you have information about practices that are known to work?"

There was a quick response. "Oh, I agree that we should be looking for good ideas everywhere and getting all the information we can about how they have worked in as many places as possible. My point, however, is that you should never grab onto some such idea and think it will work for you. In other words, investigate your own situation first—in careful detail—and see what changes make sense. In the process, consider all kinds of ideas from whatever source as a possibility for your situation. And if the idea has been successful in other settings, it obviously deserves more thorough consideration than an untested idea. My point is adaptive change grows out of your specific context."

When the final assumption appeared on the screen, Swen dispensed with it rather quickly.

- Cooperation and competition held in healthy tension is most adaptive.

"This one obviously relates to the differences we have been talking about. The creativity that differences generate comes about by people developing a balance between cooperating with each other and competing with each other when some of their ideas are strongly held but not shared by others. So everyone should expect there will be tensions, but also adaptive benefits."

Swen then announced that he was ready to give them the promised example of a *process* he found useful for facilitating adaptive change. He noted three aspects he would elaborate after presenting the process: 1) it can be used for a variety of purposes, 2) it is adaptable to all sizes of groups from small to very large, and 3) though not complicated, it requires significant competency on the part of the facilitator for it to work smoothly. For an example of a situation to which the process could be applied, he presented a brief case study involving worship music.

CASE STUDY
Ascension Worship Music

THE APPROXIMATELY 150 PEOPLE who typically attend the worship service at Ascension Church each Sunday are diverse in age. In fact, they are similar to society as a whole, including individuals across the age span from infants to very elderly. The music in their worship is quite traditional, depending heavily on a hymnal and a piano. In recent years, this traditional approach had been modified a bit with occasional praise songs, sometimes accompanied by a guitar. Those people who favor the traditional music tolerate the occasional break from tradition, hoping it will satisfy the people who favor more contemporary music. At the same time, they fear this occasional variation from established practice might start a movement away from the traditional mode of music they love. On the other hand, many of the youth are impatient with what seems half-hearted attempts to accommodate their musical taste.

Swen said—as he had been advocating throughout the day—this situation had to be addressed in its totality with full attention to the nature of worship, but for illustrative purposes he would describe his process as applied to the music aspect. He portrayed a group of ten people from the congregation—representing a cross-section of age, musical taste and related matters—gathered together to examine the issue. The facilitator would take them through a six-stage process.

1. *History.* The process begins with the facilitator asking each person— one by one—to describe the history of the situation as they perceive it. Each person is encouraged to give a complete picture—without interruption from anyone else—including personal history pertaining to the situation, such as personal history with worship and music. As the person speaks, the facilitator lists key aspects on the newsprint of a flipchart. Each person takes considerable time since the facilitator encourages the person to elaborate and checks to make sure the words on the newsprint are an acceptable record. After the process is complete with one person, the facilitator moves on to the second person and repeats it. In the Ascension music example, the individuals talked about various kinds of music, how it connected to worship for them, and how it related specifically to experiences at Ascension. This stage of the process takes a long time—possibly longer than any other stage. While it will vary with the topic and the size of the group, it could take hours rather than minutes. It is a critical stage and the facilitator works hard to develop a full history that reflects the perspective of everyone. Because it is part of the learning of everyone in the group, the facilitator works hard at keeping everyone engaged, taking breaks as needed and maintaining the integrity of the process.

2. *Interests.* The leader of the process now moves on to the various interests each person perceives are at stake in the situation, in other words, the reasons people have for resolving the issue at hand. Again the facilitator goes one by one, giving each person a full opportunity to express the interests at hand in detail—as they understand them for themselves as well as others. Key points again are recorded on

the newsprint as the facilitator patiently draws out full descriptions of the perceived interests. Among the many interests in the Ascension example are personal satisfaction, engaging in discipleship, drawing people of diverse ages, temperaments, and commitments into worship, and praising God.

3. *Options.* The next stage of the process again takes the people back into the familiar pattern with the focus this time being on identifying the various options that could bring about some resolution. It is done in a "brainstorming" fashion and options presented are not evaluated at this point but simply recorded on the newsprint. As in the previous stages, there is an emphasis on getting a full expression of each person's views without interruption and making a record of these options on the newsprint. The Ascension example included a large number of approaches to the music—and combinations thereof—and its role in the worship.

4. *Weigh options.* By this stage, the process has moved into more of a free-wheeling discussion with careful consideration of all the options, combinations of options, and modifications of them. Again the facilitator is listing them in a visible way with sufficient detail to insure some clarity as to what actually is under consideration. Care is taken to identify potential consequences of the various actions to gain some perspective on what can be expected from them. This stage may be fairly quick, or it may require a lot of conferring with other people and thus an extended time for weighing the options. In the Ascension example, the discussion explored the implications of the options in terms of technology to be purchased, the training of personnel required, their interaction with aspects of liturgy, and much more.

5. *Chose best options.* While much time may have been spent weighing the options and identifying their implications, some choices eventually must be made. At this point, the best options often are fairly obvious and there is a clear consensus. If not, it may be necessary to cycle back to an earlier point in the process.

6. *Implement the decisions.* Assuming the persons responsible for implementing the decisions have been part of the discernment group, the stage is already set for moving toward implementation of the options chosen. By and large, however, this stage probably takes

place mostly outside the group context in which this process has been conducted thus far. In the Ascension example, implementation required the participation of the pastor and everyone else involved in the worship of the church, along with ongoing communication with the congregation.

After presenting his description of this process of facilitating adaptive change, Swen turned his attention to some general considerations about the process. He noted that while his interest in the process is mainly for its use in facilitating adaptive change within congregations, it can be used in many settings for a wide range of purposes, such as conflict resolution, collective bargaining, budget planning, and more. He also emphasized that it had to be adapted to the given purpose and to the context in which it was being used.

In response to a question about the size of the group with which it could be used, Swen claimed that with the appropriate adaptations, it could be used with very large groups. The example he gave involved over 200 people who gathered, mostly as observers, to watch the process being conducted by a select group of eight people. It also included provision for anyone from the audience to come into the inner circle and take a designated vacant chair and actively participate in process under specified conditions and at designated times. His key point seemed to be that it could be adapted in many ways as long as key elements were maintained, such as taking time to hear each other out—without interruption and counter arguments—and working to accommodate and foster differences, not suppress them.

One of the participants finally raised a question. "As you have described this process, it seems to take an incredibly long time. How can you realistically find this much time?"

"If the matter is important, you can find the time," Swen responded. "Remember it doesn't have to all happen in one session. It may require many sessions in some cases. A key is to be focused and stay on task, but not rush or short-circuit the process."

When asked if facilitating the process took special skills, Swen said it does not require unusually special abilities, but some training and experience under a mentor enables a person to become adept at making the process work as intended. Certain actions are important, such as preserving the newsprint listings from one session to the next, debriefing at the end of each session, and identifying resources, data and additional people who will be needed at the table for the next session. It is not a highly sophisticated process, but one that needs to be conducted carefully, thoroughly, with respect for people, and with an expectation of letting differences grow into adaptive change.

With his description of the process completed, Swen addressed a couple of worship items in the time remaining. First, he wanted to address the interconnections between the sermon and other aspects of the worship service. He was convinced this interconnection has great potential and he jumped right into it by saying he was an adamant advocate of the pastor having at least the key elements of the sermon ready a week ahead of time, specifically by mid-week, prior to polishing up the sermon for the coming Sunday and in time for the worship team—assuming the church had such a group—to know the focus of the sermon the week before their final rehearsal for a given Sunday.

As Swen was completing his short pitch, Kevin heard sort of a snort from a guy in the front row followed by a comment, "It's obvious, Mr. Consultant, that you have never had to meet the pressing demand of having a sermon ready every Sunday, week after week, month after month." It was said with a smile and Swen obviously did not take offense. Another voice in the back chimed in saying, "Swen's right; it's the only way to go."

With a chuckle Swen responded, "If I were a betting man, I would offer you a sizable wager that if you did what I am suggesting, consistently for a month, you would never go back to your old ways. I made this suggestion at this point in our seminar because of its potential for producing a more fully integrated worship service, but I think its main benefit is for the preacher in terms of taking off some of the emotional pressures of having a sermon ready each Sunday and of having a sermon that is more coherent and grounded. In my book, it is the only way to go."

Kevin did not see people ready to argue further with Swen over the matter, with the exception of one person who suggested that this approach did not seem to leave sufficient room for the Holy Spirit to influence the sermon.

Swen responded, "I don't see why the Holy Spirit cannot be influential the week before as well as the week leading up to the sermon. If the concern, however, is that working on the sermon ahead of time will lock the preacher into something that can't be changed, I don't see the connection. Whether you are working on a sermon ten days ahead of time or three days ahead of time, things may suddenly unfold in a way that demands sudden change—whether that be events or the movement of the Spirit. For example, when that big tornado swept through the McKenzie subdivision on the north side of the city on a Friday evening a couple years ago, I imagine most every sermon in the city that Sunday was altered."

With a glance at his watch, Swen said he had one final worship topic and launched into it with a question, "To what extent do you think you should choose your worship music with the intent of attracting youth to your worship services?" Seemingly recognizing that this question had been lurking within both of the case studies used today, he would finally give it direct attention.

The ensuing discussion ranged widely but quickly focused on the word "attracting" in Swen's question. One of the more youthful participants said, "I'm deeply involved in music and I know that kids in their late teens and early twenties have particular tastes in music that are strong and you have to recognize this fact if you want to attract them."

Another person countered with, "Unless you are buying into the entertainment focus I think most of us rejected a bit ago, I think you need to look at the total worship experience, not just the music. Sometimes youth surprise us in that regard. My understanding is a lot of young people today are attracted to some of the older forms of worship music—music that is a sharp contrast with their secular music preferences."

Swen finally attempted to wind up the day's event with some concluding comments. "I am among those who are skeptical about trying to attract youth simply by changing the music. I have seen lots of failures in this regard. I sort of set you up by talking about attracting people. I would go back to our earlier focus on processes for adaptive change and urge you to be sure you are including youth in the process so their interests and tastes are included in the community decisions about how the community will worship."

With a sense of finality, he continued, "When you are trying to reach out beyond the building walls to identifiable groups of people, there is a place for the idea of attracting and it may even have an entertainment element to it, but it probably is best if it takes place at special times and often in venues other than a traditional church building. Furthermore, they actually may become worshiping communities of an unconventional sort. At times congregations need to break out of their established patterns in rather assertive outreach efforts, but that is our topic for next week. See you then. Have a good week."

chapter 12

Communities of Disciples

Waypoints

A case study is given of a congregation whose pastor has concerns about the degree of their outreach.

Three additional essential principles of an effective church are explored:

- Their ministry is unbounded by their building.
- At least half of their budget is spent on mission to others.
- They are missional, i.e., they reach out as a result of the love of Christ.

A theme that connects the twelve essential principles is developed: Churches are renewed when they become communities of disciples of Jesus.

Regarding effective programs found in other churches, leaders should:

- adapt them rather than adopt them;
- experiment with them rather than implement them.

Actions a pastor can take to foster self-organizing include the following:

- Preach on people initiating actions on their own or in unofficial groups.
- Encourage new groupings and spontaneous actions.
- Encourage the expression of differing viewpoints.

- Foster dialog within multiple, unique settings.
- Encourage experimental ventures.
- Encourage the emergence of new "containers" (physical, organizational, behavioral, or conceptual).
- Recognize that in a self-organizing system, the impetus for change occurs in many places and in an unpredictable pattern.
- Work to establish a culture where the above behaviors are valued.

As KEVIN AND SWEN entered the room for the final seminar, most of the usual "early birds" were there. As always, the room was already set up to Swen's specifications, and he had only a few preparations to complete before joining the clusters of people catching up on what had taken place in their lives during the previous week.

When the session got underway at the appointed hour, Swen announced that they would begin with a case study which he distributed efficiently throughout the room. Following the usual instructions about reading the case closely and preparing to discuss it with others, the room became silent as the reading began.

CASE STUDY
Lakeview Church

LAKEVIEW CHURCH HAS WITHIN it some people committed to evangelism and others committed to various forms of social outreach beyond the walls of the church. These two clusters of people do not have a lot of overlapping membership and, unfortunately, many people in the congregation do not have a significant overt connection to either one. These groupings within this church are not in conflict with each other; they tend to speak positively about all the outreach programs, but most gravitate toward involvement in one or the other type of endeavor. If one would enter into a discussion about the nature of the church with any of these individuals, it typically would become apparent what they personally see as the most important form of outreach for a church.

Pastor Nemick is concerned about the modest nature of the outreach of the congregation. On the evangelism side, he is pleased with the quality of the Alpha program they have been conducting, but the number of participants they have brought in from the outside has been disappointing. A couple small groups of people conduct what they call an evangelistic Bible study in their respective neighborhoods, but the number of unchurched people in them is not large. In terms of social outreach, he is pleased with ongoing donations of food and other goods that members of the congregation contribute to the "pantry" they maintain with other churches, but is frustrated with the difficulties of getting enough volunteers to staff the ongoing cooperative program for homeless families operated by this same group of nine churches. On a rotating weekly basis, they provide for homeless families in their area. When their church's turn comes, volunteers staff an operation that houses these families each night for one week in the church. Although these families are gone from the church during the day—typically for school, work, or to search for employment—volunteers provide an evening meal and then breakfast in the morning. A volunteer is present through the night and various forms of assistance are provided. It is a great program that serves a desperate need for such families, many with small children, but getting sufficient volunteers is an ongoing problem.

Many questions come to mind when Pastor Nemick reflects on the situation. Why is the evangelistic outreach of the congregation seemingly so ineffective? Why is it so difficult to get sufficient volunteers for the program for homeless families, especially given the size of their congregation and the fact that it only comes up about once every two months? Is the level of discipleship in the congregation just that low or does their discipleship take other forms? Is the apparent separation in interest in the two forms of outreach natural, or are we doing something wrong? What should I be doing as pastor to enhance our outreach?

The ensuing discussion, first at the individual tables and then with the total gathering, was subdued and not especially engaging. It appeared that this case was not an unusual situation at all; in fact, it resembled the situation found in several of the congregations represented at the seminar. The discussion gained some traction when it focused on the questions that troubled Pastor Nemick, but few exciting suggestions were being offered for him.

Swen rather quickly shifted his focus and said he wanted to present the final *essential principles* for the group's consideration. Up until this point, he had given them nine of the dozen principles and he had three more, all ones he claimed were especially applicable to the case they had just examined. He launched into his explanation as the first one appeared on the screen.

Essential Principles

8. *Unbounded by a building.* The church is located wherever its people are found, such as at their homes, their places of employment, the local coffee shop, or the place where their hobby group meets. The church is not a set of activities located in a building, it is what goes on in the lives of the members of the congregation, all week long, wherever they find themselves.

While theoretically, few would argue against the principle that the church is people and not a building, and that they are still the church even when not collected in the same place, in practice most church members do not conduct their lives as if this principle were true. Swen made this point as he pressed the group to come up with examples of what the lives of their congregations would look like if they really believed and followed this principle. At first the examples were slow in coming, but as the participants' initial suggestions stimulated the thoughts of others, lots of examples began to emerge. Examples included two mothers from one church whose presence in a neighborhood preschool play group brought the love of Christ to other mothers, some of whom were living in very difficult circumstances. As with this example, many instances included two or more congregants living a "with-God" presence somewhere in their community. Other examples were of individuals living out their faith at home, at work, in community activities and social settings.

Among the specific examples were a retired man who tutored boys who lived in difficult circumstances through the local Boys and Girls Club, three people in their twenties whose social time included hanging out in a local coffee shop where they could engage other individuals in conversation about spiritual aspects of life, the middle-aged couple whose lives were transparent to others as they created pottery in a local artist group, and a group who devoted noticeable effort to building Habitat for Humanity houses. Swen commented on the examples in a manner which emphasized being the church was not limited to a location and the manner in which one lived was central.

In response to an example of an informal group which, through special arrangements with its owner, met in a local coffee shop on Thursday evenings for a time of singing and discussion focused on their Christian faith, Swen noted there seemed to be a growing number of such "worshiping communities" showing up in unconventional places around the country. When pressed, he said he had no way of knowing whether such groups would ever become conventional churches, or the extent to which this was desirable. He was emphatic, however, in asserting that in our constantly changing society, such occurrences should be encouraged, not discouraged. The language of complex adaptive systems showed up as he argued for fostering new forms of worshiping communities in unconventional settings whenever they appeared.

Swen got a bit passionate as he chipped away at the idea that church consisted of activities conducted in a designated building, but moved rather quickly to another essential principle.

Essential Principles

10. *Budget.* At the most, one-half of the tithes and offerings of this Christian community should be directed to supporting the faith community itself, that is, to fostering their own spiritual growth. The majority of their giving should be directed outward, with much of this money ideally directed through ministries in which these believers themselves are actively involved. Inevitably, this approach will require the reduction of some programs now provided in many churches.

This principle did not produce a lot of discussion and at first Kevin wondered if people agreed with it, disagreed with it but were reluctant to say so, or agreed with it but were reluctant to talk about it because they knew their own church was a long ways from this ideal. Eventually Kevin concluded that essentially no one disagreed with it in principle, but most of the congregations represented at the seminar were not very close to this budgetary ideal.

Swen emphasized he was more interested in how people spent their time than their money. He wanted to channel much of the money to outreach endeavors in which individuals were personally investing their time. He seemed to be more concerned with the people themselves than with their money, a matter related to the next principle to appear on the screen.

Essential Principles

12. *Missional.* The community, individually and collectively, reaches out in love to others as an outgrowth of their relationship with Jesus Christ. Their *doing* is an outgrowth of their *being*. Their sense of mission reflects a concern for all dimensions of human life, including physical, psychological and spiritual.

When Swen addressed this principle it was almost as if he began to preach a sermon—a sermon delivered with deep conviction. His main focus was the part of the principle that said, "Their *doing* is an outgrowth of their *being*." He even used some systems language in making his point: the congregational system would not be the same if the outreach was not an outgrowth of people's relationship with Jesus Christ.

He then referred back to the case study they had read, noting the pastor was concerned about a lack of commitment to the various outreach endeavors of the congregation. Swen said the answer was *not* to promote the outreach programs, either those pertaining to evangelism or service. The answer was to help the people to develop as disciples of Jesus Christ. A disciple-forming congregation will naturally foster outreach as a result of its people becoming disciples. He repeated his key point: their *doing* will be a result of their *being*.

Swen was soon interrupted by a question, "Of the three dimensions of human life mentioned in the principle, physical, psychological, and spiritual, which do you think it is most important for a congregation to address?"

Swen seemed surprised by the question but hesitated only briefly before responding, "It is impossible for me to come up with a generalization that answers the question. Each situation is different and the answer would be contextual. I would say, however, be sure you don't ignore the spiritual dimension. I have seen an occasional church endeavor that addressed physical or psychological issues but ignored spiritual matters. A church program is fundamentally different from a government program both in terms of what motivates it and in what is included."

At this point, another question was raised. "You have given us twelve so-called essential principles for renewing a church. Is there one theme that ties them all together?"

This question caused Swen to pause. "Wow. I never really thought about it quite that way. Let me toss this question back to you as a group. I'll put the entire list up on the screen and scroll down through them so you can read them. You can think about what may tie them all together. In fact, afterwards I'll give you a chance to talk about it for a few minutes at your tables before we address it as a total group."

The ensuing discussion was vigorous and Swen soon broke into it to announce, "In ninety seconds, I will ask each table for a consensus phrase or sentence that is your answer. I'll then list all of them up here on the board and we can see what commonality there is."

Swen was soon collecting phrases and sentences from the tables, some of whom had not really achieved consensus, resulting in debate the entire room listened in on and even joined; in one case, it may have been closer to heckling. When all were listed, the discussion continued as the alternatives were debated, though the debating was more about alternative wording than it was about alternative concepts. Finally Swen wrote in large letters on the board CHURCHES ARE RENEWED WHEN THEY BECOME COMMUNITIES OF DISCIPLES OF JESUS. "That's my answer and I'm sticking to it."

At that, a participant near the front stood up, took a pen in hand and began to write on the board as he said, "I would prefer to express it from the vantage point of my own congregation." When his pen stopped the new statement said, WE WANT TO BE A DISCIPLE-FORMING CONGREGATION.

Swen had a pleased expression as he said, "That looks great to me and maybe that's a good transition to my next topic—what a pastor needs to do to make some of this happen."

Soon after Swen began his presentation of ideas related to pastors' promotion of various types of outreach, he was asked about the merits of adopting established renewal programs that have been used successfully in other places. The questioner said, "Why should I spend lots of time and money developing a new approach that somebody else has already figured out?"

"You want to use all the resources and ideas you can locate from all sorts of places," Swen responded, "but how you use them is the big issue. When I hear someone say they have *adopted* Program ABC from Church XYZ and are *implementing* it in their congregation I usually get uneasy—very uneasy. If they said they were *adapting* this program rather than *adopting* it, and they were *experimenting* with it rather than *implementing* it, I would feel a whole lot better."

He then began describing the value and role he saw for established programs that are presented as possibilities for export to other locations. First, he emphasized that he appreciated the help such programs could be and said he went out of his way to learn about ones which seemed in some way applicable to situations he was facing. He next emphasized if there was one such program, there probably were a number of them and he would want to check out all of them, or at least many of them if the number were truly large.

His big point was the use of any such program had to be done with full attention to local unique conditions and situations. His preference was not for moving such a program (even if modified) into the new setting, but for incorporating major elements of it into an endeavor which is custom built for the situation.

This point raised an objection from the previous questioner, "Some very successful programs work well only because of some small but critical aspects that are essential for success. If you just pick and choose parts of the program in some loosey-goosey manner, you may be destroying the impact of the program and setting yourself up for failure."

With a chuckle, Swen said, "I didn't say anything about doing this in a loosey-goosey manner. What I am saying is if you use some established program, in either its original form or in a very modified form, it has to be made to fit the unique features of the new situation. Great effort must be devoted to fully understanding the program, what its various features are, and why these features work in various contexts. It takes serious work."

He continued by harking back to their earlier conversation about systems. "What is really important is allowing for self-organizing. You want to be sure you are bringing in these new programmatic elements in a manner that has a focus on adaptive change. You want conditions under which self-organizing is not only allowed but encouraged. You want to understand why the various parts of the original program worked so they can be introduced in the new setting both with integrity and possibilities for self-organizing to shape them."

As Swen talked, he wrote on the board: AMPLIFY DIFFERENCES. "You want differences to be recognized, honored and encouraged. Just as you don't want to press a program into a situation it doesn't fit perfectly, you don't want to seek consensus as you pursue renewal. Differences are generative; they become an impetus for change. Different giftedness is important and you want to let the different gifts come into play. These differences are important not only for generating productive change but for preventing problems resulting from hidden differences. Get the differences out in the open."

He then tied the discussion back to the case study they had read, noting that the last sentence of the case was a question, "What should I be doing as pastor to enhance our outreach?" Differences were a part of his response to this question.

"There are many kinds of outreach, but I'll assume for the moment that the outreach he is referencing is evangelism. Basically it is a simple matter of communication across differences. I like the old metaphor of it being similar to 'one beggar telling another beggar where to find bread.' Differences between people generate discussion. If one perceives a need, it becomes a basis for conversation. The disciple of Jesus who tells his story is simply communicating what has happened to him personally; it is not a matter of trying to convince someone of something."

A question came from the left front table. "You seem to not want to try to convince people of your position. It sounds as if you are afraid of being accused of proselytizing. Can you really defend such a stance biblically?"

"You used the word proselytize so let's start there. By definition this word conveys the idea of trying to influence or persuade someone. I have difficulty with that word as a descriptor of evangelism on two counts. First, I don't think it is a good descriptor of our role; persuasion is the role of the Holy Spirit. Second, trying to persuade someone in this sense seems to violate a norm of our society which places a high value on tolerance. As a result, trying to persuade someone often is counterproductive. If not persuasion, what then is our role? Our role is to be open about who we are and what Jesus has done for us. It means being transparent and being prepared to explain our hope when someone wants to know. I have no responsibility for persuading someone, but I do have a responsibility for being open and expressive of the impact of the Christ on me."

Swen continued his response by tying it to self-organizing. "When a follower of Jesus engages with someone who does not have this allegiance, they are engaging differences that cross a significant boundary. They are creating connections that promote productive engagement, but have quite unpredictable outcomes. They are participating in a relationship which has no certain outcome. It is not part of a scripted plan and is self-organizing."

Swen pressed on to address more directly the matter of what a pastor should be doing to foster self-organizing among people in the congregation. In doing so, he tied it back to the idea that such a church would be a *disciple-forming congregation*. If such a community of people acquires its character, outlook, and practices from being disciples, one would expect it to be self-organizing in many ways. With this introduction, he projected on the screen a series of pastoral actions under the heading of actions which probably would be true of a pastor who is fostering a self-organizing community of disciples. As each action was projected, he added a brief commentary.

If a congregation is self-organizing, the following probably are true:

- The pastor preaches on people initiating actions on their own or in unofficial groups.

"Real disciples are not just participating in the programs and activities the congregation has established. A disciple's relationship with God results in actions, both individually and in concert with other, which develop outside of the church committees and offices. The preaching encourages it. Many of these activities take place independent of the formal structures of the community, but the people are not just a group of "Lone Rangers"; they are in community with each other, share information on what they are doing, get feedback from each other, and to a large extent operate as a support group for each other."

- The pastor encourages new groupings and spontaneous actions.

"Whether in hallway conversations, committee meetings, individual counseling, talks to groups, or phone conversations, the pastor encourages people to have a life of prayer and openness to the direction of the Spirit, such that they are ready to connect with new people and engage in new actions that are not prompted by formal actions of the institutional aspect of the church. Congregants are aware that the pastor values such developments, encourages them and offers his endorsement when they emerge."

- The pastor encourages the expression of differing viewpoints.

"The pastor is not under the illusion that everyone in the congregation agrees on all important matters, and in fact, makes every effort to encourage the expression of their differences. A climate is sought in which differences can be expressed without rancor and with love toward others of differing persuasion. This is *not* a climate of "relativism" in which convictions are unimportant, but one in which people of differing persuasions are valued. Their value as persons is high and takes precedence over viewpoints others may consider wrong or inappropriate."

- The pastor fosters dialog within multiple, unique settings.

"The pastor not only goes out of his way to support his vision of a disciple-forming congregation in many settings, but encourages dialog among everyone he encounters about these same matters. Whether in formal or informal settings, people are encouraged to discuss their values and commitments. These are not like the private "parking lot conversations" that follow some formal meetings, but open, respectful, and loving dialogs among people with differing ideas but a common commitment to being disciples of Jesus. They take place wherever these disciples gather."

- The pastor encourages "experimental" ventures.

"Initiating fixed long-term plans typically is only done with careful review and approval of all the gatekeepers. The resulting endeavors provide limited encouragement of self-organizing. On the other hand, initiatives labeled as experimental, and thus potentially open to easy change, are much easier to get started and offer greater opportunity for self-organizing. Experimental ventures, large and small, are encouraged at every turn."

- The pastor encourages the emergence of new "containers" (physical, organizational, behavioral, or conceptual).

"Whenever parts of a system are altered, opportunities for change are enhanced. The pastor encourages new physical arrangements within a church building to meet changing needs. New organizational structures, for example, new ministry teams, are promoted when needed. New behavioral covenants, like the operating guidelines of a board, are formed to meet changing understandings and circumstances. New and emerging conceptual understandings of the mission of the church are fostered as a result of study of the Scriptures and observation of changes in society. The pastor encourages self-organizing that maintains vitality and a vision for the future."

- The pastor recognizes that within a self-organizing system, the impetus for change occurs in many places and in an unpredictable pattern.

"This leader does not promote change according to a fixed plan because such plans typically do not accommodate the unpredictable patterns that naturally occur in a church system. Self-organizing change occurs in numerous and unexpected places in the system. Recognizing this reality and embracing it are important aspects of leadership."

- The pastor works to establish a culture where the above behaviors are valued.

"A key role of any leader is nurturing the culture of the community being led. The pastor is the 'culture-keeper' of a congregation and works to establish a culture that values these items related to self-organizing and fosters related behaviors. The intent is that they become part of the DNA of the congregation."

Swen then referred back to the "Lakeview Church" case study, noting that it addressed two forms of outreach—evangelism and service to people in need. Since the case had people who mostly expressed interest in one or the other, and generally did not become significantly involved in both, he wanted to be sure he expressed his conviction that both were important. He asserted that a congregation attending to only one of them probably was not adhering to the gospel narrative. In addition, the message emanating from such a church probably becomes distorted. For example, if a church is concerned only about evangelism, rather than both evangelism and service, it gives the impression of only being concerned about power. It conveys an image of wanting to grow in size and become more powerful and influential in our society. It appears self-serving— very different from the image of a church that is truly reaching out to serve people in need.

A question came from one of the tables in the back, "I buy your point about both being important, but I have a question about evangelism. I have been hearing some people advocating planting new churches as a form of evangelism. Do you buy that?"

"Yes, I do—as one form, not the only form. I am convinced by the people who tell me that multiple studies of new churches show on average close to three-quarters of the people in such new churches were not part of a worshiping community prior to joining the new church. In contrast, studies of established churches—those that have been around a couple of decades or more—show that most of the new members they acquire have moved from an existing congregation."

The questioner followed up. "Do you think the fact that so many people joining new church plants were previously unchurched has anything to do with self-organizing?"

"Absolutely, and I think the fact that you asked this question is an indication that these ideas about self-organizing and complex adaptive systems are becoming part of your conceptual framework. A new church plant does not yet have as many established ways of doing things. It can accommodate the differences among unchurched people who connect with them. It more easily self-organizes and incorporates people who do not come in with a "churchy" set of expectations about how everything *ought* to be done."

Swen pressed on. "Contemporary culture has an openness to alternative forms of doing things, such that some people want to be part of a community of faith but have some reluctance about becoming part of what our society thinks of as a church. Some denominations today are broadening their terminology and are not talking about planting new *churches* but rather are establishing new *worshiping communities*. As the terminology implies, they are establishing communities of people who are in relationships with each other, and worship together, but may never become a church in the formal sense. There is an openness to letting things self-organize."

Suddenly one of the participants who generally was rather quiet was waving a hand and actually interrupted Swen, saying, "We are almost at the end of the last one of these seminars and I have a question you need to get to before we end."

"Sure," Swen responded. "What is it?"

"It has to do with styles of leadership. I have gotten the impression that with all of your emphasis on a leader influencing events rather than controlling everything, you want a leader who is collaborative and uses group decision making. I think I understand that but it makes me nervous, probably because I once worked for a boss like that where everything got talked to death in our team but somehow nothing ever got done. At some point, someone has to take charge if things are going to get done. I'm still not sure what kind of leader fits both your theory and the real world of churches."

Swen paused briefly before responding. "First of all, I think I need to challenge what appears to be the premise of your question, that there is one particular leadership style that should be followed. I think that a leader who uses only one style of leadership will soon be in trouble. Things are more complicated than that."

"Well, I wasn't wrong then about my thought that you favor collaboration and team decision making."

"No, certainly not. It probably is obvious from our time together that I depend upon multiple ways of influencing events that may seem indirect, and I trust in self-organizing as an important factor in shaping events. But this does not mean a leader shouldn't take a lot of decisive actions. Many of the ways of influencing self-organizing require lots of direct initiative from a leader. And once decisions are made, actions have to be taken and this means a lot of direct actions on the part of the leader. And of course there is what some of us have taken to calling "the vision thing." The leader who is promoting a vision—however determined initially—is taking direct action to promote it in many settings, from quick conversations, to committee deliberations, to sermons. So, to repeat myself, the leader who has only one style of leadership is in trouble. Leadership is an art of using a variety of styles that fit the context of the moment as one follows an overall trajectory of influencing events."

By this point, time had run out and Kevin could see the usual signs of people preparing to move on to where their calendars were calling them. Since this was the last seminar of the series, when the end point was reached, it didn't all end as quickly as usual. Closing conversations between Swen and the participants dragged on a bit longer than normal. He found himself reflecting on the series of seminars in their totality but realized that his reflections would have to wait a bit as he said goodbye to a couple of new friends and helped Swen pack up his materials and equipment.

chapter 13

Bottom-up versus
Self-Organizing Change

Waypoints

Bottom-up change and self-organizing change are fundamentally different; they have some commonalities but are not the same. These relationships are illustrated in the following pairings:

Bottom-up change	Self-organizing change
organizational change	cultural change
revitalization	transformation
program development	people development
Restart	*My Story*
institutional perspective	spiritual perspective

Cultural change—and the transformation of people—requires attention not just to behaviors and artifacts, but to values and beliefs, and even more basically to underlying assumptions.

Activities that often promote and foster transformation include:

- Prayer
- Bible study for transformation (not just for information)
- Engaging in spiritual disciplines

- Participating in spiritual direction
- Engagement in ministry (service to others)

IN THE DAYS FOLLOWING the last seminar in the series, Kevin found himself reflecting on the many seminar concepts and the specific events in his life that had led to his odyssey. His reflections found him harking back to the meeting with his church board where he started to wrestle with the relative merits of top-down and bottom-up change. The differences between the two had become starker, but at the same time he was seeing more sharply some similarities.

His understanding of top-down change was still about the same. The leaders of an organization make plans for changes to be initiated and then set about putting them in place. Depending upon the complexity of the changes sought, the process of implementing the changes potentially could be quite elaborate, or on the other hand, not very sophisticated. Simple or elaborate, it had a particular orientation.

Similarly, bottom-up processes potentially could be developed in simplicity or complexity, but he also had become aware that the two could be joined in some instances. Plans for change could be developed at the grass roots and once formulated they could be initiated at the bottom, *or at the top*. Kevin had come to see planning and plan implementation as activities that could be initiated at the top or the bottom and in various combinations. He was aware of one church, for example, where a detailed grass roots planning process that permeated the congregation resulted in plans that the leaders then put in place in a very directive top-down manner.

It was increasingly clear to Kevin that all of these planning processes have in common the development of plans (whether crude or sophisticated, whether done at the top or the bottom) followed by efforts directed toward putting the plans into play. Change is planned and then attempts are made to put them into practice. Whether done from the top or the bottom, this approach is based on deciding what changes are needed and working at putting these specific changes in place. Predictable change is the goal.

Swen's tutelage had introduced him to complex adaptive systems and the idea of self-organizing change. As he reflected, Kevin realized that for some time during his odyssey *he had tended to equate bottom-up change and self-organizing change, but had come to see that they were fundamentally different.* The most significant distinction was between making predicted change happen and letting change emerge from the scene in an unpredictable manner. Even so, it was easier for him to envision self-organizing change as part of a bottom-up process than one directed from the top. Furthermore, he still had questions about the interface between bottom-up change and self-organizing change. What are the major distinctions between the two? To what extent are they compatible or in need of separation? The more he ruminated about such matters the more he was inclined to focus on yet an additional question: To what extent does each one reflect the biblical principles that should guide life in a faith community? This latter question was the main one that kept coming to mind in his reflections about his interactions with his board and congregation.

* * * * *

Kevin's reflections continued at various points over several weeks of active engagement in ministry. The ongoing, irregular pattern of pastoral care, resourcing of committees, engaging with his board, teaching classes, sermon preparation, and leading worship contained numerous reminders of his questions about change, how it comes about, and his role in it. Finally in one of those seemingly rare occasions when he found himself in an extended time of reflection, he began to make a two-column list of what he thought were distinctions between bottom-up change and self-organizing change.

The list was amended and expanded on a few occasions over several weeks and a desire grew for discussing it with Swen. A phone call resulted in an agreement to get together. As the day approached, he found himself feeling a bit of excitement about the upcoming occasion, again lunch at Goolsbys. They hadn't seen each other for several months and he realized that their bond was grounded in similar convictions and compatible personalities.

Updating each other on what had been going on in their lives took a while, but eventually Kevin pulled his list out of a folder.

Bottom-up change	Self-organizing change
organizational change	cultural change
revitalization	transformation
program development	people development
Restart	*My Story*
institutional perspective	spiritual perspective

As he placed the list in front of Swen, Kevin said, "This list has a lot of stuff in it that really comes out of your seminars, but I had to put it together for myself to help me think through the differences between bottom-up change and self-organizing change. In doing so, however, it became clear that they aren't two distinct perspectives. They overlap and the differences are not always sharp and clear. Sometimes it was only a shade of emphasis. And by the way, number four is a pairing of two different programs from our denomination that seem to me to exemplify the two orientations. I'll have to explain them."

"I think there will be a lot to discuss here," Swen said. "Like you said, all the distinctions aren't that sharp, but some of them are interesting and enlightening. Why don't you start with number one and tell me what's behind what you put in your list."

"Okay, here goes. I concluded that if I see a situation in which someone is pursuing change and they seem to be zeroed in on making changes in the way an organization is organized or structured, it is not likely to be an attempt at encouraging self-organizing change. Certainly someone could be pursuing organizational change as a means of encouraging self-organizing in the system, but it would seem to be unlikely because it is not one of the leverage points commonly thought of as being effective in causing self-organizing."

"That makes sense, but when I first saw this line in your list, I didn't think of them as *means* of encouraging change, but as *goals* of your endeavors. I thought of it this way because cultural change is more likely to occur due to self-organizing than it is from many bottom-up change endeavors."

"Yeah, that rings true also," Kevin quickly agreed. "Cultural change and self-organizing seem to go together and you are left with sort of a chicken and egg question. Which comes first? The two are together in my list partially because in my way of thinking cultural changes are deeper and more significant. We are talking about changes in people's values and beliefs and, of course, they are both hard to achieve, and when you get them, they are of more consequence."

"I'm totally with you. And I think this is especially true in a church context. Fundamentally, we are concerned about changes in people. Organizational changes are of little consequence unless they are an aid to enhancing people's lives and relationships, both with other people and with God."

"All of this relates to the second comparison on my list," Kevin interjected, "so let me go on to it. I think the difference between bottom-up change and self-organizing is clearer here than with anything else on my list. Again, it has to do with what's going on with people's lives."

"I don't think it will be hard to persuade me."

"When you hear someone talking about revitalizing a church, it generally has something to do with the way it operates, the mission of the church, its programs, staffing, and other such matters. Transformation refers to changes in people, individual by individual. The difference is huge. What happens under the label of revitalization may or may not have a significant impact on who people are becoming. Church change may or may not result in change in the people who make up the church. On the other hand, it is hard to imagine a congregation with many people being transformed in which the church overall is not significantly changed."

"Absolutely," Swen added, "and my reading of the New Testament reinforces what you are saying. You don't read much there about the sort of activities that go on in our churches under the name of revitalization. Strategic planning, visioning, building campaigns, stewardship programs, committee development, and the like are a reflection of modern society and the way it operates. The New Testament oozes with thoughts about transformation. Romans 12, for example, makes specific reference to being 'transformed by the renewing of your mind,' Colossians 3 refers to being 'renewed in the image of the creator,' and the gospels have Jesus using the word, 'repent,' on an ongoing basis. This word means to change, of course, and in spite of the tendency in some circles to think of it as a singular—almost one-time—event, Jesus was referring to something more ongoing. This should be obvious from looking at what we call the Lord's Prayer which was given to us as a pattern for prayer."

Kevin was quick to agree but also to extend these thoughts. "You are right on target, but I don't see a lot of my church family who are as committed to transformation as you are suggesting. I'm afraid that when people pray the Lord's Prayer and ask that their sins be forgiven, they are not asking to be transformed. They so often are asking forgiveness for something they have done, with little thought as to how they want their lives to be transformed so the particular sinful tendency will disappear. If we took the Sermon on the Mount seriously, we would be committed to transformation."

"So your preaching," Swen asked quietly, "is becoming more focused on transformation?"

The response had some hesitation. "You know, I wish I could give you a more emphatic yes, but I must acknowledge that I am struggling with this a bit. I am working at it, but given the nature of our society, this is truly a countercultural message. I'm struggling with how to communicate this message to people seemingly entrapped in a way of life shaped by our modern culture. And if I am really honest, I have to admit that I may be hesitant because I want to be liked and I may be trapped in our consumerist society as well. After all, I do have that mortgage to pay."

"I appreciate your struggle, truly I do, but I don't have many answers for it. If I were in your situation, I suspect that I would have some of the same struggles. But tell me more about why you put transformation in the self-organizing change column of your chart. I fully agree that it belongs there, but it is your chart so I would like to hear your thoughts."

"Well, I guess you could make a lot of arguments for this association," Kevin began, "but the idea that really keeps coming back to me is from one of your seminars. You identified the most influential leverage point from Meadow's list as changing people's paradigm or mindset. That's transformation. You said that one's mindset is a person's deepest set of beliefs and assumptions. Transformation involves challenging our deepest beliefs about what it means to be a follower of Jesus, as exhibited in our daily lives. So it seems as if transformation and promoting self-organizing almost become synonymous."

"This says a lot about your struggle with preaching. Trying to get people to change their deepest beliefs and assumptions is a huge challenge. I'm sure you would agree with me, though, that the answer to getting this sort of preaching lies in helping people see the linkage between the biblical narrative and our culture, or rather, it may be seeing that there is a lack of such linkage. It probably involves helping people construct their own narratives to live by, narratives that reflect the biblical narrative and provide direction for how they will live the desired life within the context of modern society."

"So true, and your comments remind me of some books that have been a good resource in that regard, books written by James Bryan Smith, his *Good and Beautiful* series. They are designed to be a basis for group study, and maybe more important, a guide for individual action between group meetings. They emphasize both revising one's personal narratives and engaging in a variety of spiritual disciplines that have the potential of leading to transformation."

"Yes," Swen responded, "those are great books, I am familiar with them. It also reminds me of the fact that the transformation we are talking about needs attention from multiple directions, not just through preaching. It needs attention on multiple fronts, which also reminds me of a connection here between bottom-up change and self-organizing change. A systematic planning process could be used to put in place a range of activities, such as the group sessions you just described, to foster such transformation."

"This brings me back to a point I was making when we first started looking at my list, namely that the two columns in my listing are not sharply divided. There are some linkages. A person could be promoting bottom-up change—or even top-down change—that is intended to foster self-organizing."

"Yes, that is such a key point. Although I like your list because of all it displays, self-organizing for me is such a key phenomenon that we need to highlight it and delineate how we can utilize it. In my experience with other people in the church consultant business—and in reading their books—it seems that many of them acknowledge self-organizing as something that occurs—and maybe they stress its importance—but they usually give little attention to how to utilize this knowledge. Your listing is a small step toward helping get a handle on it."

"That is the matter that I am wrestling with," Kevin said, "How do I make use of the self-organizing phenomenon in my work as a pastor who is attempting to lead a faith community?"

"Speaking as a guy who consults with churches, I would say that a key starting point is recognizing that the phenomenon exists and that it is a powerful vehicle for making change. Trying to initiate change—either bottom-up or top-down—as if self-organizing didn't exist, is a way to really handicap yourself."

"On the other hand," Kevin responded, "I think that a pastor who is focused on fostering transformation among the flock, is actually fostering self-organizing without understanding at all what this phenomenon is. So I am inclined to zero in on transformation as the central goal of my ministry and not worry too much about articulating self-organizing as what I am about."

"Oh, I certainly can't argue with that. You know, it suddenly occurs to me that your use of the word transformation is relatively new in our conversations. I think there has been an evolution in your terminology. The first statement of the essential principles you got from Elroy had 'a spiritual focus' as the leading essential principle. That quickly became discipleship and now it seems that that has become transformation. Is this a change in terminology, has your thinking evolved, or am I lumping things together that you did not intend?"

"Well, I think all of this is on the same track. I suspect that my change in terminology is not a move off in a different direction, but a matter of going deeper. True discipleship involves going deeper and deeper; it is not just a matter of following Jesus year after year in the same way. It is a relationship and if the relationship isn't growing, it is deteriorating. A true disciple is continually changing in lots of ways. My goal is not simply to have people show up in church Sunday after Sunday, put an offering in the plate, and say 'nice sermon, pastor' on the way out. I'm afraid a lot of churches in this country give the appearance of this orientation, judging by all the indicators that so many are in decline or plateaued."

"I couldn't agree more," Swen responded, "but this brings my mind back to our interaction about the struggles of preaching. Obviously, there are many pitfalls here and we really need to be careful about what we adopt as our measures of success, including those subliminal ones that shape our actions. You already mentioned some, such as having a need to please people, or having a need for security that makes you timid about preaching what may be unpopular."

"Certainly there are many pitfalls. Another one that may occur among our most gifted preachers is an ego thing about being seen as creative and original. But the real goal is something else—the transformation of people. There are a lot of things that can get in the way of being sharply focused on the transformation of our people and we have to be ruthless in keeping our focus. You find some preachers who are not flashy but have a profound impact on their people."

"Agreed," injected Swen, "But let's not forget the earlier point you made about groups, such as those using the Jim Smith books in your church. There are so many activities that can have this transformation focus which—if we aren't careful—can become social or self-indulgent in focus. Here is a place where the connection to bottom-up planning can be important. Church boards, committees, task forces and other groups can address this matter directly and give prayerful attention to how various activities can develop this transformation focus. It is not just a matter of the pastor setting the agenda but getting other leaders, especially the board, involved in developing this emphasis. It should become their passion as well as that of the pastor. The pastor, of course, can serve a powerful leadership function here by constantly directing attention to this basic goal of the faith community. And thinking back to those key leverage points for self-organizing from Meadows, remember that the second from the top was setting the purpose or goals—the vision thing. Leaders need this awareness."

"This makes me think again about all the different things we can be doing in a church that have this transformation focus. It includes spiritual direction, pursuing various spiritual disciplines, appropriate youth activities, and, of course, various service activities that are an outreach to marginalized people, both within and outside of the church community. Service to the needy is not of value just to those served; it is often a vehicle for transformation of the people serving."

"I think it may be time," Kevin suddenly suggested, "To move on in my list."

"Go for it."

"The third item on my list is a contrast between program development and people development. Actually, I think we already have talked about many of the basic ideas found here. The contrast between revitalization and transformation resembles the contrast between program and people development. Rather than working on program change, the self-organizing focus is on change among people—not prescribed, specific changes, but ones aimed toward self-directed processes of prayerful discernment that lead to changes in basic beliefs and assumptions. As with the transformation emphasis we have just been examining, it is grounded in Bible study and prayer. So I am not sure there is a lot more to say that hasn't already been said."

"Okay," allowed Swen, "Let's go on to the fourth item then. You said earlier that this one referred to a couple of programs provided by your denomination, so I suspect you will have some specifics to talk about here."

"Yeah, these two programs, *Restart* and *My Story*, are ones I really like and have participated in. They are different in focus, however, and in some ways they seem to exemplify the two orientations we are talking about—bottom-up and self-organizing change. I guess I better describe them."

"Yes, I have been wondering what they are."

"Let me begin with *Restart*. It is a program for leading a congregation through an assessment and visioning process that will give them new direction for the future. Although intended mainly for churches that recognize they are plateaued or in decline, it sometimes is used simply at a transition point, such as preparing to call a new pastor. The process begins with an outside assessor who comes in and spends a day doing a comprehensive evaluation of the church based on conversations with its leaders, review of financial and other records, examination of facilities, and so on. After reading the assessor's preliminary report, a representative group of the congregation and its leaders enters into an appreciative inquiry sort of session with the assessor in which they give their recollections about the best parts of their past ministries, express some of their wishes for the future and suggest new initiatives. All of this is followed by a half-day training session for selected leaders who will lead small group meetings with the congregation which truly constitute a bottom-up planning process."

"It sounds like," Swen noted, "the sort of thing a lot of us in the church consulting business do in one way or another."

"I'm sure it is, although in this case it is run by our denomination as a packaged program that a congregation can buy into. They tell people from the beginning that the outcome could be one of many things including relocating to a new building—possibly smaller, restarting with a new vision, initiating a more gradual change process, or even closing the church."

"And I'm sure it is in your listing because it is a classic bottom-up planning process."

"Of course," Kevin agreed, "And it provides a good contrast to the other denominational program, *My Story*, that I put in the other column. This program does not seem to me to be typical of the work church consultants do, even though I think it typifies the self-organizing change you keep touting. Actually, it looks more like an evangelism program in that it focuses on helping people articulate their personal story of God's influence in their lives."

"So, how does it work?"

"Basically, it is a small group program that includes Bible study and focuses on helping people articulate their personal story, both in written and conversational form. It encourages the participants to move outside this small group setting and share their personal story in natural ways in various settings both within and outside their faith community. The intent is to help people bring out in the open who they really are and articulate what God is doing in their lives. In a nutshell, that's what it is, although the small group study materials are fairly extensive with many facets."

"Say more about the self-organizing association you are making," Swen interjected.

"Sure, and I probably would tie the transformation idea in here also. The purpose of the program is to get people to focus on their personal relationship with God, express what it is, where their story comes from in terms of past events in their lives, and what is happening with them on an ongoing basis. It is hard to do this without, at the same time, opening yourself up to further change. What direction this further change will take is rather unpredictable, and I think deserving of the label self-organizing."

"I'm with you on that," Swen interrupted. "The outcomes are unpredictable, but if it really proceeds on a deep level, over time it could lead to significant change for individuals, and if the number of such people is large enough, to significant change for an overall faith community."

"Exactly, and here is where I want to note again the potential connection between the two columns in my list. A bottom-up change process, such as *Restart*, could result in putting the *My Story* program in place in a church, leading to changes nobody saw coming out the specifics of the original planning process."

"As I look at your list," Swen said, "I'm noticing the final line, the one that has 'institutional perspective' on one side and 'spiritual perspective' on the other side, that is, the self-organizing side. I suspect this contrast brings up a lot of the things we have already talked about. Or is there something else here that is not immediately obvious?"

"Probably not, but I guess I added it to my list because of my personal uneasiness about some of the planning work I see people in your business doing in churches. It is easy to enter into a planning process—either bottom-up or top-down—that is based on social science knowledge, group processes, organizational theory, and such without taking adequate account of the spiritual dimension of this organism we call the church. You see, I tend to use a label like 'organism' for the church more readily than 'institution.'

"And obviously, you tie this to the self-organizing idea."

"Certainly," Kevin responded, "And most important, transformation. Churches are in the transformation business and I don't want that to get lost. The Spirit has to be at the center of all our attempts at change."

"I couldn't agree more and this makes me want to consider some more your personal connection to all of this. As a pastor, you are in the midst of all of this in a way that I am not. As a consultant, I really am an outsider. You are in the thick of it. At times it must be a bit stressful."

"Well," Kevin laughed, "I sometimes wonder if I have the temperament for this job. My odyssey has led me into this self-organizing stuff which I am convinced is powerful and valuable, and I thank you for your part in this journey, but I sometimes find all of it unsettling. Am I suited to the ambiguity and uncertainty of living with this understanding of change?"

"I'm wondering if a need for control isn't a key aspect of what you are dealing with."

"Of course it is and that is what reminds me of one of your key ideas—that the way to exercise leadership is to loosen up on the control aspect and begin to influence in multiple ways the self-organizing that is underway."

A long pause in their conversation emerged as both Swen and Kevin reflected on the matter. Swen finally broke the silence. "We have been working off of your list and it strikes me that there is an aspect of it all that may be something I should say some more about. You have used the word 'culture' several times and I tend to notice since the concept of culture is prominent in my work."

"I suspect you may have some more sophisticated understandings of culture."

"Maybe so. Let me start by distinguishing between culture in the broad societal sense and culture as it pertains to an organization—in our case a church. Just as a given society has a culture—and various subgroups have their subcultures—organizations have a culture. Thus, people in my sort of work often talk about organizational culture."

"I suspect," Kevin broke in, "that you may need to be more specific about what you mean in this context when you say culture."

"Okay, although I am not sure there are a lot of differences worth highlighting between general societal notions of culture and organizational culture, I do need to be clear that any given organization has a culture. Oh, I suppose you could have a collection of people that constitute some kind of organization who didn't have any pattern of relationships with each other, and thus don't have shared meanings and ways of relating, but that doesn't seem like any real organization I know. So, organizations have a culture."

"I get it, but you still haven't really explained what culture is, especially in an organizational context."

"Okay," Swen continued, "let's go back to a basic definition. Such definitions usually begin by referring to the behaviors of people and the various products or artifacts that they create. In a given church context there are common understandings of desired ways to behave and relate to each other. These understandings vary from one setting to another, for example, Sunday worship, the women's circle, or the youth group. And all churches are not the same. Each church has its understandings."

"Yeah, what we do in Sunday worship would not make people happy at the neighboring church down the block from us, and vice versa."

"Of course, but to really get to an understanding of culture we have to go deeper. It is not just these visible features—behaviors and artifacts—it is the underlying values and assumptions of people."

As he was saying this, Swen began to sketch a rough diagram on the bottom of the sheet with Kevin's list. It was simply a straight horizontal line with a nondescript object that was partially above this line but mostly below it. As he looked at it Kevin was thinking that the part below the line looked to be about ten times bigger than the part above the line.

"My little sketch," Swen continued, "is supposed to represent an iceberg. As you know, when you see an iceberg in the ocean, what you see is only a small part of it. What is below the surface is much larger than the part that is visible. It is a commonly used illustration of culture."

As he talked, Kevin added words to his sketch. On the small portion above the line, he wrote the words, BEHAVIOR and ARTIFACTS. Below the horizontal line he wrote VALUES and BELIEFS and further down below them he wrote ASSUMPTIONS.

"My iceberg is supposed to illustrate culture. The part that is readily visible is the behaviors of people and the visible products of their creativity. But of course, you have to look beyond the visible to understand a culture. To understand the culture of any organization, such as a church, you have to understand the shared values and beliefs of the people who make up the church and the shared assumptions about what constitutes their reality."

Kevin seemed hesitant as he said, "Given the similar basic Christian beliefs of churches, you would expect them to have more in common with each other than they appear to have. There seem to be huge cultural differences between churches, even ones in the same denomination."

"In any denomination, even one with a very tightly defined set of doctrines and practices, there is considerable variation in the assumptions people make about the Christian life."

"For example?"

"Well, here's one. Talk with a group of pastors who are together in a setting where they feel comfortable to be somewhat vulnerable and raise the question of whether they ever have a sense that they have to be careful of what they do, think or feel because if it isn't right, God will 'get them.' You'd be surprised how many will admit to that."

"Aw, come on, they don't really believe that do they?" Kevin interjected.

"In most cases, no. They quickly say that is not how they read the New Testament, but at the same time, many will acknowledge that this outlook is at least part of their inner compass. And the point of my example is simply that people's behaviors are shaped by their underlying beliefs, values and assumptions. If you want to understand a culture, you have to get a handle on some of the underlying beliefs and assumptions of the people. Many are never identified or spoken."

"A moment ago you used the word 'shared' but a lot of these underlying assumptions are not the same for everyone in a church."

"Granted, but there are a lot of them that are shared, even though they are never stated as such and they become determiners of the way things are done in a church."

"Okay, I get your point," Kevin said, "but we have been talking about change in churches and I want you to talk more directly about what this has to do with change, specifically changing the culture of a church."

"Yeah, it probably is time to rein me in a bit. Okay, the basic point is that we have been tying together the ideas of self-organizing change, cultural change and transformation and we had zeroed in on the cultural aspect. So let me be more specific about changing organizational culture."

"Exactly; that's it."

"Cultures," Swen continued, "including the cultures of churches, are constantly changing in an incremental manner and we want to channel this self-organizing. Cultural change can't be mandated or forced which, of course, ties back to your focus on transformation."

"So back to those leverage points of establishing vision and fostering a change in mindset."

"Certainly, but transformation was your word and obviously you have been thinking about it a lot, so I would like to hear more about where you are going with it."

"Sure," Kevin agreed, "but I probably should start with some of my basic beliefs and assumptions. After all, a moment ago you were big into those two words."

"Agreed," Swen smiled, "you can use my words."

"To start with, I believe God wants us to be transformed and I assume transformation is possible. There you have a form of both words in one sentence. But I want to go beyond my belief that God wants us to be transformed and my assumption that it is possible to be transformed. I also believe that God did *not* create us to pursue transformation to *earn* his favor. He created us to have a relationship with him; he planted within us a desire for this relationship and thus a desire for transformation."

"Sure, but you know there are an awful lot of people in our churches who seem to have gotten caught up in a way of living that seems to be driven by a different narrative."

"I don't disagree," Kevin said, "but it isn't just what they think things should be in theory. In many ways, they have let themselves be captured by a pattern of living that is formed by the broader societal culture we live in—more so than a biblical or faith community culture."

"Okay, I think we really are in agreement, but I want to hear about the specific steps you are taking or considering pursuing."

"Before I describe anything that looks like a plan of action, let's talk about things we know from past experience in the broader church that work—that have proven to be effective in moving people toward transformation. There are five things I want to zero in on in some way—all things that you and I have discussed before."

"Let's hear them."

With that comment in his ears, Kevin began hastily scratching out on his paper a list of five items:

- Prayer

- Bible study for transformation (not just for information)

- Spiritual disciplines

- Spiritual direction

- Engagement in ministry (service to others)

"I'm sure I don't have to justify the first one on my list for you. We have oodles of indicators of prayer being the foundation of a relationship with God. I listed it first because the others all, in some sense, foster this posture of prayer which, of course, exhibits itself in a seemingly endless number of modes. It is the foundation of transformation."

"Yeah, I'm with you."

"And the second one, Bible study, is another obvious one. All kinds of studies have shown that it, along with prayer, is correlated with spiritual growth. The REVEAL study, for example, that we talked about months ago, shows this in a striking fashion."

"Yes," Swen agreed, "and I noticed you wrote that this was Bible study for the purpose of transformation. I think this is the actual goal of most Bible study, but you do see a lot of instances where it seems that people are caught up with gaining knowledge or information for its own sake. Increased knowledge is great as long as its pursuit doesn't get in the way of scripture serving as a vehicle for our transformation."

Kevin charged ahead. "The third one is really a collection of a large number of practices, essentially all of which are intended to foster a life of prayer and closer relationship with God. For example, fasting, living simply, solitude, journaling, humility, and meditation all are pursued to encourage prayer and submission to the Holy Spirit in our lives."

"Your next one is spiritual direction. Do you have many people engaged in it in your congregation?"

"No, and given our culture, I doubt that it will become very common in its classic individual form. At its core, however, it centers on one's relationship with God and transformation of that relationship. A spiritual director typically listens and asks an occasional question, but these questions can at times lead to new insights and new steps in prayer. I know you are familiar with such questions, but a couple of the common ones really stand out in my mind as valuable. 'How has it been with you and God lately?' and 'How do you pray?' Conversation about such matters really is a focus on transformation."

"You said you did not expect individual spiritual direction to become common in your congregation, yet you included it in your list," Swen interrupted.

"Yes, but my list did not specify individual spiritual direction and, as you and I have discussed before, the most common form of spiritual direction in the church historically has been group spiritual direction. The first example of it that people tend to mention is John Wesley's cell groups in England a couple hundred years ago. The standard question they asked each other was, 'How is it with your soul?' Group spiritual direction of this sort is very much a possibility in our church circles. I have real hope for it in small groups."

"I agree with your assessment of their potential but this means creating groups where this really is the focus. Not all groups are the same. But keep going; you have one more on your list."

Kevin continued. "The fifth item is engagement in service ministries. A lot of people are pushing such activities because of the great needs of certain people—needs of many different kinds. Certainly ministry is important for this reason, but it also has an impact on the people serving—not just those being served. So service can be a vehicle for transformation of the people engaged in service."

"I'm with you on this, but I think it might contribute more to the transformation you are seeking if you incorporated with it a bit of your previous item—group spiritual direction."

"Absolutely, and I think you could say much the same thing about all five. Engaging in them in some combination enhances their potential."

"It is clear we are on the same wavelength about your items," Swen continued. "We probably established that a long time ago, but your items have come up again in the context of our discussion about bottom-up change and self-organizing change. I really would like to hear more about what you plan to do in your congregation and how you see all of it in terms of these two orientations toward change."

"Certainly, but first let me say a bit more about the changes I would expect if these moves toward transformation have an impact. First of all, I would expect the transforming changes in people's lives will be highly varied—not predictable. Individuals are not all the same and it seems that the Holy Spirit influences people in highly varied ways. Second, I expect that these changes will permeate each person's life. Transformation does not result in superficial changes; I would expect some of these changes to be truly life-changing. And finally, I would expect that the pace of change at some point would pick up. The REVEAL study we talked about a moment ago showed that as the impact of prayer, Bible study and other discipleship processes took hold in people's lives, the pace of transformation increased, often exponentially. I hold out hope for real transformation in people's lives—at least in a substantial number of people."

"Yeah, I realize you are hoping for substantial transformation, at least in some people, and that you have reason to think it will happen. Clearly, it is a serious matter of prayer for you."

"Yes," Kevin agreed, "it is both a matter of prayer and a serious focus for my ministry work. But that brings us to the point you wanted me to address—what specific actions I am pursuing *and* how they relate to the bottom-up, self-organizing distinction we have been talking about. We have already talked about preaching for transformation, so I'll zero in on other steps, ones we know have been effective in many instances in other places. High on my list is setting out to foster the spiritual disciplines among our people."

"You said earlier that this was high on your list. So, what are you planning to do?"

"We are in the process of initiating some classes on the spiritual disciplines, setting up some mentoring sessions for people who have expressed an interest and offering some training sessions for those of our small group leaders who have expressed an interest in pursuing this in their small groups."

"So," Swen asked, "is this an attempt at self-organizing change or what?"

"I think it is a combination of approaches. It is an attempt at promoting self-organizing change in that—as we talked about a moment ago—engagement in the spiritual disciples is an avenue to self-organizing change and transformation. But I am getting there through some pre-planned initiatives."

"In fact, from what you have said it appears to be a top-down endeavor."

"Yes and no," Kevin responded. "I am sure at first blush it appears to be very top-down, but actually the plans came out of a lot of bottom-up discussions. We have committees in charge of both education and small groups and both were a key part of the planning for all of this. Our board was deeply involved as well. We had numerous in-depth discussions about these plans, including discussion about the self-organizing change we hoped would result. And I can't leave out the discussions we had in some town hall meetings we set up with whoever was interested to talk about where our church should be headed. So, In spite of its appearance to you, I think it was more bottom-up than top-down."

"Is there more to your push for transformation?"

"Oh, yes. Our education committee is focusing on adult classes next year that are mostly focused on some aspect of transformation. And the small group committee is doing a pilot test of group spiritual direction in a new group set up just for that purpose."

"That sounds like an awful lot for a church your size."

"Yes, it is, but there is one more item. Remember *My Story*, the denominational program I mentioned? Well, we have a small group of people who are pilot testing the first part of their curriculum and getting started with telling their personal stories in various settings. Yes, there is a lot going on and it is a combination of bottom-up and self-organizing initiatives."

Swen paused, seemingly pondering the overall picture he had just been gaining. "It strikes me that all you have been describing seems in some way to be connected. It is not just a random collection of activities that have popped up. Am I right?"

"Definitely. They have grown out of lots of discussion in committees, town meetings, and the board—and these discussions have been focused on the concept of transformation."

"What about self-organizing?"

"Yes, that too, but when I am talking with members of the congregation I find it easier to connect with them about the concept of transformation than self-organizing. But when we start talking about the action of the Holy Spirit in their particular individual life, we are touching on self-organizing at times without using the word."

Again Swen paused before continuing the conversation. "It seems to me that you must be doing a lot to cast a vision of what this is all about for your congregation."

"Without a doubt. You really convinced me about setting a vision as being only second to developing a mindset as a leverage point for affecting our system. I come to every committee or board meeting prepared to promote this vision. The same is true of my meetings with individuals, casual hallway conversations, and certainly with Sunday worship. It is hard to imagine a Sunday morning where I don't fit it in, either in the sermon or somewhere else."

'I'm impressed. It also reminds me of a recent conversation with a denominational executive in which we were talking about individual congregations that are thriving—and there are a lot of them in spite of the many that are plateaued or declining. In talking to such people, one gains the impression that across denominations these thriving congregations have a clear spiritual focus. So it seems you are on a path that experience shows to be headed in the right direction."

"I think we are on a good path," Kevin allowed, "but I have some concern about staying on it. What if a bunch of these initiatives fizzle? People are on board now, but I wonder if failure of some of our efforts could kill it all off. I've started a caravan down this road unlike anything I have attempted before and I am afraid of serious breakdowns. "

"I certainly understand the concern, but it seems to me that you are off to a great start and with some key safeguards along the way it should get you to a place you want to be—even though at this point you don't know exactly where that is."

"Easy for you to say, mister consultant; you don't have to live with the consequences of all of this like those of us who have to really work for a living."

Swen did not take the bait and continued on. "Let me describe a situation that bears a bit of resemblance to what you are doing that, in fact, did fizzle. It may be a useful comparison to point out some key differences. Let's see if I can provide some encouragement by talking about something that fizzled."

A smile came with the response. "Okay, let's see if you can be Barnabas by telling me stories of failure."

"I'm familiar with a pastor who set out to move people toward transformation by setting up five short classes—two sessions each—that addressed different areas of discipleship, one on the spiritual disciplines, one on identifying your spiritual gifts, one on Bible study for transformation, and I forget the other two. Each was conducted by a different person and, as I said, was a short intensive. All apparently were well done, but the number of people who actually took them was very small. After offering the set of five intensives two different times, he dropped the endeavor and concluded that it had been a failure."

"I'm waiting for the encouraging part."

"Patience, o ye of little faith. First of all, I want to point out some differences between what you have already done and what this fellow did not do. Then looking ahead I want to recommend some future actions to you that he did not take. To start with, this pastor basically designed the approach on his own. Now, he did have the input of the people who taught the five classes. Although he identified the five topics and recruited the five instructors, he had each of the five people design and prepare their own classes. They were all very competent and did a good job. He did not, however, have the buy-in of the other leadership in the church. Certainly the board knew of the plans and agreed to them, but they had no real part in developing the vision that was the basis for offering the classes in the first place. It was on the pastor's shoulders. If the classes succeeded, he would get lots of credit. When they fizzled—as they did in terms of enrollment—he just let them fade away and no mention was made of them again."

"Okay, I think I finally heard some encouragement. It sounds as if what I have been doing to build a common vision among our leaders, especially the board but throughout the leadership, will be important as we move into the future."

"Exactly," Swen responded, "and you have been creating a climate where self-organizing has a much better chance of flourishing."

"You seem to think I have done some things right. Now it seems you also want to give me some advice about future actions."

"Yes, and to do so I will keep using this same problematic example. When enrollment in the classes didn't live up to expectations, he just dropped the project rather than carefully evaluating it. Why were enrollments so low? Was it the nature of the classes themselves? Was the promotional material at fault? Did people not understand the vision that was behind this endeavor? Or did they understand it but reject it? With some changes, the endeavor may have been successful. And if this program was not to be continued, what would be done to reach the goals they were pursuing? In all of this I am convinced that the evaluation should be collaborative. Those who were part of shaping the original plans need to be part of evaluating them."

"I hear you and it is a reminder that leadership is not about up-front persona and an image of being creative and one who gets things done by the force of one's personality."

Kevin continued. "It also reminds me of something we have discussed before—something I really buy into. It is the idea of treating a new initiative as a pilot test or an experiment."

"Yes, when something doesn't work, we want to take a different approach but not abandon our goal. Our goals should have been carefully considered enough that we are quite tenacious in pursuing them. We may need to step back and regroup, or come up with a different strategy, but we still want to maintain our focus."

"It also brings to mind this idea of measures of success that we have talked about before."

"Definitely," Swen jumped in, "and I would emphasize distinguishing between intermediate and long term measures of success. If this fizzled project is abandoned because the immediate goals were not attainable, you still want to keep the long term measures of success clearly in mind. We need to know why we are doing what we are doing and keep on keeping on."

"And for me that means keeping on in fostering a culture of transformation, something I think I can best do by fostering self-organizing through ongoing attention to vision setting and shaping the mindset of the congregation through my preaching and everything else I do."

chapter 14

Associations of Churches

Waypoints

Any approach used at the *regional level for a collection of churches* must fit the context and take account of the following:

- Any approach is only as good as its implementation.
- An initiative must engage the personal spiritual lives of the people involved—it must have a focus on personal transformation.
- Even a district-level program should attend to creating within each congregation a culture of personal transformation.
- It must proceed on a broken front with attention to the leverage points of vision and mindset.
- Encourage pastors to pilot test various programs that fit their context.
- Help church boards to become spiritual communities.
- Support and prepare their pastors, their most important role.

Two potential metaphors for a pastor are engineer and artist. Regional leaders should promote with their pastors the metaphor of artist.

"HEY KEVIN. THIS IS Swen. We need to talk." The voice on the phone was friendly and calm.

"Why? What's up?"

"I just got a call from the guy who is the head of your district of churches, Leon Rigirozzi. Obviously, the two of you have been talking about change in churches, including self-organizing change. At any rate, he was asking if I could help your district do things that would be supportive of positive change. I have done quite a few workshops for church leaders that have been sponsored by regional associations of churches, but I have never consulted with such an association about how they should organize and conduct their own affairs to be supportive of change in their member churches. It sounds like an interesting challenge and I told him I would like to consider the possibility, but before I work out something more concrete with him, I thought it would be helpful to have a chat with you, since you have a good handle on this change business and you know the workings of your denomination's sort of regional association—districts, I guess you call them."

"Well, my friend, I have a hunch this is going to cost you a lunch at Goolsby's."

"I already figured that would happen," Swen chuckled, "so I guess it is just a matter of picking a time."

* * * * *

The conversation in a window booth on their usual east side of Goolsby's took quite a while to get to the intended business, but finally Swen launched into it. "Tell me about your denominational polity, most specifically, the structure and role of the district apparatus."

"I suppose it is sort of an in-between arrangement. We don't have someone like a bishop who assigns pastors to churches. Individual churches conduct their own search for their pastors but the district has a strong hand in the process as well. Any new pastor has to be approved by the district as well and the district actually has a role in locating candidates for the churches to consider. The polity is based on a notion of what is often called connectionalism. The individual churches expect to collaborate with each other on many matters and they try to work together on mission projects and help each other on various endeavors."

"That fits with what Leon told me. Although he wants me to do a series of workshops on change for pastors—somewhat like the ones you attended—he also wants the district to be able to provide other support for churches as well."

"I assume," Kevin said, "he wants to foster self-organizing change and a culture of transformation much like you and I have spent a lot of time talking about."

"We could hope so, but I find that pastors and their regional leaders rarely have a solid grasp of all of these concepts, so I would never start out by assuming such understanding. They want help in making change but are not sure what it takes to get the change they want. So they tend to latch onto the latest fad or whatever someone makes a convincing case for."

"Are you thinking that that is where Leon is? That after hearing my raves about your outlook, he wants you to come in and do your thing here in our district and make everything better?"

"Maybe. I'm not sure," Swen said. "But I am nervous about letting myself end up in the position of being the guy who is going to fix things for someone else."

"I sense that there is a lot of stuff that goes on in the consulting business that you are not totally on board with, or am I just imagining that? I have never heard you running down other people in the consulting business, yet at the same time I have picked up your reservations about a lot of the stuff that gets promoted for making change. It seems that there are a lot of things you would not want to do."

"That's probably true, but it is not so much someone's particular technique or program, but how and where it is used. The context is so critical."

"Okay then," Kevin expressed with some vigor, "tell me some of the things you would *not* do here in our district and why."

"I imagine that list could get fairly long, some simply because I don't think much of the approach, but in most cases because I don't think it is what is needed at this time in this place."

"Even so, I would like to hear about some of them and why."

After a long pause, Swen said, "This may be helpful. I'll start with one we have talked about several times before, appreciative inquiry, an approach that I like and use on occasion. I find it a useful tool, but only as one tool among others used in a holistic manner in settings where it fits. What I shy away from is its use as a program that is supposed to stand on its own. I know of one denomination, with districts a lot like yours, where it seemed to sweep through the districts. It seemed that everyone was doing workshops to train pastors and other leaders in the use of appreciative inquiry. Too much was promised. By itself it couldn't do that much."

"What about strategic planning?"

"You have a similar problem there. There are a hundred and one kinds of strategic planning and you find various names given to it, mission studies, visioning, discerning the future, focusing, and so on. As with appreciative inquiry, such planning can be quite helpful. I guess it better be, because much of how I make my living is by helping churches do this sort of thing. The problems come when it is used as a stand-alone tool. It so much depends on the context and how it fits in."

"Say more about that. What does the context have to do with it?"

After a brief pause, Swen said, "When I conduct such a process with a local social service agency, for example, it is not the same as when I do it with a church, because the purposes of the groups are so different. Even when I am working with a church that does a lot of social service, it is different. You can find churches where such service seems to drive the system, so to speak, but if they lose their mooring in the gospel of Jesus Christ they tend to go into decline."

"It sounds as if you are talking about what at various times I was calling a spiritual focus, discipleship and ongoing transformation."

"Exactly. Things need to be grounded in who you are, namely, in the case of Christian churches, being disciples of Jesus Christ. A church engaged in strategic planning has to constantly be asking itself, 'Is this what Jesus would have us be doing?' Pursuing this question is a matter of spiritual discernment and you would expect it to be grounded in individual and corporate prayer. And sometimes it takes quite an extended period of time. Contracting to do a strategic planning process over a defined number of months may not give ongoing prayerful discernment sufficient influence. It is giving the planning process itself a bigger role than it deserves. It potentially can keep you away from being authentically who you would like to think you are."

"To use your current example of social service, I imagine it could mean doing either more or less of it."

"Sure, as I implied earlier, it is possible for a service or activist oriented church to lose its spiritual moorings, but there are oodles of churches with an apparently spiritual focus that have become isolated from the world Jesus wants them to be serving. It is easy to find downtown churches whose members mostly had moved to the suburbs who found new vitality when they began to reach out and serve their immediate neighborhood."

"Yes," Kevin added, "but a lot more of those churches have just died."

"Unfortunately, I think you are right. But the point of all this is that a church is made up of a particular group of disciples of Jesus and that identity should determine what the church is, not some planning process."

"So, I'm getting the message that you wouldn't encourage our district to set up a process of strategic planning for each of its churches on some mass basis, but what about helping churches on a more nuanced basis, such as our denomination's program called *Restart*, which we have talked about before?"

"Sure," Swen responded, "from what you have told me about it, it sounds like a solid program incorporating elements of both appreciative inquiry and strategic planning in a reasonable manner. I am aware of a number of denominations that have programs of this sort. My only cautions would be that it be used for those churches where there is a felt need for it on the part of the congregation and that it be done in a manner that gives due attention to prayer and spiritual discernment. It would not be a district-wide program for all churches, but one for those where it fits."

"I've heard of programs that sound a bit like *Restart*, but seem a lot more heavy-handed. An outside team comes in, does considerable fact-finding, and then presents a plan to the congregation to either accept or reject as a total package. If accepted, the leadership of the church then begins to put the plan into action, usually with considerable help in the form of coaching, workshops and other support. Some of these plans are pretty dramatic, involving major financial commitments."

"I know of quite a number of churches that have gone through such a process. They are usually referred to as an *intervention* to distinguish them from a strategic planning and implementation process. They are really very much top-down operations as I have seen them in practice."

"So, what do you think of these interventions?" Kevin asked.

"Well, let me think how I want to put this. I know that there are really positive examples of the process, especially in those places where the people who developed the approach were in a position to shape and refine the process they had invented. Those instances I have seen up close have had decidedly mixed results. The one district where I have seen it up close gave a lot of positive feedback about the pastor support and study groups that went with the district program, but, in most of the churches, it is hard to see that much positive impact of the interventions themselves. There isn't a residue of bad feelings about the program, not at all, but you don't find many people talking about all the great things that came out of the district's commitment to this program of interventions. I have seen up close one example that turned out very badly. It was an individual church that went through such a process independent of any support from a district or regional association. The church made some rather sweeping changes and within two years, it closed and the building was sold."

"Why the dismal failure?"

"That is hard to be certain about, but I have enough personal friends who were a part of that church that I feel quite confident of my judgment on this one. The church had declined from thriving to somewhat desperate in a short number of years and was without debt. The intervention included acquiring some debt and making significant changes, changes that probably were appropriate and potentially positive. The difficulty came in the implementation. It was basically in the hands of the pastor who it turned out was insensitive and incompetent. I think there is something about any strongly top-down approach that makes it vulnerable to an authoritarian leader who is not up to the task. Possibly it would have turned out differently with some district level support, but I doubt it."

"It appears," Kevin said after a long pause, "that you have a lot of evidence to support your hesitance about such interventions."

"No, no, no. I have only my personal impressions. If there has ever been a thorough evaluation or a research study of such interventions that really gets to the underlying dynamics of them, I am not aware of it. I guess my reason for even getting into this topic at all is to emphasize two points. First, any approach is only as good as its implementation. So much depends upon how it is done. Second, whatever is done, it needs to reach down to the personal spiritual lives of the people involved. Personal transformation growing out of a relationship with God is foundational."

"You won't get any argument from me on that last point. This conversation has been headed down a path focused on things you wouldn't suggest our district do. Are there other things you don't intend to suggest to Leon?"

Swen quickly responded. "The first thing people like Leon usually expect from a consultant like me, is a proposal that I come into the district, do some sort of study, and then lead them through some sort of processes that will result in new initiative, new enthusiasm and new direction. I have done that with lots of churches and I could do something of that sort for your district, even though I haven't been engaged to help a district transform itself before. But I am not inclined to do that for the many reasons we have discussed in our recent conversations. I am convinced that the only truly effective transformation of your district must be grounded in the transformation of people in your various churches."

"I guess we need to move on to what you really will do, not just talk about what you won't do. But first, let me ask about something that has been discussed in our district. As I mentioned earlier, we make a point of being connectional. It has been suggested that we should try to strengthen these connections by agreeing to have more joint endeavors that connect our churches, various mission projects, boards of neighboring churches meeting together for support, pastor support groups, study groups that connect several churches and the like. What do you think of this?"

"In summary, I would be completely supportive, go for it. I would not, however, expect dramatic results from them, especially if they did not grow out of a grass roots initiative. Your district certainly could create some structures to support this connectionalism, but there has to be an underlying desire for it if it is to thrive and have a significant impact."

"Well, with all of these matters out of the way," Kevin said, "I think we should zero in on what you actually *would* do in our district."

At that point their server interrupted their conversation by asking if they wanted to order dessert. As usual, she was recommending the peach cobbler. Again as usual, they declined dessert, but accepted the offer of refills on the coffee and diet cola. Swen then returned to Kevin's question.

"My bottom line starting point as to what should be done in your district would be a focus on individual transformation. Earlier we were talking about creating a culture of transformation in a church as a starting point for self-organizing and creating a climate within which people would grow under the influence of the Holy Spirit. I would say something analogous for your district—your collection of churches in this geographic area. We would want to develop a culture of transformation at this level which establishes as the norm that transformation is expected and everyone is looking for evidence that it is flourishing in the churches."

"I certainly am not surprised that this would be your starting point but Leon probably will be wanting to know how you are going to put wheels under it."

"As in a church, I would start with the leverage points of vision and mindset. I would want to instill within your pastors and everyone who is part of the district organization a vision for churches with a culture of transformation. I would hope to create a mindset among these leaders of transformation being both possible and desirable. The question, of course, is how you go about doing so."

"Okay, so that is the question," Kevin responded, "how do you respond to it?"

"I would proceed on a broken front, doing a lot of different things at the same time, looking for places where I could get traction. I would try to make transformation a common topic of conversation, see how people respond to these ideas, take every opportunity to do teaching on it, and start various activities that may create movement in this direction."

"So what would some of those activities be?"

"Well, how about starting with those two denominational programs you have talked about—*Restart* and *My Story*. *Restart* probably is a program for only a subset of the churches in your district but its presence can be talked about as an example of the district's push for transformation. It may only be a tiny thing in this big picture but it is something concrete that illustrates where the district wants to go. The last time we got together you had *Restart* on your list as an example of revitalization more so than transformation. I agree with this characterization, but you can promote transformation within this program and communicate to everyone in the district that it has this potential and everyone should be happy to see it going on for that reason, not just because an institution—a church—may be revitalized."

"What about *My Story*?" Kevin asked.

"Well, you identified it as a program with power for transformation and I think that is true. You said it was an evangelism program but it does have this transformative potential for participants because it engages people in reflecting on and communicating their own faith journey and thus bringing attention to what Jesus has done for them."

"How big a part do you see this program playing in creating a culture of transformation?"

"That's hard to say. In a few cases, maybe quite a bit, but if nothing else, it becomes one piece of the total picture being presented to people, that of a collection of churches committed to transformation of people."

"Sure, I can see it as a part of an attempt to create an ethos that includes the desired vision and commitment to a new mindset," Kevin said. "So, what else is part of this broken front approach you mentioned?"

"I have never done this, but I can imagine doing some seminars for pastors and lay leaders on the topic of creating a culture of transformation. It would also be possible to include such discussions into whatever form of meetings your district has. However it is done, I think it is essential to have ongoing group discussion of how such a culture can be attained—one that is stable but continuously self-organizing."

"I think this conversation would be important, but don't you have to have something more participatory, something that really involves a significant number of congregants in meaningful activities?"

"Oh, sure," Swen responded. "A good place to start, I would think, is by teaching classes of some kind for people in the congregation using curriculum materials that are focused on transformation. I imagine this *My Story* program would include some materials that would serve this purpose. The Jim Smith books we were talking about, *The Good and Beautiful* series, would also seem to be prime candidates."

"Would you start a district-wide program of such classes?"

"I would *not* do that. The people in charge of such things in your district apparently have not tested out how any of these materials would work with your people—and there is the possibility that some would work well with some sorts of groups but not others. I would do pilot tests of several materials in different settings. The old notion of treating something new as an experiment is always good."

"So you would start pilot-tests of a whole bunch of such programs in different settings. The more the merrier?"

"Well, within reason," Swen responded. "You are checking out how these programs work with various types of people, you are gaining insights on how best to use them, and you are spotting some of the challenges you will have to overcome to use them on a more extensive basis."

"So then you would set up a district-wide program using one of these sets of materials?"

The response came with a chuckle. "You really haven't abandoned those top-down approaches as much as you been saying, have you? Or are you going to claim that since a lot of pilot testing was done, such a district-wide program would be a bottom-up approach?"

With just a hint of defensiveness, Kevin said, "Whether it is top-down or bottom-up probably is beside the point. Have you got a better idea that is more self-organizing?"

"Hey, I didn't say such a district-wide program is a bad idea. I just wouldn't commit to such an approach until I had the benefit of learning from the pilot-testing of multiple materials in varied settings; that's all. And whether such classes are uniform across the district, or a potpourri of many different ones, I think a case could be made for viewing them as part of an attempt to encourage self-organizing change. After all, transformation is different for each person and none of the programs we are talking about have a set of behavioral objectives that define exactly what behaviors each participant is supposed to display at the end. This is but one part of a more sweeping set of initiatives intended to develop a mindset among congregants as to what it means to be a disciple of Jesus and create a vision of what could be in your faith communities."

"So whether you think of it as top-down or bottom-up, some instruction of this sort may be important. Once we have settled on some classes or group studies to use, I would think it would be important to provide some instruction or mentoring for the people teaching the materials."

"Certainly," Swen responded, "but just what and how extensive this support should be would depend on the materials, the background of the people you have as teachers or facilitators, and other factors."

"So what else do you have in your broken front approach?"

"Well, one thing that I can't help thinking about often is something we talked about months ago—helping church boards become spiritual communities."

"I recall that," Kevin replied. "I suppose doing so would vary a lot depending upon the polity of the denomination."

"I'm not so sure of that. I think it is less the polity and more the culture that has developed with a particular church as well as across a denomination. Certain shared meanings develop about what it means to be a member of the board that are far more important than the formal polity. The shared meaning that has developed in many places is that the board is to do the business of the church and make the major corporate decisions—with little attention to spiritual discernment and being spiritual leaders of the people. I see this even in many places where the formal polity of the church says that they are to be spiritual leaders, including determining what the pattern of worship will be."

"I'm with you on this matter of spiritual leadership—especially when I start thinking about creating a culture of transformation in a church. The board is a key part of making this happen, and unless they themselves are in the process of being transformed, there is a sharply reduced possibility of leading in this direction. So, what do you think can be done about this?"

"A couple of things. One is to hold meetings or retreats for boards— either for a given church or a group of churches—in which the focus is helping them to become such spiritual communities. I think there is real potential in doing this, although I have encountered a disappointedly large number of such so-called training programs that are focused on operating according to denominational polity, with inadequate attention to forming a spiritual community."

"And the second one?" Kevin asked.

"The second thing I would do is provide education for pastors on how to lead their board in becoming a spiritual community. My guess is that this second idea may be more influential than the first one. After all, the pastor is with the board on a continuing basis and is in a better position than anyone else to lead this renewal of the board."

"What's the district's role in this?"

"The district can provide this education for its pastors and, possibly equally or more important, foster a culture in which this matter is treated as something important and where pastors are discussing among themselves their progress in this regard—how much progress they are making, the obstacles encountered, and what has worked for them in providing this leadership."

"Since we are talking about assistance for pastors," Kevin asked, "what else would you suggest providing for them?"

"At the top of my list is making provision for spiritual direction for pastors, more specifically group spiritual direction. I see limitations, however, on what a district can do for its pastors in this regard. First of all, they have to want to be involved in it; it has to be truly voluntary. Second, the composition of the groups is critical. A group has to be made up of people who want to be together—people who trust each other or at least have the potential for building this trust readily. In some cases, pastors find it easier to get this cohesiveness with a group that does not include any other pastors who are part of their district. In other words, these pastors are from other denominations. So, what I am leading up to is the conclusion that the district may not be the best place to expect initiative on this matter."

"I'm not totally convinced of that. The district may be able to encourage a norm that says everyone should be in spiritual direction but not expect that the district would provide this opportunity for everyone. In addition, it could provide this opportunity for pastors who wanted to enter into such a process with other district pastors. It also could provide support of some type for pastors who want to enter into such a group process with pastors from other tribes."

"I hear you on that," Swen responded. "Some person or entity has to take the initiative in making all of this happen, and, more importantly, push for it to be the real thing. Being in a support group typically is not the same as being in a spiritual direction group. Certainly a support group can have this orientation, but almost by definition such groups are supportive to the point of not asking the pointed questions that may be needed, such as, 'Where do you see God in this troubling situation?' 'How do you pray?' and 'How is it with your soul?' Another way of saying some of this is that a group therapy group is not the same as a spiritual direction group. Also, it can be said that without education and a facilitator, the typical pastors support group lacks many of the elements of spiritual direction."

"You don't have to convince me on this point. I have been in a spiritual direction group for three years now. It has been very important in my ongoing transformation. In addition, this experience probably is crucial for pastors setting out to foster spiritual direction within their own congregation."

"It sounds like we are both on the same page on this matter, so maybe we should go on to another item in what I have been calling a broken front. As we have discussed on previous occasions, involvement in mission or service projects can be an important part of transformation for some people. I know we are in agreement on that point. The question at hand, it seems to me, is what part the district itself should play in a district-wide transformation initiative? What part can or should the district play in fostering these mission projects?"

"That's obviously a key question," Kevin said. "So, what do you think?"

"In a nutshell, I think the district can be a help, but—as with many endeavors—the main action is in the individual congregations. There is real merit in a collaborative mission project involving a couple of churches, a cluster of churches, or even an entire district. The big advantages I see in these broader endeavors are that some valuable projects are just too big for some churches; there is a cross-fertilization of ideas and reinforced passion in collaborative endeavors; and there is an opportunity to process some of the experience in an enriched environment.

There was a chuckling response from Kevin. "There were a lot of high-dollar words in that last sentence. What do you mean by 'process some of the experience in an enriched environment'?"

"Okay," Swen laughed. "Let's see if I can get real. The main transformation impact of mission endeavors is the experience itself. We have abundant testimonials about that. There is some additional benefit in many cases when people interact with others about the experience. So I am simply saying that if the district is sponsoring collaborative mission project, they should provide lots of time for prayer, study and also for participants to share with each other how their time together is impacting their relationship with God. Is it causing any personal transformation?

"Now that we have that out of the way," Kevin said with a smile, "Let me say something about the nature of mission projects. Some projects are organized by a church, a district or some other group, and then they solicit participants. Many of these projects are great endeavors and I have nothing against them. They are somewhat different, however, from a mission endeavor that grows out of individuals' interface with the world around them. Such people are influenced by the environment they live in and as a byproduct of the experience—under the direction of the Spirit— they respond to the need they are sensing first hand. Typically this is a different sort of experience from one where a person just signs on for a project someone has organized for them."

"And your point is….?"

"I think Jesus wants disciples who are sensitive to the needs around them and respond to these needs as they experience them. As they are transformed, I am convinced that people become more sensitive and also responsive to these needs—directly, not always expecting that there is some program for it. So I would encourage mission that emerges from such responsive lives. I am looking for lives transformed by their mission experiences."

"No argument from me on that point. I think that is what we want," Swen said, "and I think we have now covered enough examples of my broken front."

"You know, in some ways it looks like a motley collection of activities. It doesn't appear to be part of a coherent overall plan."

"I am sure it has that appearance, especially to the person who is big time into planning and hopes to control events. It probably is not what you would get in most strategic plans, *but* remember how this conversation started. I think we agreed that the transformation of the lives of individual disciples of Jesus was our bottom-line goal. We also agreed that we would like to see considerable self-organizing and that the leverage points of vision and mindset were our most profitable focus. It is bound to look a bit messy and we will expect our plans to evolve over time, actually to evolve continually."

"I'm wondering how you might convince the hesitant person who expects careful planning—convince this person to get on board with you." Kevin interjected.

"I may not be able to, but I would try by giving two images and asking which one is the best fit. The one image is that of an engineer who creates a product by drafting detailed engineering drawings of his product and then has the product built according to specs. The other image is that of an artist—a painter let's say—who begins with an overall design in her head and begins to paint. The painting evolves as the light reflects off the first bits of paint applied to the canvas in unexpected ways and as new images arise in the mind of the painter. Both images are important modes of creativity. I would simply ask, which is the best metaphor for the transformation process we are attempting to foster?"

"I think you know which one I would pick, but it brings to mind another matter. The painter in our situation—more than anyone else in most cases—is the pastor. Many of them struggle with this. Your engineer metaphor fits their approach to their work more than that of the artist. It strikes me that they would be helped by a person who could come along side of them as they do their work—a coach or mentor. Couldn't the district play a role in providing this help for them?"

"Absolutely," Swen responded. "I think this really would be valuable."

"I've got another question. We have been talking specifically about our district—right here at home. If something of the broken front plan was to be initiated here, who's going to do it, Swen? You or Leon?"

"To me the answer is quite obvious, it's Leon. So far, I only know him based on a phone conversation, so I don't know if he is up to it or not. I imagine you have an opinion on that matter, but I am not going to ask you for it just yet. I think I have a potential role in this process as well, but I doubt that it is what Leon envisions at this time. It appears to me that he has the more conventional expectation that I will come in, be his engineer and prepare a set of plans that he and/or I could implement. I am inclined to think that my first job is to help him understand the stuff you and I have been talking about today. I am speculating that the next thing would be for me to work with him and a small team of others from the district to develop an overall map of an endeavor focused on transformation for the district—nothing like engineered drawings, but a preliminary map for a journey through unexplored territory where we have only a few landmarks to go on. Another role I could play would be to do some of the educating of groups along the way. Finally, I potentially could serve as a coach to Leon in this process. I would come at this endeavor not as a person with generic coaching skills, but as someone with these coaching skills and a fairly deep understanding of the dynamics of change and the transformation being sought."

"I like it, yes I do."

"One other point strikes me," Swen continued. "You could be a really great resource in all of this. If Leon is convinced to form a small planning team as I just suggested, I would campaign for you to be part of it. The closer we come to having a critical mass of people on this team who have a commitment to transformation as a goal, the easier the job will be. Am I right in thinking you would be eager to do so?

"Let's go for it."

chapter 15

Church Start-ups

Waypoints

Launching new worshiping communities is key to the growth of *the* church overall. Several realities about this situation must be acknowledged.

- Both society as a whole and institutional churches have been changing substantially in recent decades.

- Growth in established churches is mostly through transfers of people from other churches. New church plants gather the majority of their people from the ranks of the unchurched.

- New models of church planting have emerged. There is more tendency for a new faith community to be embedded within some aspect of the broader community. Bi-vocational pastors are more common. A wide variety of new forms of worshiping communities are appearing.

- Successful church planters tend to be entrepreneurs, who are risk-takers, and are ready to try untested approaches.

- Planters of new churches increasingly are supported through assessment centers, coaches, internships and training programs.

Important principles pertaining to establishing new communities of faith include the following:

- Successful church start-ups tend to depend on God's agency rather than human agency.

- Fostering self-organizing and depending on the initiative of the Holy Spirit are compatible.

- Three focal points of forming new worshiping communities are encouraging relationships, fostering discipleship, and promoting vision.

- Three crucial aspects of new faith communities are ongoing worship, community, and outreach.

The essential principles of effective churches apply to new church start-ups as well. Building spiritual community is the primary means of *influence* and is in contrast to exercising control.

AGAIN A PHONE CALL—THIS time from Kevin to Swen—put the two men together at Goolsby's. Since they last met, Swen continued his work with the regional group of churches to which Kevin's church belongs and bits of information about this work found its way to Kevin. He was especially intrigued by the news that an initiative for planting new churches was about to begin.

After the usual catching up, Kevin said, "I heard from Leon that he and you are talking about an effort to plant more new churches in our region. Apparently, that is a particular interest of yours."

"Yes, it is a growing interest. I have spent lots of years helping churches revitalize their ministries—and that has been fulfilling for me—but I am coming to realize that the church world keeps changing and it is more and more apparent that planting new churches is the way the church overall is growing."

"Are you talking about how our churches are changing or the society in which we live is changing?

"Well, really both," Swen continued, "but I am especially aware of how the circumstances of institutional church life have changed. More and more congregations can't afford a full-time pastor, especially in rural areas. Bi-vocational ministry is becoming more common, and it seems to me that along with this is an increase in the number of pastors who are not seminary graduates. I hadn't been all that aware of these changes because my work rather naturally has been mostly with larger, established congregations. Working with Leon and your association of churches has made me more aware of life across the full sweep of churches—all kinds and sizes of congregations."

"I have the same sense of these changes, but what does that have to do with planting new churches?"

"I'm not sure; maybe my interest in planting new churches is realizing that this is the main way the church overall is growing. The big Protestant megachurches get lots of media attention and that tends to obscure the fact of lots of new congregations being formed."

"I seem to recall," Kevin interjected, "in a previous conversation, we talked about the fact that in some denominations which are growing, the majority of the growth is in newly formed congregations, not in older established congregations."

"Yes, and most important to me is that growth in established churches tends to be from people moving from one church to another, while newly planted churches tend to engage a lot of unchurched people, about 75 percent in many of the studies I hear about."

"Yeah, I have to admit that most of the new people who have come to our church since I have been there were transfers from other congregations. I'm afraid that is typical."

"So, if we want to reach unchurched people," Swen continued, "it seems that forming a lot of new churches is the way to go. And this is not just theoretical; there are denominations where this is happening. They are fulfilling the Great Commission—making disciples—by forming new faith communities. It is a conscious and deliberate effort."

"I can see how that would be, but I am not sure how it addresses what I think is one of the problems faced by smaller churches—a lack of funds to support a small church. The overhead in terms of salaries and facilities is a real problem for little churches and this is just creating more small churches with lots of overhead costs."

"But the whole church planting scene is changing. It is not being done the way it used to be. Think back to the 1950s and 1960s. Okay, don't give me that bit about you being too young to remember the 1950s. You probably were born in the 1960s and that is close enough that you have knowledge about how church planting was done in that era."

"Sure," Kevin responded. "The denomination bought ten acres in a growing suburb and hired a hard-charging young pastor to go out there, organize a congregation, get them established enough to borrow money to construct a building and they then had another church. I guess it was sort of a 'build it and they will come' approach."

"And when was the last time you saw that work?

"I guess I can't think of one from the last decade or so."

"If you had more time you probably would come up with one," Swen responded, "but certainly that is not a common approach today. It would be a lot easier to come up with examples of such attempts that have failed."

"Well, what is the approach for all these church plants you are talking about?"

After a long pause, Swen responded. "I guess I see about four approaches, including the one you just described. I'll call that one the 'old model.' A second one I'll call the 'modified old model.' Again you have a seminary grad who is provided with some salary who sets out to form a congregation, but in this case he or she goes into a definable neighborhood, connects with some of its people and begins to build relationships and a presence. There is no thought of acquiring a building at this point. Once they form some community, they may gather for worship, spiritual dialog, or whatever in some existing space, a home, a company cafeteria, a community center or other space that they can use on a limited basis."

"OK, it sounds like the only difference is whether or not they build a church building. Is that it?"

"No, no; it is fundamentally different in another sense. It is not the 'build it and they will come' approach because in today's world the unchurched mostly won't come, no matter how the program is packaged. The approach I am talking about is one of going into a neighborhood, establishing relationships with people in a variety of settings and gradually building a community of people—a faith community. The community is built through relationships—a growing network of relationships."

"OK, that is your second model," Kevin said. "What's next?"

"A third model in my classification system is the bi-vocational church planter. This person acts much like that person in the previous model except he or she has a 'day job' and is doing the work of building relationships and community 'on the side.' The approach this person is taking is much the same except there is less time to do it. On the other hand, this person has a running start because of existing connections with people, especially if the job and home are close together."

"This one resonates with me," Kevin was quick to say. "I have a cousin, Linda Felpski, who is doing just that. She is a seminary grad and has a full-time job as a loan officer in a credit union. Her work hours are fairly stable, she doesn't have to do a lot of overtime, and she is planting a church. I don't see her often because this is several hundred miles away, but the last time I saw her we had a fascinating conversation about what she is doing. She is supporting herself through her job, but her denomination is supporting her church planting effort in other substantial ways. She is provided with a coach and she is part of a small network of church planters who support each other in various ways under the guidance of a person who is the facilitator of the network. I think she would be a great example of what you are talking about."

"Definitely. That's it. Sometimes they result in a full-blown church of the kind we usually think about, and sometimes they continue long-term as a vital worshiping community that is never chartered as a formal church. In either case they are an expansion of the kingdom."

"You said you had a fourth model. Is it a variation on number three or something radically different?"

"Maybe something in between," Swen responded. "The approach is much the same as the previous one, but the background of the church planter is different. In my previous models, the church planter was a seminary grad, but in this case the church planter doesn't have this formal preparation for ministry. It is a matter of seeking out people who apparently have a giftedness for this ministry, and a passion for it, but have not had the desired education. The idea is to help them start into a process of gathering people into a faith community and at the same time give them some of the education they need."

"This sounds like a real stretch to me. Where are you going to find people who can do this?"

"I admit such people are not super abundant, but they do exist. The secret is to identify them, help determine if the passion is there, and provide the needed education and support. The bottom line is determining if God is calling them to this ministry. If so, there are ways to support and help them."

"You haven't convinced me yet," Kevin responded. "There are parts of my seminary education that haven't seemed that important to me, and lots of stuff that I didn't get there that I have needed, but still there were many parts that have been valuable and have been necessary to my work as a pastor. Seminary was important."

"I am not going to deny the value of seminary, but even your denomination, with its high value on an educated clergy, has a program for preparing lay pastors. Leon filled me in on it. As I understand it, your denomination has provided such education, without formal academic credit, to lay persons who will play a ministry role in existing churches. Over a couple years or so, they have been given enough education that your denomination has seen fit to put them in ministry roles in existing churches, sometimes as the solo pastor of a small church. What I am talking about is having such persons begin a new faith community from scratch. There are places where it is being done, and given what we have been talking about with the changing state of institutional churches in this country, I think we will be seeing more of it."

"If I grant for the moment that this is possible, I still don't see how you are going to know who really has what it takes to plant a new church."

"Well, you have the same problem with any of these models," Swen replied. "Everyone is not cut out to be a church planter, but a new twist has come on the scene in the last couple of decades or so, something generally called an assessment center. Typically operated by a denomination, they are set up for the specific purpose of evaluating candidates to make a judgment about their potential for being church planters. It is a rigorous process, taking two or three days, that includes written tests, individual interviews and group interaction."

"We church people are nice to each other," Kevin interrupted. "They aren't going to tell a bunch of seminary grads that all that time in school was wasted and to just forget about it."

"Hold on. They aren't deciding if a person is qualified to be a minister; they are making an assessment of their potential for going out and starting a church. And actually they are very rigorous and discriminating. The numbers I am hearing from such groups is that they only endorse about 25 percent of the people who go through the process; that's one out of four that get their stamp of approval."

"So what about the other 75 percent?"

"It is suggested that they are better suited to taking a role in established churches, or being a chaplain, or some other ministry role. Planting a church takes a unique skill set and this process is designed to identify people with this specific giftedness."

Kevin's body language indicated he accepted this response, but another comment followed, "Your fourth model was church planters who had not been to seminary. Is an assessment center going to take on evaluation of people like that?"

"It depends upon which assessment center you are talking about, of course, but, yes, it is a possibility. What is being evaluated is not the depth of their education in Bible or theology, but their giftedness for going out into some corner of society, establishing relationships with people, and bringing them together to form a community. They are looking for people who are evangelists and entrepreneurs. One person who is part of one of these assessment centers told me the first thing they look for is whether or not the person being assessed has had experiences that included starting something new. The word 'entrepreneur' really describes something they are looking for."

"When you say entrepreneur, are you talking about the type of person who in the business world sets out to develop new products and start up new businesses?"

"I think I'm referring to a similar sort of person in terms of some personal characteristics," Swen continued. "An entrepreneur is the kind of person who will explore and consider many alternatives before really deciding on a course of action. A church planter has to do that. There isn't a ready-made plan to follow; novel approaches have to be considered and you don't just act on the first idea that comes along. When you initiate some of these novel ideas, of course, you have to expect the unexpected. You have to be ready for the unexpected and deal with whatever comes along."

"It sounds like you want the kind of person who thinks outside the box."

"Absolutely. A church planter has to be ready to take unusual actions and create things that are out of the ordinary."

"It also sounds," Kevin continued, "like you are looking for a Lone Ranger kind of person who can charge ahead and get things done without depending on other people."

"No, not at all. We want the kind of person who has initiative, but who also collaborates with other people. This person does a good job of networking with other people outside the community he or she is trying to develop and within this emerging faith community cultivates a lot of collaboration."

"OK. I get your point. Anything else about your entrepreneurs?"

"Well, Swen responded, "I guess I would just add that this person depends on God, and is a person of prayer who really is committed to discerning God's will in all that is being done. We are looking for a person who is willing to try new ideas and take risks, but who does it in a prayerful and thoughtful manner."

As Swen paused, Kevin started to say something, apparently thought better of it, and hesitated. Finally he said, "These new approaches to planting churches seem to be saying something about the world in which this church planting is going on. The unchurched do not have the same outlook about churches as when I was a kid. The scene really is changing."

"I agree. I think the church as an institution is becoming less prominent in our society and that may not be all bad. Some would say the
church is becoming less significant in today's world—it's on the decline—
but I would like to think that, as the institutional form of church is losing
prominence, something more like the early church is emerging. I would
like to think that our ministers—paid and unpaid, ordained and unor-
dained, designated as such and informal—are moving out of buildings
labeled as church into the broader society in a way that may resemble
a bit more what Jesus did. He gathered people together in all kinds of
settings, drew attention to the reign of God, formed circles of people who
bonded as friends, cared for each other, and reached out beyond their
circles to care for others and tell them the story of their personal lives
with God. That is the authentic church and a building called church is not
necessarily part of the picture."

"I can't disagree, but I find it sobering, maybe because my life is
so tied to an institutional church. But I guess this may be a prod to my
thinking. We need to really work hard at breaking out of our current
mindset—a mindset which has our building and our programs at the
heart of so much of what we do."

"Yes," Swen responded. "I think such a change in mindset pertains to
people leading both established churches and church plants. There are all
kinds of inadequate concepts we need to move away from. For example,
one we were just talking about is the consumer mentality of many people
in our churches which results in people switching churches because they
think a different church will have more of what they want—and what
they want is almost never help and support in serving Jesus more fully
and reaching out to other people around them."

"And I have to admit that we pastors get sucked into this as well. It
is so easy to slip into doing what we think will please people, rather than
helping them to become better disciples of Jesus."

"So it is, but this isn't the only conceptual shortsightedness we have.
People in both established churches and church plants tend to give ex-
cessive deference to charismatic leaders. I guess it often is related to the
consumer mentality we were talking about. Such leaders create an excitement about church that may or may not be about discipleship."

"As long as we are on the topic of inadequate conceptual bases for
growing a church," Kevin inserted, "we probably should add that the
structures we create are not the secret either. I know we have talked about
this more than once, but it obviously fits in here."

"When I try to summarize the sort of things we are talking about, I usually say this is about God's agency, not human agency. It is so easy to fall into a pattern of depending upon human effort, planning, and persuasion. If we really were committed to God's agency, we would devote ourselves more to prayer and discerning the direction of the Holy Spirit. And that, of course, is why I have been so adamant that church boards need to be spiritual communities and not just organizations conducting business."

"I like your summary—it is about God's agency, not human agency. Like planting a church, leading a congregation is a matter of following the leading of the Holy Spirit. I am surprised, however, at one thing."

"What's that?" Swen asked.

"Systems seem to be such a big part of your thinking, especially self-organizing, but I haven't heard any mention of them today."

"Well, it hasn't come up specifically in our conversation, but it certainly is part of my thinking about the topic we have been on, that is church planting, and the distinction between God's agency and human agency. In my mind, there is a relationship of some sort between depending upon God's initiative and leaving room for self-organizing."

"I think I know where you are going with this," Kevin said, "but I suspect that some of my fellow pastors who are big into careful planning, both the top-down and bottom-up types, would object and say they approach all their work prayerfully and seek God's direction in their planning."

"Of course they would, and I'm not contesting that. I'm simply saying proceeding in a manner that encourages self-organizing in essence gives more opening for the Spirit's influence to shape the actions of everyone who is part of the picture, not just the person who is in the planning role. And maybe I am especially sensitive to this matter in the context of church planting. Some church planters seem to want to follow a particular strategy that is all mapped out ahead of time. And many of these strategic approaches are good; I like them. Every context is different, however, and I think it is important to be responsive to everything there."

"What does that mean in real world terms?"

"For starters," Swen said, "I want it to be a grassroots approach that empowers the people being served. This isn't something being done for them, it is something being done with them. Many of these people are not tuned into the typical church culture. They may not even like the idea of being part of a church, but they are open to someone coming along side of them and engaging them in a wide range of activities that in some way connect with the spiritual dimension of life."

"I take it that you are talking about entering into a relationship and having fellowship with them in a deep way. Relationships are the foundation of ministry, not programs."

"Absolutely. It is not a matter of doing something to attract them, but relating to them and listening. It is about listening, listening, and keeping on listening."

"Agreed. And I am finally, really waking up to the fact that people have a lot more to say when I am asking open-ended questions instead of constantly giving my opinion on everything. Instead of being the preacher when I am in personal conversations, I find it really opens up the conversation when I ask questions such as 'What do you think God is like?' or 'Why is everything around us so messed up?' and really want to know what the other person thinks."

Swen was quick to respond. "I think what you said about really wanting to know what the other person thinks is key. Questions that are designed to give you an opening to make your speech, whatever that is, don't really open up a conversation."

"I guess if you are trying to build a new community of people, you have to build real relationships with people, one by one," Kevin added.

"Some of that is getting close to individuals, but it can also have a community focus. One good approach is to do what some people have called a neighborhood exegesis that is based on interviewing people to find out what the neighborhood needs are."

"That makes all kinds of sense, but after doing this sort of careful assessment are there any focal points that you would hope everyone would attend to?"

After a brief hesitation for some reflection, Swen responded. "Whatever this neighborhood exegesis produces, I see the response having three focal points or foundations that I would label with three words. They are relationships, discipleship, and vision."

A slight smile appeared on Kevin's face as he saw Swen falling into his usual reflex action. On his napkin he was writing in block letters, RELATIONSHIPS, DISCIPLESHIP, and VISION.

Swen continued, "The first of these is something we have just been talking about a lot; relationships are key to all the rest of it. In a small faith community where most people quickly get to know the others, people expect that relationships will be central. If they didn't they probably would not be there. It is one of the key foundations for everything else. Relationships are the foundation of a new faith community, not programs."

"And I assume the second one, discipleship, is the same as the discipleship we have talked about so many times in the past with regard to established churches."

"Certainly. It needs to be the central purpose of the new faith community that is being formed. Things will happen that probably are, to a considerable extent, for the purpose of fellowship. Other activities will focus on service to others, both those in this faith community and to the broader neighborhood or community within which they are located. But taken together, everything that happens there is tied in some way to helping people become more competent and engaged disciples of Jesus.

"And I'm sure the third one, vision, also is the same vision idea we have discussed many times before."

"Yes," Swen responded. "Discipleship is the key outcome of this vision, but the vision presents a picture of how it is hoped this outcome will be reached. Creating a specific local vision requires first of all living in that locality to gain a deep sense of the context. From this foundation, a vision can be created of how, in this specific faith community, life can be fostered that will result in a greater level of discipleship."

"I know you have been emphasizing this vision is specific to a particular faith community and that you would expect this vision to vary a lot from one place to the next, but aren't there some facets of this vision that you would expect to be the same from one place to the next?"

"Yes, in a broad sense, but the specifics probably would vary a lot. There are three connecting points within most every new worshiping community that I would expect to see. They would probably look quite different from one place to the next, but I would hope that most any such community would have provision for everyone who is part of it to engage in worship on an ongoing basis, to be part of a holistic small group, and to be part of various outreach ministries—service endeavors that reach out beyond the faith community itself." On his napkin, Swen was adding another triad of words, WORSHIP, GROUP, and OUTREACH.

"I assume," Kevin said, "that these three—worship, small group experience and outreach ministries—are about the same as we have talked about in the past regarding churches in general."

"Yes, although in the case of a new worshiping community, I may have more expectation that the outreach ministries would be tied to the community where this new faith community is being planted. In fact, I can imagine this new church tying some of their outreach work into extant community projects rather than creating their own."

"I take it you mean finding service projects that already exist in a community," Kevin said, "joining them as a group of people from your faith community, and becoming a significant part of making them go."

"Sure. There may already be a community garden project there, for example, or a project to help single parent families. The new faith community may increase its connection to the broader community by becoming actively involved in these projects rather than creating their own. It all depends."

"I'm sure this is another place where it would be helpful to be conscious that self-organizing occurs and capitalize on it."

"Sure," Swen responded, "and I would emphasize again that decision-making needs to be at the grassroots level. They go together."

A pause in the conversation emerged and shortly Kevin said, "I'm thinking about that list of essential principles that I got from Elroy and that we tweaked a bit as you used them in your seminars. Would that list look somewhat different if it were being applied to a church plant or would it stay pretty much like we had it? I'm guessing it would stay largely the same but I'm wondering if there wouldn't be a few differences."

Swen seemed to ponder the comment a bit and finally said, "Why don't we go over the list quickly and see what we think. I think I have a copy of them with me in this folder."

Swen quickly located the list and Kevin shifted positions so both of them could look at it at the same time. Finally Swen spoke up. "You know, I think I'd stay with the list as it is, but somehow I think it would be easier to adhere to these principles in a start-up church than in an established congregation. What do you think?"

Kevin continued to examine the list and finally said, "I agree and I see about four of them that I think would be easier to follow in the church plant."

"That's close to the same number I have, although I imagine we better look at each of them separately to see if we are on the same wavelength. The first one I picked was personalization."

"Same here."

Swen continued. "I think this one would be easier, if for no other reason than that a startup church is small to start with and almost has to be very personalized. But I think it is more than just the size per se, people likely are not going to be drawn into a new group unless it is very personalized."

"I agree and your argument for considering this one easier in this context is similar to what I would say about another one: church-as-community. Size, the newness of the situation, and the initial lack of institutional structure means the natural tendency will be a focus on community."

"So far we are two for two and I suspect there is another one we would agree on, namely the principle of being unbounded by a building. Almost always, it would seem to me, a new church does not own a building and so wouldn't be encumbered by everything that goes with owning and maintaining a building."

"Yes, but it is very possible that a group is so committed to the idea of needing a building that they constrain everything they are doing by putting a lot of their energy into raising the money needed to get their own building."

"Your point is well taken," Swen commented, "but it doesn't have to be that way. If they want to do it, it should be easier to be unbounded by a building in a startup context than it would be in an established church."

"Agreed, so it appears that we now have three principles where we have a similar perspective. Have we got a fourth?"

"Okay, let's see. I think the notion of the staff being there mainly to prepare others to reach out and minster, rather than doing all the ministry directly and being the only minister in the group, would be easier in the church plant setting. I have to grant, however, than even though it may be easier to pull off in this context, I'm not sure it will happen. I think the notion of doing ministry themselves is so ingrained in pastors, so much a part of their self-identity, they find it difficult to really buy into this principle."

"I had the same hesitation," Kevin responded, "but I agree it would be easier in this setting for the pastor who has this commitment."

"That's four, and that is the number you picked, but I had a fifth one, budget. The idea was that more of the community's budget should be directed toward ministry outside the group, than inward for their own spiritual formation. It seems to me that if a church planter is to be successful, his or her activities must largely be directed toward people who are not yet part of the community, so their resources will be largely focused outward."

"Maybe, but a new group is so focused on itself that even what they do as outreach has a strong self-serving aspect. They are reaching outward largely out a motivation of bringing people into their group. So I suspect that most of the money you have regarded as being devoted to outreach is as much based on a desire to strengthen their group as it is devoted to outreach for the sake of the people being served."

"I get your point," Swen responded, "but I still think it is easier to do in this church startup context."

"Maybe, but I think it is obvious that we think these principles apply to a church plant just as much as they do to an established church, and that by and large, it should be easier to stick to principle in the new situation."

"Yes, I agree, but there is another question that is interesting to think about. What about self-organizing? Is it easier to make use of self-organizing in shaping the future of a church that is just developing or is it harder?"

"Well, we were talking about this just a few minutes ago," Kevin noted, "and I think we already agreed that in a fluid situation such as a church start-up, it is natural for self-organizing to come into play."

"Yes, but this doesn't mean every church planter is ready to make use of it. Some people want to come in with their plans and make them happen rather than letting them emerge. The service projects we were talking about can be a good example of the distinction I am making. The best outreach efforts will reflect the passions and values of the people in the new faith community, and when these passions coincide with needs of their surrounding context, self-organizing may bring good results."

"So it is a matter of God's agency, not human agency."

"Of course," Swen said, "but I'm not sure that all that many people recognize this reality. The Spirit is operating in the lives of Christ followers and we need to encourage people to live in this reality. Using the concept of self-organizing as a descriptor in this context is most appropriate in my way of thinking."

A long sigh preceded Kevin's response. "This perspective challenges some people's notions of leadership, as we have discussed before. For many people, a strong leader is someone who gets plans put in place and gets everyone organized to turn the plans into reality. I think both of us see this ability as part of the skill set of a leader, but it doesn't capture the essence of leadership."

"Certainly not, and I am convinced that systems-thinking helps us get a handle on the essence of true leadership in all settings, but especially in a new church start-up."

"I'm sure we agree on that point, but since you are in the midst of helping our regional group of churches zero in on planting new churches, I would appreciated hearing you spell out how you see this leadership in such settings."

After a brief pause Swen responded, "I guess I would come at it from two perspectives. First, recall that a system has three components: elements, interconnections and a purpose or function. The leader of a new church start-up is the key determiner of what this new system will become by setting the purpose for it. Much more than in an established church, this leader can pin down just why this new group is forming, so a major part of his or her leadership is helping this community identify their purpose for existing. Second, recall when we were talking about leverage points for making change in a system, one of the top two leverage points was the matter of goals, purpose, and functions. In other words, whether you are the leader of an established church or a new church start-up, this leadership needs to have a constant focus on why it exists. And then, of course, there is that most influential leverage point of all—constant attention to shaping the mindset of the people in the community—that is shaping their deepest beliefs and assumptions. This is the basic stuff of leadership; it's not organization and management."

"Your summary reminds me of a recent radio broadcast I heard in which the speaker was emphasizing the importance of a leader not starting with what was being done, or how to do it, but focusing on why it was being done. It is all about purpose."

"Certainly. And knowing something about systems helps us understand why it is so important to zero in on purpose, or why, before getting consumed with action items."

On his napkin, Swen had written, WHY, WHY, WHY, one above the other as if it was a list. Kevin's fleeting unspoken question was whether Swen thought it was so important it needed to be emphasized or he was just writing things in threes today.

Kevin seemed satisfied with where the conversation had taken them thus far, and his body language indicated he was thinking of a transition. "We seem to be on the same page in terms of what you might call a philosophy of leadership, but I am wondering how your new church planters will operationalize all of this"

"That isn't a simple question, but there are some key matters a church planter has to attend to, and more specifically, engage the emerging flock in addressing in depth. Together they need to identify their vision, core values, and mission."

These three items were spoken effortlessly as he simultaneously wrote on the back of the napkin he had flipped over, VISION, CORE VALUES, and MISSION.

As Kevin started to think that here was another list of three, Swen added another item off to the side, RULE OF LIFE, and said, "Here is another one, rule of life, that I will come back to, but first let's deal with these three, They are standard items you probably have heard people talk about at various times."

"Yes, been there, done that."

"Certainly. They are so basic, but the point is that an influential leader needs to put a lot of energy into helping this emerging faith community come to some understanding on them, both as individuals and as a community. They become the subject of sermons, group discussions and informal conversation. The vision thing, we have talked about over and over again. The core values are equally important. Some of them may be reflected in the essential principles we have been using, but it is more broadly based in the principles by which individuals expect to live."

Kevin jumped in on this point, "I have recently given this a lot of attention in our congregation. Our leadership group came up with a list of core values based on a New Testament study and we presented it to the entire congregation for consideration. The list was discussed in various settings and we massaged it a bit based on this discussion. It is now something that gives us guidance as we go about our work."

"Of course, and what we are talking about is not that different for a start-up congregation. It is just basic leadership stuff. It is the same with mission. The vision for this new congregation has to be translated into more specific endeavors for their particular context."

"Okay, I see that this matter of operationalizing everything is really the stuff we have talked about many times, but what about that fourth item you wrote down, 'rule of life?'"

After a pause, Swen responded. "I like this label but I sometimes hesitate to use it because the word 'rule' is so easily misunderstood. The word has a rich history, being rooted in monastic life from many centuries back. A rule of life is simply a set of guidelines by which a group of people agrees to live, both individually and corporately, but in an individualistic culture like ours even something we call guidelines is a tough sell."

"That's for sure! Phrases like 'challenge authority,' 'I'll do it my way,' and 'it's mine,' are everywhere. You can't preach the New Testament authentically without finding out that our culture is individualistic to the extreme, and I probably should add, consumeristic.'"

"I see I have struck a responsive chord, and, as you know, I am not just talking about preaching. I'm talking about everything we do to help people address how they live and a life of apprenticeship to Jesus is clearly countercultural."

"We are right back to the basic matter of discipleship, or personal transformation, we seemingly always get to," Kevin said. "In the last couple of months I have found myself really attending to it in my ministry. I have been encouraging people to focus on several questions that have been brought to our consciousness from various sources. From the cell groups of John Wesley a couple of centuries or so back we have the classic question, 'How is it with your soul?' Spiritual directors are inclined to ask, 'How do you pray?' Our study of John 15:7 highlighted the question 'What should I pray for?' And our project to help people in our neighborhood prompted the question, 'Jesus, what would you have me do or be?' This matter of personal transformation really has started to permeate my reflections on ministry."

"I was struck by your focus on questions. It was just a few minutes ago that we were talking about the importance of listening to people and engaging people with questions. It is obvious that you have been doing this."

"And don't you want to tie this back to systems ideas as well."

"Of course," Swen replied enthusiastically, "and the obvious connection is to mindset. The most important leverage point for influencing self-organizing, as we have said many times, is to focus on mindset, our most basic beliefs and assumptions. And that is exactly what you are doing when you zero in on such profound and basic questions. You are shaping people, who in turn will self-organize activities within your congregation in a way that your best plans and management will never do. I am sometimes asked how to influence mindset and you have just given a good example."

"And I hope I can do this, just as I would hope a church planter is trying to shape the mindset of people gathered into a new church. I would hope that both of us would be helping and supporting our people in serving Jesus more fully and reaching out to other people around them."

"Absolutely. And it reminds me of a way in which some church planters today see their mission. Some see a key aspect of their mission to be forming yet additional churches. They want to form a new worshiping community that in turn will want to plant another church. They set out to fulfill the Great Commission, not just by making new disciples, but by forming new communities of such people; that is, starting new churches in all corners of society, not just in buildings that sit on a prominent street corner."

"I'm impressed with this perspective," Kevin responded. "It seems to me that this is really grasping what the Great Commission is all about—making disciples and forming communities of these disciples."

After a brief pause, Kevin continued. "I keep wondering how the stuff we have been talking about for churches in general over these past months differs for church start-ups. In terms of your systems ideas, it would seem that they are the same in both contexts."

"I agree. The concepts are applicable to all social and organizational systems. I am not so sure, however, about the essential principles for churches that we have been massaging and using."

The degree of jest in Kevin's rejoinder was unclear. "You're telling me your systems ideas, built on social science, are firm but you are not so sure about our essential principles, principles which are biblically based."

"Hold on. You are mischaracterizing those essential principles. There is a reason Elroy didn't simply label them as biblical principles. Biblical ideas were applied to a specific cultural context—institutional churches. The list of principles is for churches. Certainly they have a biblical foundation but the application is to a specific context. They are always a work in progress because the context keeps changing. After all, we had our discussion about whether the principles applied to new church start-ups because that is a different context than the one in which we originally were applying them."

"Okay already. I was jiving a bit, but you made a serious point. Since these essential principles are a work in progress, everyone using them should treat them as such. In fact, a useful process for any congregation would be a review of the principles to decide how they fit their specific context. It could be a useful vehicle for studying both biblical concepts and the context to which they are being applied, that is, one's own congregation."

As they stood to leave, Swen said, "That probably is a good note to end on. Our work of fostering positive change is always a work in progress and we need to be evaluating what we do on a continuing basis and not think we have the final word."

Appendix A

Essential Principles

THESE ESSENTIAL PRINCIPLES ARE a work in progress. They are deriving from careful reflection on the institutional church as found in contemporary society and the biblical basis for its desired nature as well as means of its revitalization. They are presented as a starting point for others in their consideration of their particular situation and means of moving forward.

1. *Discipleship focus.* The church should focus on developing disciples of Jesus Christ. It should not attempt to have "comprehensive" programs at the expense of this central spiritual purpose.

2. *Simple goals.* The church's goals should be simple: that each believer master the spiritual disciplines most central to that individual and develop the spiritual gifts needed to reach out beyond him- or herself to further the Kingdom in accordance with the direction of the Spirit. These goals should apply to all believers, although the means to the goals will vary as these believes themselves vary.

3. *Personalization.* Teaching and various aspects of spiritual formation should be personalized to the maximum extent possible. To that end, a significant portion of teaching should take place in small groups with peer leadership, and spiritual formation on an individual level should be common. Decisions about programs, use of time, teaching approaches and modes of spiritual formation should rest with the people engaged in these activities rather than a governing group not engaged directly in the ministries themselves.

4. *Believer-as-kingdom-seeker.* The governing metaphor of the church should be believer-as-kingdom-seeker rather than the more traditional metaphor of teacher or pastor-as-deliverer-of-spiritual sustenance. Coaching and spiritual direction should be prominent, to

help believers learn how to examine their own lives and foster their own spiritual development in the context of Christian community.

5. *Church-as-community*. The church as a community of believers should be the guiding image rather than the church as an institution. Church is the stuff of relationships, prayer and worship rather than programs, budgets and management. This community, with its focus on relationships, prayer and worship, should not be constrained by, or dependent upon, an unresponsive institution.

6. *Tone*. Within the context of the community's basic statement of faith, the tone of the church should be explicitly and self-consciously one of accepting diversity in the way the Spirit directs the lives of the community's believers. Given the fundamental importance of this direction of the Spirit in individuals' lives, the community as a whole should avoid collective actions that do not have full community support. On the other hand, as a true community of believers it should have open communication about fundamental matters of faith and practice in a manner that provides both mutual support and encouragement of individuals' prayerful examination of themselves and give subgroups within the congregation the freedom to follow the direction of the Spirit for them.

7. *Measures of success*. The measure of success of the church should be growth in discipleship. It can be assessed by individuals in the context of community interaction. The primary focus should be on *being*, that is, who we are as person, not on *doing*, that is, the work we accomplish. Numerical growth in the size of the congregation should not be basis for measuring the spiritual growth of the congregation.

8. *Unbounded by a building*. The church is located wherever its people are found, such as at their homes, their places of employment, the local coffee shop, or the place where their hobby group meets. The church is not a set of activities located in a building, it is what goes on in the lives of the members of the congregation, all week long, wherever they find themselves.

9. *Staff*. All members of the community should see themselves as ministers and in a role of ministering to others, both inside and outside the community. Although paid staff members devote more of their

time to serving the community itself and preparing others to minister, ministry itself is done by all.

10. *Budget.* At the most, one-half of the tithes and offerings of this Christian community should be directed to supporting the community itself, that is, to fostering their own spiritual growth. The majority of their giving should be directed outward, with much of this money ideally directed through ministries in which these believers themselves are actively involved. Inevitably, this approach will require the reduction of some programs now provided in many churches.

11. *Worship.* The worship done in community is focused on telling the story of God, celebrating it, and responding to it. The community is reminded of God's purposes and concerns and celebrates them in a manner where this content takes precedence over style and other matters of taste. Individuals are enabled to acknowledge their brokenness, repent, and open themselves to God's redirection of their lives. The community gathers—as disciples, not consumers—and then is sent out renewed.

12. *Missional.* The community, individually and collectively, reaches out in love to others as an outgrowth of their relationship with Jesus Christ. Their *doing* is an outgrowth of their *being*. Their sense of mission reflects a concern for all dimensions of human life, including physical, psychological and spiritual.

Bibliography

Friedman, Edwin H. *Generation to Generation: Family Process in Church and Synagogue*. New York: Guilford, 1985.

Hawkins, Greg L. and Cally Parkinson. *Follow Me: What's Next for You?* Barrington, IL: The Willow Creek Association, 2008.

Jones, Jeffrey D. *Traveling Together: A Guide for Disciple-Forming Congregations*. Herndon, VA: Alban Institute, 2006.

Meadows, Donella H. *Thinking in Systems: A Primer*. White River Junction, VT: Chelsea Green Publishing, 2008.

Olson, Edwin E. and Glenda H. Eoyang. *Facilitating Organization Change*. New York: Pfeiffer, 2001.

Smith, James Bryan. *The Good and Beautiful Community*. Downers Grove, IL: InterVarsity, 2010.

——. *The Good and Beautiful God*. Downers Grove, IL: InterVarsity, 2009.

——. *The Good and Beautiful Life*. Downers Grove, IL: InterVarsity, 2009.

Steinke, Peter L. *How Your Church Family Works: Understanding Congregations as Emotional Systems*. Herndon, VA: The Alban Institute, 1993, 2006.

Willard, Dallas. *The Divine Conspiracy: Rediscovering Our Hidden Life in God*. New York: Harper San Francisco, 1998.

——. *The Spirit of the Disciplines: Understanding How God Changes Lives*. New York: Harper & Row, 1988.